STRAIGHT OUTTA COMPTON

My Untold Story

Antoine *"DJ Yella"* Carraby

STRAIGHT OUTTA COMPTON: My Untold Story

Copyright ©2021, by Antoine Carraby.

Cover Art Design by Raymond Canody.

Front cover and page 8 photo by Michele Poorman.

Edited by Johnnie Goolsby.

ISBN: 9798506023630

DEDICATION

I would like to thank God first, my wife, our kids, Javanne and Terrence, and little Tovah, Bryson, Elijah, and Kris. Next, I want to thank my mother and father, Mary (R.I.P.) and Joseph (R.I.P.), my grandmother, Luci (R.I.P.), my brothers and sisters, Carlos, Joseph, Keith (R.I.P.), André (R.I.P.), Arnett, Sherreé, René, and Monique, all my nieces and nephews, and my wife's sisters, Gina, Sis, and "Bye, Felicia."

I want to thank all my childhood friends, Dedrick, Big Chuck, Derrick, Larry, Mike W., Mark, Jonathan, and Sidney (R.I.P.), my up-north cousins, Playboy T and Nicole, Mark "Big Man" Rucker (R.I.P.), Weed, Kisha and Deon, the Rucker boys, The Twins, Lil E, E3, and Erica. I want to thank Allen J. and wife, Sharon C., Debbie, Marvin, Marilyn (R.I.P.), and Wellington, Monescia, Pastor Johnson and wife, his brother Alonzo and wife, Pastor Raymond and wife, and the Jesus Is The Answer church family.

I would also like to thank my old school Wreckin' Cru buddies, Lonzo, Cli-n-tel, Shakespeare, Unknown, and Greg Mack from K-DAY.

Special thanks to Johnnie Goolsby, the Ruthless family, Arabian Prince, The D.O.C., Bone Thugs-N-Harmony, JJ Fad, ATL, Menajahtwa, and T. Woods.

Xtra special thanks to my N.W.A Friends4Life...
Who would've thunk it? That our love for music back then would have brought us this far. We started from nothing— we had nothing. Through all the ups and downs and the craziness, we eventually made history together. I love you, Dre, Cube, Ren, and Eazy. (R.I. P.)

If I left anybody's name out, I am so sorry.

2

FOREWORD

Every few years comes a story of change, survival, and transitions. What you are about to witness is the life and times of Antoine "DJ Yella" Carraby. He was a member of the rap group, N.W.A, which also featured Eazy-E, Dr. Dre, Ice Cube, and MC Ren. N.W.A was labeled "The World's Most Dangerous Group."

This man's life began in Compton, California, a city known back in the 70s through the late 90s as having one of the highest crime and death rates in the USA. As a product of his environment and love for music, his path was destined to merge with other beginning musicians who would excel in the evolution of a new genre of music. This group of young men would take the impact of this unique style of music (which had begun in the early 1980s) to another level and style known as gangsta rap. This group was deemed the pioneers of the West Coast sound, and Eazy-E gained the title, "Godfather of Gangsta Rap."

When these young men from Compton came together, they could've never imagined they would wind up in the **Rock and Roll Hall of Fame** (2016) and make music history. Their music turned the world upside down as they were able to bring the underground rap style to the commercial market and influence audiences of all races and ages. Antoine will share his journey from the halls of Compton High School as a student and band member, to the clubs and skating rinks of Compton, then to the fame and notoriety of N.W.A. This story will amaze, shock, and motivate you as he shares his powerful story. So, get ready to join him as he takes you on this journey to inspire artists and people, both young and old.

Hopefully, this book will enlighten you and help you through your struggles and disappointments. May you find an answer that can change your life.

Bishop Dr. Ernest Johnson, D.D.
Senior Pastor of Jesus Is The Answer Church
Host of JITATV.ORG

CONTENTS

INTRODUCTION

From the beginning of time, there was a plan for my life, even before I knew who I was. I used to be a member of a group that was and is still known worldwide. I once thought that I had it all, but I discovered I didn't. This is my story—about somebody that went from rags to riches, back to rags, and then to a brand-new way of life.

As you read this book, I would like to point out two things. First, the words that are in parentheses represent my personal thoughts. Second, some of the words written are informal (It's my own way of speaking.) In other words, they are not meant to be written and spelled formally.

After you read this book, I also hope that you will find this new way of life. Why? Because it is there where you will discover the greatest love of all.

Antoine "DJ Yella" Carraby

MY JOURNEY BEGINS...

CHAPTER 1: IN THE BEGINNING

As I'm sitting here, clicking the side of my water bottle, and taking a deep breath, I'm sitting back thinking about my life— all the things I done and all the things I should have done. But where do I start?

Let me take you wayyyyy back. How bout' 1965?

Let's start at age 4. (That's the furthest I can remember, LOL.)

I was born in LA County (Compton). My parents' names were Mary and Joseph, and I had 8 brothers and sisters.

Let me see if I can get this order right...

Starting from the oldest, there is Carlos (Corky), Joseph (Beany), Keith (The Wild One), André (The Hustler), Arnett (Sweet Pea, named after the character in the *Popeye* cartoon, AKA—The Smart One), Sherreé, René, me, and Monique.

(L-R) Keith, Carlos, André, Joseph, and the little one is Arnett.

All nine of us were by the same parents. That's almost unheard of these days. They were married for many years.

But the sad thing was, after all the kids, they ended up getting divorced later on after my baby sister was born.

I was just 4 years old, so I missed out on having both parents in my life. I didn't get to hang out with my brothers and have that brotherly time or fatherly and family time. How did I know this? Because me and my younger sister had no baby pictures.

After the divorce, my mother packed up, then took us younger kids and moved from Compton into my grandmother's house in LA.

A couple of weeks later (it was early one morning), I woke up and didn't see my mother. I walked all around my grandmother's house looking but couldn't find her. Finally, I ended up walking out the front door. I was still wearing pajamas and house shoes. I started walking and just kept on walking and walking and walking and walking. Eventually, I walked up to a house. Out stepped a lady that reminded me of the character Samantha on the TV show *Bewitched*. She was a nice lady. She invited me into her house. Then she called the police. That was my first encounter with the law.

The police arrived and took me to the station. While I was there, they even gave me some candy.

They called my mother, and she came and got me. I didn't know it at the time, but my mom had taken Arnett to school in Compton. My mom told me later that I had only walked around the corner. But being a kid that young and in a new neighborhood, I felt like I had walked forever!

My mom eventually rented a house that was located just around the corner from my grandmother.

Here's another memory...

When I was in the first grade, I was walking home from school one day. I went into the house through the back door. I turned the knob and stepped into my mother's room and, *SHAZAM*!!!!

I had just stepped into some grown folks' business.

I remember the scene in great detail...

The silhouette of two bodies...

One of my older brothers was having sex with this girl.

I backed out the door without them hearing me.

10

I didn't think about it that much, but that moment was a rude awakening. One that I never forgot.

Early 70s

We moved back to Compton, and then my mom bought us a house. Now it's nine kids and my mom. She worked extra hard to put food on the table and a roof over our heads. I remember the color of the house being dirty beige. It had 3 bedrooms and 1 bath. We also had plenty of bunk beds, including a triple bunk bed! We even had grass in the front and back yards! And yea— we were "PO"! (That means broke and poor.)

We had some cool neighbors. But the embarrassing thing for me was that we only had one parent in the house. Everyone else had their mother and father—and a nice house.

My family was well-liked in this neighborhood. My neighbors to the right were the Wayne's. They had a son named Charles, but I called him Big Chuck because he was tall.

(He eventually grew to 6'7"!)

My neighbors to the left were the Merrietts. They had a son named Derrick. My neighbors across the street were the Carters, and their youngest son was named Larry. To the left of them was the Gates family. And then down the street was Mike Ward, Dedrick, Mark, Aaron (Chubby), and Homer (R.I.P.). This was my crew. We hung out in the streets. We played baseball, football (in the streets), rode motorcycles, minibikes, go-karts (no motor), and bicycles together. (Unfortunately, I never had a new bicycle.) I always got the hand me downs. Or, I had to put together my own bike using spare parts. But we had great fun playing outside. It's something they don't seem to do too much these days. I was the only one out of us that played a sport, which was little league baseball. I did that for 5 years in a row. The only bad thing was no one came to my games except for Corky. He came to ONE game when I was 15. (I was playing in the senior league.) That was it.

My mother had a good reason for not coming to my games.

She worked so hard to make sure all of her children were taken care of. She was a nurse who worked a 3-11 shift.

My father, even though he lived across town in LA, never came to my games.

11

The crazy thing is, when I went to sign up to play, my dad wasn't taking me to sign up, but he was taking my brother Arnett.

I got signed up because I just happened to be there. But it turned out that I did pretty well at the tryouts.

The coaches said that I had a great arm, so they made me a pitcher. Now there was some good things that I remember while I was growing up. You know we was "PO", but we got a few treats.

Our once-a-year treat was Mickey D's.

(If you don't know what that means, it's McDonald's.)

That was one of the biggest joys for us growing up! Our second biggest treat was going to a drive-in movie!

I can remember it just like it was yesterday. I can just taste it now...

What was it? A medium buttered popcorn and medium Coke. AND THAT WAS GREAT!

1974

(L) My mother, Mary and (R) my grandmother, Luci.

It's 1974, so for right now, let's stop with the nice stuff. Let me take you to something more serious.

When I was in the 6th grade (Ralph J. Bunch Elementary), I remember talking to my brother Keith. He was in the bathroom shaving. I came in to use the bathroom. (I had to take a #2 of course, LOL.)

Afterwards, I was about to walk out when he said, "You're not going to wash your hands?"

I looked at him like he was crazy and said, "NO!"

He broke it down to me why I should wash my hands. So, I washed them and left.

Speaking of bathrooms, I can remember another kinda weird moment. This took place when I spent the night over my father's house after the divorce. I was about 4 or 5 years old. And for some reason, my father let me take a shower with him.

No funny stuff happened. But that just didn't sit right with

13

me—even till this day. Take it from a kid's point of view.

Looking at that "hairy monster" just felt wrong.

So, parents, I don't recommend doing that. Please don't take baths or showers with your kids. Now back to the timeline.

Later that night, I was asleep, and something woke me up. I went into my mother's room. She was sleeping, so I laid down on the end of her bed. Moments later, I was awakened by the sound of a single gunshot from the house in back of us. The time was 1:45 a.m. I drifted off to sleep. The next morning, I heard my mother crying. I found out my brother Keith was accidentally shot in the neck and killed at his best friend's house at 1:45 a.m. He was just 21 years old.

Later, I found out that his best friend was sitting in a chair, facing a mirror, pointing the "empty" revolver, and pulling the trigger.

Click... click...click ...click... click...

Amazingly, as my brother was going past the mirror to pick up something, the last "click" fired, striking him in the neck.

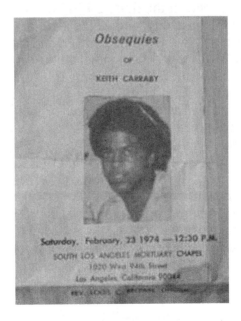

My brother Keith (1954-1974) (R.I.P.)

14

So, they say that he laid there for 15 minutes before he died.

When the police arrived, my brother was able to motion to them that it was an accident.

I remember all the funeral stuff. We wore the same blue jean suits— with chrome studs all over each outfit.

I remember being there and viewing the body. That was creepy— I mean, really creepy. I even remember the smell of the hairspray that was put on his hair.

Sometimes, when I wash my hands, I think back on that meaningful conversation with my brother Keith that I had in the bathroom that day. It led to me waking up and hearing that single gunshot. It also led me to being the last person to see his body as they closed the coffin. After that, I was afraid of the dark for the remainder of my childhood. Enough of that—back to the nice stuff.

I just graduated from the 6th grade. My mother sent me up north to Oakland to visit my cousins. I stayed there for one week. It was my first time being out of town and smoking weed.

Now let me explain. When I got there, my cousins did one thing— smoke weed all the time. 24-7.

The momma, the daddy, and all the kids.

I had never smoked weed in my life. But that was all they did. It was fun for that week— being high all the time. But you know, I learned a life lesson... Weed is not my thing.

Now I am in the 7th grade. Don't get it twisted—We're still "PO." (That means I had to buy my own school clothes and come up with my own lunch money.)

Other words, I had to get a J-O-B.

My first job took place at my school (Enterprise Jr. High) during the summer. It was through the C.E.T.A. Program.

That means you work five days a week all summer, and you get one check, which was great for me. That meant Swiss cookies and milk in the morning.

You're going to like this one. I got me a second job. But check this out. I worked Monday through Saturday, 5 hours a day at the local dairy market in the evenings. Now I'm buying more Swiss cookies, more clothes, and customizing my bike. That means show lights, mirrors, an 8-track player, and car speakers.

And guess what? I'm doing all this on a small budget....

$1 an hour, and that's if I get paid. The crazy thing is most of the time I didn't get paid! So, they owed me about $250, which was about 250 hours of work. And I'm going to say "WOW" to that!

My show bike (Mid 70s)

And this went on for about 3 years. So, I'm going to say "WOW" to that, too!

Speaking of show lights on my bike, I remember I had a little buddy. Let me think of a name for him...

(I'll call him Blue Boy.)

He was from a neighborhood near me called Taco Flats. He had a cold blue Schwinn Stingray bike. The sad thing is I heard somebody broke into his house, then killed him for his bike.

Because I was so young, I didn't really feel the significance of my little buddy dying.

But I do miss that "Bye, see you tomorrow," as he rode away on that cold blue Schwinn...

Hold up, let's stop here. Let me back up a little bit...

Both my mother and grandmother went to church every Sunday. But I (Mr. Bad A**) didn't attend regularly.

What I mean by regularly is... I DIDN'T GO AT ALL.

The neighbor to the right, Mr. Wayne, invited me to Sunday school one time. And I do mean ONE TIME.

16

So, I went, but the only thing I remember was the dollar breakfast that his church sold. That was my church history.

Now here's a little more history...

One day my brother Joseph asked me to DJ for his wedding. Me being a young entrepreneur at the age of 12, I turned this into a real gig. (Of course, no money changed hands.) But during that time, we didn't have no playlists, computers, or things like that. So, I had to do it the old school way. I had to cue up the 8-track tapes the night before. But during the wedding, I had to play one tape at a time because there was no mixing and no scratching in them days. And it's crazy that this event would wind up becoming my destiny.

The Garage

While we're in the backup mode, let me keep it backed up. Let me talk about our **infamous garage**. A lot of lives were changed there. I'll start off first by saying, my brothers nailed the garage door shut. (Then they cut out a doorway.)

This turned the garage into three different things:

1. A sanctuary for the homeless.
2. A studio/rehearsal hall, and...
3. A clubhouse.

Let me explain why.

On the sanctuary part, my mother always took in my brother's friends because they had no place to go. She showed them love by housing and feeding them, and that went on for many years.

Now let's talk about music. My two older brothers (Corky and Joseph) had a Top 40 band. They played all kinds of music by groups such as Santana and War. I used to listen to them rehearse all the time. While they were practicing, I used to "set up" my toys on the bed and play them like they were drums.

One day I went into the garage when no one was there. I got on the drum set and started playing, even though I never had a lesson.

I sounded pretty good. As a matter of fact, I started my own band with Mark on the bass, and Big Chuck on the guitar. (All they knew how to play was one note, LOL.)

Our so-called band lasted one rehearsal. My brothers' band split up. Corky went one way, and I started playing drums for my

17

brother Joseph's 3-piece band. So, they set the garage up like a recording studio. I guess I played well enough, so they wanted me to record with them all the time. But I didn't really like to because it was messing up my playtime outside on Saturdays.

Now let's talk about the clubhouse. Me and some of my friends had a game where we would all be in the garage. One of us would cut the lights off, then start socking each other in the dark. Why we played that kind of game? (I have no idea.)

So, that was our hangout spot. I used to work on my show bike, while my brother René and Dedrick used to gather up all the roaches and make one big super joint.

("Roaches" is what's left of a joint after smoking it.)

By the way—my two older brothers were the ones smoking the joints.

Not to change the subject, but this event happened in the garage also. One night I was in the living room listening to some music.

My brother André came into the house and said, "I got something for you outside in the garage."

I said to myself, "*Hmmm*, what could that be?"

So, I went outside, opened the door slowly, and then—WOW!

I jumped for joy! There was a naked girl standing there! She lived in the neighborhood. Let me think of a name for her...

(I'll call her Wild Girl X.)

Man, she really woke up something in me! And you know what's funny? That's how I learned about the-birds-and-the-bees. Now let's move forward...

Me, Larry, and Big Chuck used to go swimming all the time at the park. On this one particular day, nobody was around to go swimming with me, but I decided to go anyway.

This time I didn't go to our normal park. I wound up going to the trailer park's swimming pool, where they charge you 25 cents to get in.

Sometimes when you're young and poor bad things happen...

The horrible thing is, I had no one to talk to. I didn't talk to my father. My brothers were older, so we didn't talk. My mother was always working. So, I really had nobody to turn to and no guidance. Without going into more detail, my soul was taken for 25 cents. (That's the price of a candy bar.)

This is where I am going to put the **"Black Curtain"** up.

That moment affected me for years. From that day on, I was on my own.

High School Days: Compton High

There used to be a saying about going to high school. I can't remember what it was, but whatever it was, I didn't get it. I used to be a little popular in junior high. Now I'm in high school and it feels like starting over in first grade again. (It seemed like this kinda stuff only happened to me.)

I had a few friends, but now I am just a "nobody." So, let me see where I'm gonna start.

I'm in the 10th grade. I still have my dollar an hour job, my fresh new clothes, my Swiss cookie money—and I still got my show bike. (But that's getting old.)

Let's talk about high school. It ain't what's it's cracked up to be—at least for me, anyway. So, I have to be a little nerd for a while until I get used to this setup.

Now first things first. I was used to the desk that you could raise up and put books inside. I would ball up pieces of paper, then tape folded paper to the back of the desk. This became my basketball court. Then me and my buddies used to shoot hoops inside the desk. That was in junior high. This is high school. All you get here is a flat desk with no-frills and no thrills. (How did I learn anything?)

But let's get one thing straight. I never did homework, and I never carried books to school. All I had was what they used to call a Pee Chee folder. (It was an inexpensive folder used to store paper in.) And let me tell you— by the end of the year, "the pee done fell off the chee!" It wound up being just a worn-out folder with scotch tape all over it.

And that's the way it happened for all three years.

(That means one folder a year.) Let's get back to the 10th grade.

One day, I met this girl, and she was bad! Let me think of a name for her...

(I will call her Baby Girl J.)

I fell in love, but not "really" love. I just had a girlfriend with no hanky panky. (That means no milk from the cow.)

But...I was in love. Well, enough of that love stuff.

19

It's springtime now.

I had played my last season of baseball.

I thought I had a pretty good chance of making it on the high school team, but I had a choice to make.

Pick curtain # 1 or curtain #2.

What was behind curtain #1?

Playing baseball, going to practice every day, and being broke.

Or I could pick what was behind curtain #2.

Keep buying my Swiss cookies and having money in my pocket.

I picked curtain # 2. I kept the dairy market job.

(This is the real world. This ain't no *Let's Make a Deal*, LOL.)

11th Grade

Now I got this high school setup down pact. It ain't as tough as I thought it was. So, I had a little break.

My neighbor Larry from across the street had a sister named Nissy (Yniska). We both were in the same grade, and she was on the drill team.

She said, "You should join the marching band."

She hooked me up with this guy. Let me think of a name for him...

(I'll call him Major K.S.)

Why would I call him a major? Because he was one of the drum majors of our high school band. We hit it off right away. He asked me if I wanted to be a drummer in the band.

I said, "Cool."

Then he started teaching me all kinds of stuff— all the beats, the cadences, and how to march with the drum on.

The funny thing is I caught on real fast.

(Must I say more? LOL.)

Let's move on.

This might put a smile on your face. I FINALLY got rid of the dollar an hour dairy market job! "I'm moving on up..."

Just like they did on *The Jeffersons*! I got me a real job now.

Let me think of a name for the place...

(I'll call it the "Bell.")

It was cool, a little different.

I had to mop floors, cook beans, fry taco shells (now that wasn't fun), and on top of that, I had to wait on customers. But

20

not just customers, I also had to take orders from these so-called "captains."

But we'll call them managers. Can you believe I did this for a year? (Really?)

Anyway, one day while I was at work, I remember I was cleaning up, and somebody came up to the counter.

I turned around and said, "May I..."

My eyes looked at this guy. Then my eyes looked down.

There it was—a sawed-off, double-barreled shotgun.

Who was holding it? I don't know who the man was. But I can tell you what he said.

"Nobody moves! Nobody gets hurt!"

So, I stood there and thought to myself, "Oh... So, THIS is what you would call a robbery. A code 2-11."

But let's get back to the matter at hand. A sawed-off double-barreled shotgun was pointed at my stomach. I am looking him dead in the eye. This could turn ugly real quick.

Why? Because I had just made a cash drop, and there was only about $25 in the register. Think about it. All it took was the pull of that trigger, and my life was done.

(I hear the sound of a bell. "Ding!" Miracle!)

So, he robbed us of that little bit of money and fled.

Soon the police arrived, and I told them that no one was hurt.

(This was my second encounter with the police.)

Now let's switch gears. I'm in "love" again. But not IN love.

She was a senior and on the drill team. Let me think of a name for her...

(I'll call her Cutie Pie N.)

She was thick and sexy. I remember she had a little orange Datsun. During lunch, we used to drive across the street to the courthouse's parking structure. Always at the same time, always on the top floor, and in the same parking space. That's where we would have our hanky panky...

I got the frills, but not the thrills. (In other words, all we did was kiss.)

Now it's prom time for the seniors, and I find myself in the middle of making another choice.

"Should I? Should I not?"

Cutie Pie N asked me if I could take her to her prom. Let's see...

On one hand, if I take her, it's gonna cost me. (I ain't making that kind of money.) But on the other hand, if I say no, I wonder if she'll be mad? Well, I made my choice.

Let's get to the next subject. Did I mention she was mad?

So, my neighbor Nissy had a friend. Let me think of a name for her...

(We'll call her Lady A.)

She was a senior and a cheerleader, and she needed a date for the prom. Watch out! There's a joker in this deck.

So, Nissy kinda talked/tricked me into taking her to the prom.

The crazy thing was there was a gas crisis at the time. You couldn't buy gas when you wanted to. You had to buy it on odd or even days. If you don't know what that means, you could only buy gas based on the last number of your license plate. (The numbers were odd or even, LOL.)

That put me in a tough situation. I wanted to drive my mother's 1976 silver 4-door Ford Granada. (It kinda looked like a fake Benz.) So, here it is. Not enough gas in her car to take Lady A to her prom. Now I had two problems to solve. The first one is the car. Let me think about it...I didn't have a choice.

I had to drive my brother René's 1961 Volkswagen Bug.

Why? Because he had even license plates, and it was an even day. I felt a little embarrassed about driving his car because it wasn't as nice as my mother's car—and I dang sure couldn't afford to rent a limo.

So, we rolled up to the prom in the black Bug. We were a little late, but I was kinda glad we were. (Really didn't want nobody to see us.)

Did I fail to mention? I told Nissy and Lady A, "I ain't buying no pictures."

Now let's get to the second problem. This one was coming, and I knew it was coming. (This is when the joker pops out.)

I knew somehow I would run into her (Cutie Pie N) at the prom.

She stared right at me, gave me a dirty look, then rolled her eyes.

Well, they say, "Don't burn your bridges," but Mr. Bad A**'s burnt his bridge all the way down to the ground. Cutie Pie N never talked to me again. Was it something I did?

I thought to myself (in my Redd Foxx (R.I.P.) voice) ...

"YOU BIG DUMMY!"

Since we're on this love theme, let's talk about it some more.

I just got out of the 11th grade. It's summertime. Guess what? I'm back in love again. I met this girl. Excuse me, I mean, lady. Maybe this might be my first love. (This one had plenty of frills and thrills.) Hee hee...

Let me think of a name for her...

(I'll call her Sexy V.)

I met her one night at my neighbor Homer's house party. She was two years older than me, and she was sexy. I mean, capital "S" sexy! Now I did something I don't usually do. I told a white lie, but you can call it a lie. I told her I was out of high school, and that worked for a while. So, a week later, we went to my favorite place in my mother's Ford Granada— to a drive-in movie.

Wow! This was the first time I ever took a girl there or drove there!

Of course, I bought that famous popcorn and sodas—and did I mention I was a hero, not a zero?

(Sometimes, I just have to laugh at myself.)

Now let's fast forward the timeline...

Okay. One day, while I was at work, I remember I was cleaning up, and somebody came up to the counter.

I turned around and said, "May I..."

My eyes opened wide. It was Sexy V and her two friends!

At that moment, I wished I could just click my heels three times and disappear! (*There's no place like home, there's no place like home...*)

Did I fail to mention? I didn't tell her that I worked at the Bell and was still in high school. I felt a little uncomfortable and embarrassed.

So, we both stood there, acting like we didn't know each other.

Then I said, "May I help you?"

Senior Year: 79-80

Senior picture (1980)

It's my last year of high school and you're not gonna believe this. I quit the job at the Bell, and I got me a high-paying job. It may not be high class, but it's about a dollar more than I was making at the Bell.

(And I don't have to wear that uniform no more.)

Okay, let's talk about the job.

First: The location...

Gage and San Pedro. If you don't know where that is, it's in the hood. Did I fail to mention? It's a liquor store.

My brother André turned me on to it because he worked there—and did I say, "It goes down around here?"

(From street fights to the winos in the parking lot.)

Second: The job title...

Let me see...I was *FREEZING* my a** off going in and out of that cold refrigerator/icebox.

Plus, I was stocking shelves, mopping floors, and calming the drunks down. As you can see, there's no glory in this. But it's better than my old job. My senior year is off to a good start.

I forgot to mention, I was a drummer in the band last year in the 11th grade.

Over the summer, Major K.S. wanted me to be a drum major.

Drum major (1980)

So, I learned all the steps—how to choreograph all the moves, how to twirl the baton, and how to lead the band.

Now I just became the 1980 drum major for the Compton High Tarbabes Marching Band and that was a first in my family.

We had no cheerleaders or nothing like that and I would have to say, it was rather fun. Every Friday night, we marched at the football games.

Should I slip this in? We were UNDEFEATED and # 1 that year? But we lost the championship to a rival team from Long Beach ☹. The bummer was, just like with baseball, nobody came to see me at none of my games.

Now let's get back to the timeline. Sexy V is still being sexy, but I'm getting a little bored. Let me see...

In November, I took her to the homecoming dance. That was alright. Now it's February, and we're at the senior dance. I was kinda bored, so I took her home. (It wasn't too far from the dance.) We sat in the car, but I can't even tell you what we talked about. I know for some reason she didn't want to do the hanky panky. 😞

I looked her dead in the eye, and I asked her, "Do you want to Exit Stage Right?"

Then she looked me dead in the eye and Exited Stage Right.

That was the last time we talked.

After that, I went back to the dance. There I was, standing there all alone.

I thought to myself (in my "Old Man" voice...), "You big dummy!"

Here we go again. I'm in love once more. (Okay, get your laugh out.) This time, it's actually locally grown. In other words, she's right down the street. (Wow! It's funny because it's the same house where I met Sexy V.) So, let me think of a name for her...

(I'll call her Foxy D.)

What can I say about her? Every night after work, she meets me at the **infamous garage**.

Same place... same time... same groove. Hee hee...

Moving on...

It's prom season—again. I've already been to one. Now I'm starting to feel like a carpool dummy.

Seems like everybody wants to use me for the prom. But I don't mind because I like wearing tuxedos. Here we go...

Prom #1: My brother René's girlfriend had two sisters that were twins, but they didn't look alike.

His girlfriend asked me if I could take one of them to the prom. How can I describe them?

One of them looked like a swimsuit contestant. The other one— like Plain Jane. So, I got excited because I was thinking it would be the swimsuit contestant, but it was short-lived. Then reality hit me. I ended up with Plain Jane. She was alright, but she still wasn't the swimsuit contestant.

Prom #2: Okay, I had to take Foxy D to her high school prom. It was cool. I got to wear another white tuxedo, which I kinda liked. I actually looked pretty good in it too.

Did we take pictures? Yea, of course, we did. Let me hold off on these proms for a second.

Back to this **"Black Curtain."** The issue still hangs over me like a dark cloud. I can't seem to shake it. And there's nobody I can talk to about it. This is really affecting me.

26

Why am I getting so bored with the girls? What is it? Is it me? Or is it that d*mn **"Black Curtain"**?

Prom # 3: Finally, it's my prom. But here's the situation. On one hand, I have Foxy D down the street.

(Let me think—same time, same place.) That one works!

On the other hand, Baby Girl J called and asked me to take her to our prom. I have not talked to her since the 10th grade.

(No frills, no thrills.)

So, what should I do? Be happy or be bored? *Hmmm...*

Well, I figured it out. I'll be bored at the prom and happy at the after prom. Other words, I'll take Baby Girl J to the prom, and then Foxy D to the after prom.

There we were, "Cruising down the street..." but not in a 6-4.

I'm driving my mother's car, but now it's got some battle scars. The mirror is hanging off on the passenger's side. But you know what? She really didn't care. Of course, we was late, and yes, we did take pictures. And what did I get out of all this?

No pictures from the first prom, Plain Jane from the second prom (same place, same time), Foxy D on the third prom, and at my prom? We were so late! But I bet you we got those $60 chicken dinners!

Graduation (1980)

27

It's the end of the year, and it's graduation time.

I had enough credits.

So, Mr. Bad A** had decided to take off first period for the whole year. (I don't recommend that to nobody.)

But the weird thing was, my mother and father came to my graduation. I was so happy. But watch out! There's a joker in the deck.

I was excited because my father promised me a gold chain for my graduation. Nothing spectacular, just a regular gold chain. (But here's where the joker popped out.) I never got my gold chain—and that made me hate my father for the next 20+ years. Parents, please don't do this to your kids. (Never promise them anything.) An old saying is, "Promises are made to be broken."

Now the entrepreneur is back on it. It was My second DJ gig. (And of course, no money changed hands.)

Well, I'm DJing our graduation after party, which Nissy hooked me up with. No more 8-track tapes. I had one turntable and no headphones.

I was using my brother André's stereophonic receiver and speakers. If you don't know what a stereophonic receiver is, it's what we call a power amplifier nowadays.

(But it was nowhere near 1000 watts.) I was rocking the house! But every time I put on The Sugarhill Gang's "8th Wonder" song (of course, I played it three times), the whole system would shut down.

Then everybody would turn and look at me. And I had that dumb look on my face. (What happened?) I found out later that I was overloading the system by playing it too loud.

Now let's switch gears. I think I'm done with falling in love. Me and Foxy D done foxed our last time. No more "same place, same time" after work in the **infamous garage**.

Now back to the hood. (You know, the job at Gage and San Pedro.)

I moved up to the register, and I'm doing good now. But I did something I don't normally do. Let me explain before I tell you.

It was a Friday night. I was on my register, and my coworker was on his register, which was side by side. Then he shows me a trick that he does on his register. Let me break it down...

Somebody brings a soda and chips to the register. He charges the customer the correct price, which is $1.60. But he rings up only 60 cents. Then he takes $1.00 and slips it in his pocket. So, he does this the rest of the night. I (Mr. Bad A**) did the same thing. I knew there were cameras on, so I was slick. But I wasn't that slick.

I stood there and thought to myself, "Oh...So THIS is what you would call stealing."

Now the next day, I came in to work on a payday.

My manager called me in the back. He had a funny look on his face.

Then he said, "You already got your paycheck. And by the way—you're fired!"

I thought to myself (in my "Old Man" voice...), "You big dummy!"

The one time I followed my coworker and I got fired. I told on him, and he didn't even get fired. I learned my lesson. No more stealing for me. That was my first and my last time. Now I'm on poverty row. What the heck am I going to do now?

One day, I remember driving in my mother's car. I decided to be a fireman.

This is the only family picture with all of us (except Keith).
Back row: Joseph, me, and André
Middle row: Monique, my mother, and Arnett
Bottom row: Carlos, Sherreé, René

So, I'm thinking you can go to a fire station and get an application. But that was short-lived because when I got there, they told me that you had to go through the proper channels. Well, that career was over. Alright, let me think...

I'll go to college (Compton College). But there's a twist on it. I heard that you could get grants for going to school. All you have to do is enroll. Well, I registered. I went to college for a whole whopping three weeks. That means I never went to a class. I just hung out, walked around campus, and ate lunch. I never bought a book. I never even carried a Pee Chee folder. The problem was they gave me the check too fast. (It was only a few hundred bucks.)

One day while I was eating a burger during lunch (which was all day), I said to myself, "I don't think I'm cut out for this college stuff."

So, I finally made a decision. College was not for me. I shook the dust from my shoes and that was my whole college career. There would be no fraternities, no college activities, no nothing.

I was one grant check and done. LOL... ☺

CHAPTER 2: THA DAYZ OF WAYBACK

There's a new chapter in my life. I'm still on Poverty Row. No job and no love life. (Not at the moment.) Now here's a bright point. I just discovered credit. Wow! They gave me credit at a local department store. Here's the twist on it. My mother wanted me to have her Granada. But only on one condition— if I bought her a washer and dryer on credit. So, I'm driving MY Granada. That was easy to do. But eventually, I was gonna have to pay for it somehow.

Now it's the Fall of 1980, and I (Mr. Entrepreneur) got another DJ gig. (Of course, no money changed hands.) This time it's for my brother André's house party. He happened to be living in the hood on Gage—and I did something at the party that I never ever done again. I wrote this rap and performed it while I was DJing. I felt kinda weird rapping. (And besides, nobody was listening to me anyway.) After the rap, I figured it out...

Rapping was not my cup of tea.

So, after the party, I was on my way home when I stopped at a traffic light.

After the light turned green, something told me, "Don't move."

It was like I was frozen for a moment. I couldn't take my foot off the brake. I turned to my left and saw a Deuce and a Quarter at a high speed. If you don't know what that means, it's a Buick Electra 225. (The 2 is the "Deuce" and 25 is the "Quarter.")

Do you get it? A Deuce and a Quarter.

Now back to the story. I glanced to my right, and the Oldsmobile next to me pulled off. At that exact same moment, the Deuce and a Quarter came speeding through the red light.

And then it happened. KABOOM!

I don't know what happened to the people in the car.

But all I know is that Oldsmobile got knocked into the next block. In other words, they got tore the f**k up!

As I sat there behind the steering wheel in shock, I said to myself...

"Wow... That was supposed to be me."

(I hear that same bell sound. "Ding!" Miracle!)

Let's keep moving forward. Now I got me a car, and I'm starting to visit a couple of 18 and over clubs.

So, the first one I went to was called **The Workshop**, which was located on 91st and Western in LA. The cool thing about this one is they had a lighted danced floor, just like the one in the movie *Saturday Night Fever*. That night I met this fine girl, and I do mean FINE GIRL from Altadena.

And guess what? I'm not going to say I'm in love, but I'm in love again. (It's not real love, but maybe real lust.) So, let me think of a name for her...

(I'll call her Miss Altadena.)

What can I say about her? If you don't know where the city of Altadena is, it's right above good old Pasadena.

(The Rose Bowl...Should I say more?) But back to Miss Altadena. She was kinda sexy, and freaky. And the funny thing is we used to always make out in the living room while her mother and sisters were in the back room. But we never got caught.

Hee hee...

Now, let's get to the other 18 and over club. It was called **Eve After Dark** and was located on the second floor, which was above a barbershop, flower shop, and income tax shop.

I thought to myself, "What a strange name for a club. **Eve After Dark**?" (I didn't get it then, and I still don't get it, LOL.)

It was located on Avalon and El Segundo, near Watts and Compton— but still in LA. At the time, I had no idea this particular club would also be a part of my destiny. Now back to the club. It was cool, but it didn't have no lighted floor. Nothing spectacular happened that night for me. I didn't meet no girls...

Oh, I forgot! I did meet one. So, let me think of a name for her...

(I'll call her Sweet Chocolate.)

Sweet Chocolate with the red car. What can I say about her? Well, she was "chocolate." LOL. ☺

She had the frills; she got the thrills... It was cool. But as they say, "All fun things must come to an end." Let's move on.

It felt like I was meant to do something else in life. But I just didn't know what it was.

So, I hooked up with a buddy of mine named Cool Hand. He was into DJing parties and dances.

He also wanted me to work with him promoting his dances.

But all he really had me doing was the rough stuff, like hanging posters and loading speakers. But he never let me DJ.

(Maybe he did once or twice when he went to the bathroom.)

Speaking of hanging posters, let me describe what hanging a poster is all about. First of all, you have an almost 5-pound staple gun (about 12 inches long) and it puts out ½ inch staples. Then you hammer it like a hammer. You also have 3-inch nails with a round piece of cardboard washer, so it doesn't tear through the poster. Then you have a handful of posters. That's another 20 pounds.

(And did I say this was illegal— posting signs on city property?)

I remember this one dance we were promoting in the city of Montclair, California. We used to drive out there at about 2 o'clock in the morning. Then we would get out and hang posters on every pole. There we were, sneaking on the corners, looking like criminals hanging posters.

So, I'm sure "us" looked very suspicious in the middle of the night. (Of course, no money changed hands.)

I said to myself, "There's got to be a better way to make a buck, 'cause I ain't making no bucks here."

Oh, did I fail to mention? I also got approved for a new credit card! But... after all the swipes and making no payments, did I say that my A-1 credit turned to Z-1 credit? Should I really say why? (Insufficient funds due to the Jobless-81Act.)

I thought to myself, "Oh...So THIS is what you call bad credit."

I remembered seeing this lawyer in a commercial on TV.

Yes, TV. (No social media in those days.) I don't remember nothing about this commercial, but I remember him saying, "No Bills."

So here it is. I'm in this lawyer's office with my head down. I'm talking to the man himself— "Mr. No Bills."

I was terrified, thinking the credit police was looking for me.

It felt like it was the end of the world.

So, Mr. No Bills looked at my credit history and said, "You have about $2,500 worth of debt."

Then he said something that kinda eased my pain.

(In my mind, I was already on my way to credit jail.)

He kinda chuckled and said, "You know, they can't arrest you for this."

I almost fell out of my seat after he said that.

I thought to myself, "Oh, really?"

So, I stood up and walked out of his office with my head up and my chest out.

Then I said, "I'm baaaaack..."

Let's speed up the timeline. A few months have passed, and we're still hanging posters. (And I'm still working for free.) I didn't know it at the time, but by doing all this "free" hard work, I was laying the foundation for my future.

But the "free" hard work was not over...not yet.

Wreckin' Cru: 1981

It was a Friday night, and my buddy Cool Hand wanted me to go to this club with him and meet some people. The club? **Eve After Dark**. Wow! Didn't I just talk about this club?

So anyway, we made it there, and I met this guy named Lonzo (the "Old Man of the Cru," LOL) and a guy named The Unknown DJ. But I called him Unknown. You gonna like this. They offered me a job! But there was a catch to it. In order for me to be in the Wreckin' Cru (the DJs of the **Eve After Dark**), they challenged me to see if I would be down with the crew. They wanted me to go out and put a "rip" on the rival's posters. (The rival crew was called Uncle Jam's Army.) They offered to pay me 25 cents a poster.

Now let me explain what a "rip" is. You go out all over town looking for posters. Then you tear the bottom half of the poster off so nobody can see the date, place, and time of the party. So, I accepted the challenge. But by me being Mr. Entrepreneur, I had a plan. For 25 cents? I'm going to put the "rip" on everybody's poster! So, me and my neighbor Big Chuck hopped into the Granada. (Remember, I have a car now.)

So, we rolling and we "ripping" everybody's posters.

But then we got to this one corner on Western and Century Blvd., right in front of the donut shop. Me and Big Chuck were ripping a poster when two guys walked up on us. Let me set the scene...

"Two people without any weapons and two people with 5-pound staple guns in their hands..."

34

And must I say Big Chuck is 6'7"?

So, we was standing there looking at each other.

I couldn't believe who it was...

The leader of the rival crew! Uncle Jam's Army!

There they were, talking sh*t.

Never realized we were from Compton, not LA. Yea, they was talking that sh*t, but they didn't do a d*mn thing about us ripping their posters. (I guess we proved ourselves that day.)

The next day, we rolled back up to the **Eve After Dark**.

I told Lonzo and Unknown, "We got a trunk full of posters."

So, me and Unknown went downstairs to count them. We walked across the street. Then I opened up the trunk.

He said, "Man, whose all these posters? I didn't ask for all these..." (There was over 300 posters.)

I said to Unknown, "I did my thang."

And they sure paid me for all them posters too. I got the job. I guess I am now an official member of the Wreckin' Cru.

So, that next Friday, I was on the job DJing. I had the last slot, which was from 2 a.m. to closing (which was around 3:30 a.m. to 4 a.m., depending on the crowd).

Now let's talk about the pay. It might not be much, but I can look at it two ways. Being broke or not being broke. Having gas money or riding the bus. (Buses are not my way of life.) What was the pay? 50 bucks a night on Friday and Saturday and sometimes Sunday. Let me think about it. I DJ for only two hours—not bad. Did I also say I get paid separately for hanging posters? Okay, that works. Then there's the fringe benefits. (This is what you would call a perfect opportunity to meet girls.) That's what I'm talking about! Count me in...

Now, this was a weird thing. There was a DJ named Dr. Rock who had the prime spot from 12 a.m. to 2 a.m. (Must I say he had been there for a few years?)

I'm not gonna say it's me, but the young kid (which was me) came in on fire! After that weekend of him being the top DJ, the next week, he was gone. Suddenly, there I was, pushed into the prime slot. (That was a fast promotion.)

Later on, Lonzo told me that Dr. Rock had moved to Texas.

So, Friday rolls around again. Unknown has the slot from 10 p.m. to midnight, and I got the main slot.

I was a little nervous the first week, but now I'm kinda

rocking the house! And did I say the club was upstairs? You have 200-300 young people sweating their a** off, so we called it "The Sweat Box." The DJ booth was at the back of the club behind tinted glass. That was cool. I felt like a little star! Now I get to mix on grown folks' equipment.

I had two turntables and a mixer with a round knob for the crossfader. (Which is how you mix the song from the left turntable to the right turntable.) Plus, we had little speakers in there for monitors so we can hear the outside music. I was in Heaven now. Me and Unknown are really clicking, and it went on like this for the next couple of years. Let's get back to the present time. How can I describe the **Eve After Dark**...?

Hmmm...It reminds me a lot of the movie called *Peyton Place.*

(If you've never seen the movie, it was nothing but drama.)

Okay, let's start with the drama—not real drama, but we're just setting the characters up.

Let's get to the cast. You got Lonzo, the club owner (but he didn't own the building), and his girl, who is Lady V. (She runs the ticket booth.) Next up, we have Unknown, who DJ's and runs the bar. And may I add, his two sexy female employees who keep everybody happy by selling the chips and sodas? Then, of course, there's Unknown's girl, Queen C, who also sells tickets. (But don't forget her name.) There it is. That's the cast. Oh! I forgot about me—the new guy on the block.

Let's get back to the pay. I'm talking about the extra pay. I'm talking about the fringe benefits. First up, (I have to laugh at myself on this one.) I meet my first two girls at the club. They are sisters. Let me think of a name for them...

(I'll call them Pixie and Dixie.)

I couldn't handle both of them, so I had to call in the reserves.

I hooked up Pixie with Big Chuck. I kinda liked Dixie because she was a little thick. This girl was all about the frills and the thrills, but she could also be a little ghetto.

These are the kind of benefits that this job is offering (no 401K), and I love it.

Now me and Unknown are hanging tough.

We doing all kinds of things together, but we don't meet girls together. Why? Because I would kinda call him an L-7.

(If you don't know what that means, that's a square.) In other words, he don't cheat on his girl.

We did have somewhat of a rendezvous. Meaning two girls lived on my street. Let me think of a name for them...

(I'll call one Light-Skinned L and the other one Pretty P.)

So, we hung out at his apartment in Bixby Knolls, which was in the rich part of Long Beach, CA. Once we got there, I said, "Let's separate."

I took Light-Skinned L to the bathroom. You know, like... shower? (What is it with me and these bathrooms?) Of course, I did my thing. There was frills and thrills, but in Unknown's case, there was no hanky panky. He and Pretty P just sat and talked. Now back to the **Eve**...

It's 1981—Christmas time. We're still rocking the house. Lonzo decided to bring in a rapper for a live show. We was always trying to do something different at the club, staying two steps ahead of everybody else. (Like that Army one.) So, we had Kurtis Blow (one of the hot rappers at the time) and his DJ fly in from New York. If I'm not mistaken, this was his first show in LA. The performances went well, and I even learned a few things from them.

"What things?" you may ask.

It was the first time I ever seen a DJ "scratch" on a turntable live. If you don't know what scratching is, it's when the record is spinning on the turntable, somebody grabs it and stops it with their hand. Then, while they are moving the record back and forth, it causes it to make a sound. That's scratching. Do you get it? But before the show, during the soundcheck, his DJ (which was his brother, Davy D.) actually gave me a one-on-one lesson on how to scratch. He showed me how to take the rubber mats off the turntable and replace them with scratch pads and wax paper underneath. Then he showed me how to glue a penny on top of each needle (we used two turntables and two needles) to keep them from jumping all over the place. That was Scratching 101.

So, me being Mr. Entrepreneur, took it, and I never stopped running with it.

Where did I run to? I would say, being one of the first DJs to scratch in LA. I scratched up a storm.

So, me and Unknown were trying to think of ways to be very creative and make some extra money.

To be honest with you, it was never about the money.
(But if you mention girls? *Hmmm...*)

1982

Me and Unknown have gotten really tight. We was like a pre-Dynamic Duo, like the characters from the TV show *Batman*. (You know, Batman and Robin.) The reason why I say this is because it's crazy—that Unknown's real name is Andre. And when the real Dynamic Duo teams up in the future, his name will also be Andre. Wow! Was this some kind of premonition or something? (That makes me want to just drop the mic!)

One day we were hanging out at The Flip Store in Hollywood, California. Inside there, they used to blast the music very loud.

Remember the show *Laverne and Shirley*— how Laverne wore the letter L on her blouse? That's how the clothes were in The Flip Store. They had a small letter "F" on their T-shirts. But the funny thing is, we never bought anything from this store. It was just one of the hangouts in Hollywood.

As we walked inside, there was a song playing at the front of the store. It was just the beat bumping. It wasn't bad. Actually, sounded pretty good.

So, we walked to the back of the store. When I heard the music there, I was stunned. All you could hear was scratching—and it was like, incredible.

We asked the guy at the counter, "Who in the h*ll is that?"

He told us that it was a new song called "Buffalo Gals."

We looked at each other and said, "Wow!"

We drove all over Hollywood looking for that song and finally found it at Tower Records. You know what happened next?

On Friday night at the club, I wore that song out. As soon as I started playing it, the crowd went nuts. I could see them dancing on top of the rails. They was standing and looking inside of the DJ booth with their fingerprints on the glass.

(But no girls put "them" on the glass, LOL.)

When I said to the people, "Tally Hoooo..." they said, "Sh*t!" Then, when I said, "Tally HO Tally HOO!" they yelled, "BULLSH*T!"

I played it quite a few times, and they just loved it. How could I tell they loved it? Because Lonzo hated it.

As he was listening to it, he asked me, "Why are you playing that song so many times?"

I said, "You're just old. Look at the crowd."

So, speaking of the crowd, I did my usual fringe benefits search, and "Chi-ching!"

There she was—the cutie of the projects. Why did I say that? Because she lived in Nickerson Gardens. (If you don't know where that is, it's the projects located in Watts.)

But here's the thing. There were two girls again. This time, they weren't sisters, but they both lived in Nickerson Gardens. I had to call out the reserves again. But before I go on with the story, let me think of a name for them...

(I'll call them M + M—one Sweet M, and one Miss M.)

Now back to the reserve call. I called Big Chuck to the rescue and gave him Miss M because I liked Sweet M. Did I say this one wasn't so freely with the frills and thrills? I had to work hard for this one. And the funny thing is, later on, they ended up working at the club with us. But you know that didn't last too long. It was a little too close for comfort. (That was messing up my fringe benefits.)

But let's skip to the next meeting. This one was fine. And I mean capital "F" fine! Let me think of a name for her...

(I'll call her Pocahontas.)

Everybody in the club wanted her.

Everybody thought I had her because I played a joke on Lonzo one time. We were leaving a restaurant (Denny's) one night.

Me and Pocahontas was in my car, and Lonzo was in his car, driving next to me.

She said she was tired, so she laid her head in my lap.

This is where the joker comes in. Lonzo is driving, and he's looking in my car, and he doesn't see Pocahontas, only me. I'm making a facial expression and pointing down. When he saw that, his eyes got as big as donuts!

But in reality, there was no frills and no thrills. So, that few weeks of showing off Pocahontas came to an abrupt end.

Wow! She was really fine! How did I let that get away?

I thought to myself (in my "Old Man" voice...), "You big dummy!"

I hate to change the subject, but let's put the girls on the back burner for a moment.

39

Oh, I forgot to tell you how I got my DJ name. (Well, it all started back when my family were sharecroppers...Naw, they weren't sharecroppers, LOL.)

Let's go back to 1981. You know— the time when the wet curl was out. Remember the S curl and the Jheri curl? And everybody—including me— had at least one Prince outfit in their closet? You know the purple jacket, white shirt with the long thing hanging and the ruffled cuffs? The tight—oops— I meant the sexy leather pants? And what about the lace gloves? That was all me, except for the high heeled boots, LOL...

Wait a minute. Let me calm down before I start singing his song, "I Would Die for You." Or better yet, you do remember the Beat It or the Thriller jacket? (Of course, I had a black Beat It jacket.) I'm getting just too excited.

Let me get back to my DJ name. People don't know this, but I was originally called "The Master Rocker." That came from a song by an artist named Bernard Wright. It stayed with me until Unknown gave me a new one.

How did he come up with my new name? Well, one day, we was listening to this song on a 12-inch vinyl called "Genius of Love" by the Tom Tom Club. But on the B side of the 12-inch, there was an artist named Mr. Yellow.

At the very beginning of his song, the first thing you heard was "Yella."

After hearing just that, Unknown turned and smiled, then said to me, "Yella—That's your new name right there."

Later on, it became DJ Yella.

And that's the day we started to think of "new and different ways..."

What do I mean by that? *Hmmm*...I practiced more on my mixing and scratching. I wanted to perfect my style. I wanted to be faster and quicker on the cut than anybody. On the mic, you had to be spontaneous and quick on your feet. So, I learned a way to perfect my voice. In other words, you have to just talk on the d*mn mic. (DJs don't usually talk on the mic these days.)

Mind Blowing

Now let's get to some meat and potatoes. Me and Unknown had our thinking caps on after an all-night session playing Donkey Kong. (Not on PlayStation, because it hadn't been invented yet.) We was on a game system called Intellivision that the Sears Department store used to sell. Suddenly, an idea came to me.

I said, "You know something? We should make a mixtape of Rap and Techno music. Ain't nobody done that yet! But let's make it different somehow. Maybe I should scratch and mix for a whole 60-minute tape!"

Then he said, "D*mn boy, that's a good idea! We'll call it 'Designer Music!'"

Lonzo wanted to get in on the action. So, he bought a tape duplicator, where you have to sit there for 60 minutes and record one side at a time, Side A, and Side B.

I guess that means we have to split the profits three ways. (That would become a problem later on.) Back to the mixtape.

We started selling copies of them at the club. (Not online, but we did it the old school way— at the DJ booth.) Surprisingly, it was a big hit in the club. We sold out of Volume 1.

Now we had to make Volume 2. The problem was, you had to sit there hour by hour, dubbing the tapes.

That worked on the first volume, But, on the second volume, the hours got sh*tty. Then the money got funny. Why?

Because it's hard to split up $5 a tape, plus the price of the blank tape, and the cost of the duplicator. And that's when the problem came in. Other words, that $5 didn't go very far. I don't know if we ever got to Volume 3 or not. So, that well-planned business venture didn't last long. Since we're in this mood of rocking the club, here's another thing that didn't last long.

There was a fad called the "60s Mod Look" or something like that. It kinda reminds you of that Gothic look. This is where you wear the black trench coat, the black hat, and black boots. They do the little dance like they're marching in line. (Which was cool to look at.) Bobbing their heads while moving their hands up and down to the song "Whip It" by Devo. Here's one more thing that didn't last long.

There was this girl I met. Let me think of a name for her...

(I'll call her Freaky J.)

And here we go again. There was two of them. (What's with these two girls at a time?) Once again, I called in for the reserves.

DJing Compton High's Dance (1982)

Big Chuck came to the rescue. Let me think of a name for the friend...

(I'll call her Crazy P.)

So Freaky J had her own apartment near Hollywood or someplace like that. Now, these two was real cool. And I must say, of course, she had ALL the frills and thrills. Instead of making this story long, let's cut to the chase.

It was a Thursday. The Compton High School student council invited me to DJ during their lunch period. I was there to do some promotions. (I'm back at my alma mater. Wow! My old stomping grounds!) So, on this particular day, when I was leaving the school, I seen this girl walking home. (Just to let you know, she was 18.)

I had noticed her while I was DJing at lunch. She had her eyes on me and I did something I never done before.

I pulled up on her and said, "You need a ride home?"

To my surprise, she said, "Yes."

Before I get to her name, let me tell you about the vehicle I'm in. I'm driving in Lonzo's old school van. (It wasn't a minivan.) It looks like the van on the *Scooby-Doo* cartoon that Shaggy drove. He lets me drive it so I can carry the DJ equipment and hang posters. And me, being Mr. Entrepreneur, I added a third reason with a plan. This will become my frills and thrills spot.

So, back to this girl. I have not yet described her. Did I say she was bad? But not like the song, "She's a Bad Mama Jama." I mean bad, capital "B" bad. Let me think of a name for her...

(I'll call her PYT.)

If you don't know what that means, it's "pretty young thing."

So, I took PYT to her house. We sat there and talked in the van for a little while. I decided to invite her to the club that night.

I told her, "It's Thursday, and it might be kind of slow."

She said, "Cool. Just pick me up."

Later that night, we pulled up to the club at about 9:30. And did I say there was a joker in this deck? As we walked in (she had on some nice leather pants), Big Chuck whispered in my ear...

"Freaky J is in the DJ booth!"

At that moment, I wished I could just click my heels three times and disappear!

(*There's no place like home, there's no place like home...*)

I told Big Chuck to take PYT to the DJ booth! I needed to come up with a plan and QUICK! Let me think...

Unknown is DJing now. I could take his spot, and then he could take my spot. Then I can just put the headphones on, and I'm good. BAM! That's the plan.

I started walking up to the DJ booth very slowly. But before I open this door, I have a choice to make...

Stage Left? Or Stage Right?

I opened the door, and what did I see? At Stage Left was Freaky J and PYT! They were sitting next to each other! At Stage Right, I see Unknown, with the headphones on, bobbing his head. I made my choice...

What did I do? I ran to Stage Right. But here's when the joker popped out. Unknown would not let me DJ! He even laughed about it. He thought this sh*t was funny. Suddenly the man that had a plan had no plan at all.

I walked out of the DJ booth, ran to the mirror against the wall, and screamed. Then I turned around and looked at Big Chuck.

I thought to myself (in my "Old Man" voice...), "You big dummy!"

But this time, I wasn't the dummy. Freaky J came on her own. I didn't invite her. She got too big for her britches. That was the last time I talked to Freaky J.

After the club closed, I took PYT home. While we were parked in the van, she looked me dead in the eye. I looked her dead in the eye. Then I thought of this song by Grover Washington, Jr. (featuring Bill Withers), called "Just the Two of Us."

Hee hee... (Sometimes I just have to laugh at myself.)

And did I say she had frills and Chi-Ching thrills? But you know me... "All good things must come to an end."

Now let me give you some more history. After another all-night session of Donkey Kong, Unknown came up with this brilliant idea.

He said, "Hey! Let's do a remix to "Blinded by Science" by Thomas Dolby!"

I looked up at him and said, "Ughhhh..."

You know I'm trying to get to the next level of this game that I cannot pass.

Anyway, I nodded my head. I said, "Okay, that sounds cool."

(I'm not going to jump up and say, "Oh wee wow—Gee whillikers!") My mind is still stuck on this gorilla and the ladder.

The next day, Unknown did his research and found out the song was on Capitol Records, which was right there in Hollywood.

So, after checking it out, he ended up getting us a meeting the following week with one of the A and R people. But this time, there's a lawyer joker in the deck. I'll explain that to you later.

The next week rolled around. We were on the way to this 11 o'clock meeting. We rolling on the 110 Freeway in his little 2-door convertible Fiat.

(He must be ballin'. He lives in Bixby Knolls.)

The top was down, and we was cruising. We was excited as h*ll...

Then all of a sudden, he said, "One-Time is behind us flashing his lights." (That is what you call the po-lice.)

So, this motorcycle cop pulled us over. Our excitement came to a quick stop.

We both looked at each other and said, "What the f*ck?"

The cop walked up and said, "I pulled you over because of that bottle between your legs."

Unknown picked up the bottle and said, "Oh, this bottle? It's just root beer."

Then the officer said, "Have a nice day."

We looked at each other and said, "Did we just get rain on our parade?"

We made it to the meeting, and it actually went very well. The next day we was on it. I finished the mix, and we went back to Capitol Records. Now, this is where the lawyer joker pops out. What do I mean by that? We didn't have a d*mn lawyer.

So, this was the deal. We make the remix. Then they pay us $1200. But there was some fine print on this contract that we didn't understand.

(You know, it's those little words people never read.)

Actually, we didn't read it, and this is why the joker slapped us in the face. In other words, what it was saying was...

When we turned in the remix, we would get $200 upfront and the $1000 balance after the artist's approval...

Guess what? Days later, we didn't get the approval. In the end, we only made $200. That's why when you do paperwork, have a lawyer. That was a bummer.

All the hard work I put into that song, and it was a really nice mix. I thought I was going to be the first club DJ to make a remix on a major label. The $1200 would have been cool. But we walked away with 200 bucks. What did we do after this? We went to the bank and definitely cashed that check.

Then I said to myself, "This ain't gonna stop me."

Let's switch back to the **Eve**.

We still rocking every weekend at the club. Lonzo came up with an idea.

"Let's do a dance at the Queen Mary Hotel."

If you don't know what the Queen Mary is, it's an old boat made in 1929, and it's docked in Long Beach, California. But it's kinda high class. So, I did all the promotions for the dance. (That means hanging 500 posters.)

The dance sold out! And here it is...1100 people packed on

the Queen Mary. I'm standing in front of the turntables listening to the crowd make all this noise. And they all were staring at me.

From the **infamous garage** to the Queen Mary...

I felt right at home. Locked and loaded.

I slipped my headphones on and everything went silent. I felt like a star. (It might be just local, but still, I felt like a star.)

Then I scratched the beat of my first song, "Genius of Love." The people went nuts.

There was so much excitement on the boat, I forgot all about my fringe benefits. I didn't even catch a dead fly. I just got caught up in the moment. (Shame on me.)

If It Ain't Ruff

When it came to the Wreckin' Cru, there was a nice side, and then there was this side...

Let me tell you this tale—excuse me, this story about a DJ crew called V.P. Productions. Earlier I told you about putting a "rip" on somebody's posters. (Yea, we did that a few times.) Now this crew has totally disrespected our posters. There's not even a name for this action. This kinda action is so low it's time for an award. We call it the Smack Down Award. (In other words, "It's time to whup some a**.")

Now let me get back to this VP Productions. I was out hanging posters, and I seen something that just didn't look right. Somebody was hanging posters on top of ours.

They didn't even have the decency to pull our posters down. They just hung right over them and didn't even cover ours all the way up. All the hard work I done to hang them, and these fools straight up hung their posters over ours? Are you kidding me? So, I snatched all theirs down and took one back to the club.

We had this sit-down meeting (in a circle like we were in the movie, *The Godfather*) about this situation.

We looked at the top of their poster and said, "This is the problem— VP Productions."

Then we looked at the bottom of the poster and said, "This is the solution— the date, and place."

And what's the plan? Show up and show out at their event.

A couple of weeks had passed, and I don't remember the

46

month, but I remember it was a Saturday the 21st— the day of their dance. Let me set the scene for you. It's like a black and white gangster movie.

We loaded up two carloads of what we're gonna call "friends."

We rolled up to Los Angeles Southwest College around 4 o'clock. It was about three hours before the dance.

Now picture this: At least ten people in black walking up to the door of their event.

(Now you know there's a hothead joker in this deck.)

And that hothead was Super V. But on with the movie.

We walked right in there on 'em while they were setting up. Lonzo, since he's the oldest of the Cru, was talking s**t about them hanging on top of our posters.

That VP crew was looking quite nervous in their t-shirt and hat coordination. Now I would like to tell you it's gonna be a happy ending, but VOILÀ!

The hothead joker pops out! Super V didn't just talk s**t. He started whuppin' on them!

I know in their minds, they wanted to say, "Feet, don't fail me now!"

Since Super V started this mess, now we had to end it. Their feet sure failed them that day! They were stuck in that spot. We got to tossin' them all over the building! Hats were flying everywhere! We found out later they still had the dance that night (it turned out to be a big flop anyway)—even after the beat down. That was the last time we heard from that crew.

Let's get to some steak and gravy. It's a few months later, and the club is still being packed out on the weekends.

The clientele is starting to come from all over–from places like West Covina, Montclair, and even Orange County. And you know what that means. The fringe benefits is now a variety pack.

Not to be bragging, but I'm really starting to get a name for myself. Now I'm kinda being recognized as one of the hottest DJs in LA. People are starting to call me to do events outside the club. Here's one example. A manager at a Chuck E. Cheese restaurant (the pizza place) gave me an offer to DJ for a couple of hours every Saturday for the kids. But you know me, I had a plan. Since we have the new clientele at the club, I did my fringe benefit search one night. You guessed it. There she was across the room. Staring at me, with her blue eyes and blonde hair.

(It looked like it was blowing in the wind.) All I could think of was pointing my two fingers and singing, "I Would Die For U" by Prince, LOL. She kinda reminds me of the girl from The Brady Bunch. Let me think of a name for her...

(I'll just call her Marsha Marsha Marsha.) ☺

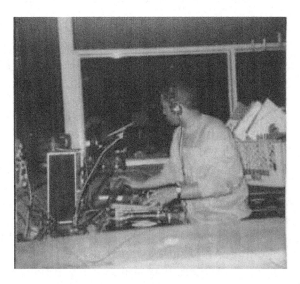

DJing at the Eve after Dark (1982)

The cool thing was, she was down with hanging out with me while I did the Chuck E. Cheese stuff. And what's so cool about that? We was rolling in the van! Hee hee...

Back to the Chuck E. Cheese "concerts."

The kids actually enjoyed me playing the music. They were breakdancing and doing all kinds of stupid stuff. The parents appreciated what I was doing because their little ones was looking up at me like I was some kind of celebrity. Deep down in my heart, it felt pretty good. I was using my talents to give back to the children.

I also did other events for free at junior and senior high schools, and they just loved it. I had a feeling I had to give back.

Funny thing, I never dreamed of being a DJ. It came naturally to me. While I was out doing all these events, Unknown, the master marketer, was hitting the pavement looking for more DJ opportunities.

He heard about some people from Motown Records that was looking for me to do some scratching on one of their artists' songs. We hooked it up, and I found myself at Motown Studios in Hollywood!

We walked into one of the control rooms and I said, "Wow! This is nice! This is what a real 24-track mixing board looks like!"

(I guess this is where the big boys hang out.)

So, I put our mixer and turntable at the end of the mixing board. When I started scratching with it, I felt embarrassed because the fader made a little noise, a static sound. I had to think fast on my feet.

I told the engineer, "Let me plug directly into your board because this mixer is not working."

So here it is. I had to scratch right from the mixing board with no headphones. That was a very unique thing to do at the time.

The other unique thing we did was we had them burn the acapella vocals directly to a blank record. That's what I used to scratch on this song. The funny thing is, I don't recall the name of the artist, but I do remember this. I finally made it to a major label by scratching. And that was just the beginning.

As time moved on, there was more drama at the club.

I met this girl one day and a funny thing, she happened to live upstairs above Unknown. That was kinda unusual. But let me think of a name for her...

(I'll call her Miss Bixby Knolls.)

This is what makes the story funny. First, we are upstairs in her place. Guess where we are? In the bathroom.

Of course, there was hanky panky. (I must have a fetish about bathrooms, LOL.) What is it, washing your hands or taking a shower?

Before we move on, let me describe Unknown. He's from Detroit, and he don't believe in locking doors. Why? I have no idea. Since I've briefed you on this, let's keep it going.

Me and Miss Bixby Knolls go downstairs to Unknown's apartment. I was about to knock.

Then I said, "*Hmmm... He's from Detroit.*"

So, I turned the knob, and of course, it's unlocked. I opened the door, and I didn't get five steps in. It looked like he just

49

appeared there, standing in front of his room door with his eyes as big as Krispy Kreme donuts. He's looking real nervous and very suspicious. Why? I had no idea.

Then I said, "What's going on here?"

He's fumbling for all these words, but he only said, "Nothing."

Then I said, "What's her name?"

I thought to myself, "This is Unknown here. He's an L7." (Remember the square?)

I asked him again, "Who's in there?" and his donut eyes got bigger!

I wondered to myself, "It can't be Queen C!"

As he stood, looking dumbfounded, we just decided to back up out of there. To this day, he won't admit who was in there.

(I have an idea.) But since we're in this mood, here's another crazy story that left me kinda dumbfounded.

One Friday night, I came to the club and didn't see Lady V at the ticket booth. I saw Queen C there.

I thought to myself, "It's kinda early for her to be here."

So, I just said "Hi" to her and kept on going. It was a normal night, nothing different, nothing unusual, and nothing strange.

Well, on this night, Queen C went home with Lonzo. (Not only did she go home with him, but they also ended up living together.)

I said to myself, "Wow, that's weird. I ain't gonna touch this one. I'm gonna stay out of grown folks' business."

Some things just make you say, "*Hmmm...*"

Even to this day, I haven't talked to Unknown or Lonzo about "that one."

CHAPTER 3: THA DAYZ OF WAYBACK 1983

The club needed a new name change. The **Eve After Dark** was now called **The Penthouse**. Now this name I get. The second floor— Penthouse.

I remember one Saturday night at the club. Unknown was on the turntables, and as I was standing there getting ready for my set, I heard a knock at the door, so I opened it. I saw one of the big ballers from the neighborhood. Alongside him was this tall young skinny kid named Andre. I didn't know this at the time but meeting him would become another part of my destiny. His DJ name was Dr. Dre, but I'll call him Dre. The big baller wanted his young DJ to battle me. He's talking trash.

I laughed to myself, "Does he know— who— I—be? LOL."

Now Unknown jumped in, and he's talking trash. The big baller's talking about betting $500.

Unknown said, "Put your money where your mouth is, son."

But the funny thing is, it was all in fun. They we're just talking trash. And you know what? That battle never happened. While they were talking trash, me and Dre just looked at each other and chuckled. Whoever would have thought at this particular moment that we would meet. The meeting was our destiny, and our working together would become history.

A week or two went by. It was a Wednesday afternoon, and I just happened to be inside the club. I was practicing on the turntables, making sure my skills were up to date—and guess who walked in?

It was Dre. He looked a little stressed about something. He told me that he was DJing a dance down the street at Locke High School. He told me his music had just died. His amp for the speakers played out.

So, I told him, "No problem. You can use one of ours."

Then I grabbed the amp and took it downstairs to his car. But hold up! There was no car!

I turned and looked at him, then thought to myself, "How did he get here? Did he walk all the way from Locke? D*mn, boy! That was a long walk!"

So, I drove him back to the dance.

We walked in, and all eyes was on us. I hooked up the amp to the speakers, and VOILÀ! The party was back on!

But the crazy thing was, from that day on, he was just like my brother from another mother. And the young kid had skills. He was pretty quick on the cut. I don't know if he was faster than me, but the boy had hidden talents inside of him.

By the next week, he was a part of the Cru. He had the last slot, which was 2 a.m. to closing. If I am not mistaken, the following week, another guy came to the Cru. His name was DJ Cli-n-tel, but I called him Cli-n-tel...

(L-R) Dre, me, Cli-n-Tel, and Lonzo, Wreckin' Cru's first photo. (1983)

He was more like a rapper/DJ/very educated kid. Now the Wreckin' Cru was set, and this is how it went on for the next couple of years, every Friday and Saturday night. But let's not forget about the fringe benefits.

Let me tell you about something I bought that would later be another part of my destiny.

It was very simple—just a plain Kodak disc camera. If you don't know what a disc camera is, you take the picture, drop the disc off at a local store to get it developed, then you wait a week before you pick up the pictures. It's not like your cell phone, where you can just talk on it, take pics, and check your IG or Facebook. This was 1983.

So, imagine this was a little movie. I met this girl at the club, and she stayed in a city far away called Indio, California. In order for me to go see her, I needed to borrow a car. I couldn't drive my car that d*mn far because that was a two-hour drive. So, I borrowed my mother's Mustang. I also took along my little camera. I really have no idea why I took it, but it came with me.

Let me think of a name for her...

(I'll call her Miss Indio.)

Why? Because I don't remember her name. (LOL.)

So, after this long drive, I picked her up. We made it to a spot (where the grown folks gets down), but this particular time I said something I never said before.

I said, "Would you like me to take pictures of you?"

Then I said to myself, "What a dumb question."

To my surprise, she answered, "Yes."

Did I fail to mention they were nude pictures? Taking the pictures wasn't the hard part.

(Later on, in life, that would become a natural for me.)

She had no problem with the photo session, either. ☺

And the hard part was not dropping off the photos but picking them up.

A week later, in front of the store, I'm thinking to myself...

"Am I going to get them, or am I not going to get them? Will I look like a creep, or will they be smiling at me?"

I walked in with my head down and my glasses on. I whispered to the clerk, "May I have order number 217?"

He said, "What did you say, sir?"

I said, "Again, may I have order number 217?"

Then he said, loudly, "Oh, you want order number 217."

Sighing, I said to myself, "Wow! Did he just put me on blast?"

Funny thing about it, there was no expression on his face. I even had double copies. As the clerk handed me my mysterious package, I thought of the theme song "Superfly" by Curtis Mayfield. I turned and took my glasses off, held my head up high, and strolled out the door, just like I was The Mac. Now let's switch reels here.

One day I was listening to this new 12-inch vinyl that came out. It was called "Carbon-Copy."

I said, "Wow, that's neat. It had all kinds of scratching and mixing on it just like the mixtape I did at the club!"

But this is what you would call a bootleg record. What do I

mean by that? It is an unlicensed published work of another person's music, which is illegal. I know there was no permission given. (In other words, it's a straight rip-off.) But that's how we do it in the ghetto. (LOL.) I brought the idea to Lonzo about making a one-sided bootleg record called "Scratch Party."

But I told him, "Let's go into a better studio that has a 4-track tape recorder in it."

If you don't know what a 4-track tape recorder is, it's a machine that records multiple tracks at the same time, but it's all separated. I can scratch on two of the tracks, and the other two I can lay the music on.

His response was, "Okay, let's do it. I'll pay for it."

Then I thought about the old mixtape from the club.

I told him, "Just pay me upfront for it. I don't want to wait on record sales." 🙂

I shouldn't have been so quick on the draw. I should have had more patience and took the record sales because it sold more than I thought. And how much did Mr. Entrepreneur make? $600. Not bad for a mix, but the money only lasted a couple of days. I thought I was cool with the money. But I found out a year later through the grapevine that it sold a few thousand units on the street.

I thought to myself (in my "Old Man" voice...), "You big dummy!"

Well, at least, I'm a little smarter this time around.

I told him, "Instead of the $600 for one volume, let me do volumes 2 and 3 for $1200."

It made me feel a little better. But I still didn't get it or understand. The record sales still went through the roof.

(Now that's what you call being YOUNG AND DUMB.)

I feel like there's a competition. Did I just say competition?

I hear there's another rival out there making bootlegs and they call theirs "New York Scratch Masters."

Now I have to turn the heat up on the mixes. They gotta be even better. I'm starting to make volumes 4, 5, and 6. Looks like my pockets are getting a little fatter! So, we come up with and make a new volume called "Scratch Dance."

Now the competition is on.

I finally find out who's making these "New York Scratch Masters." Not only are they NOT from New York, but they're also from the same crew—the Wreckin' Cru! Surprisingly, it's Dre and Unknown!

I said, "Wow... Really?" And all three of us laughed about it.

I looked at Dre and said," Boy, your pockets getting fat! They trying to catch up to mine."

We only made those records for a few months, then we moved on to bigger things. You know what's so crazy about this?

It was our first experience producing and making actual records. And we didn't realize that this was the beginning of the Dynamic Duo. Move over, Batman and Robin! There are some new heroes in town. (LOL.) Let's get back to the club.

I'm holding down my midnight slot. Dre and Cli-n-tel were sharing the 2 o'clock slot, and don't let me forget Unknown, who is still on the 10 o'clock slot. We're starting to get more popular in the city. We're starting to be the hottest DJs around.

And you know what? Me and Dre are really starting to click. We're just like the old saying, "White on rice." But this is the new saying— "Brown on rice." And you can't get no tighter than that. Other words, we are more tighter than brothers. When you see him, you see me. When you see my car rolling, you see him and me. We always ate and hung out together.

Should I mention the fringe benefits? Well...

I'll just leave that to your imagination. I'm not going to throw him under the bus, but I guess I'll throw myself under it. (LOL.)

One day I met this nice-looking girl at the club. But there was a problem. She had a friend attached to her (once again).

Let me think of a name for them...

I want to call them Heckle and Jeckle, but them were boys.

(I'll call them Betty and Wilma, like the two ladies on *The Flintstones*.)

I got Wilma's number, and she said, "Call me sometime this week."

I didn't call that week. Actually, I didn't even call her that month. But I did finally call her.

Now here's the problem. She said she would only go out with me if her friend went with her. So now I had to think of a scenario. We're going to call this a rendezvous. I called Big Chuck to the rescue once again.

I told him. "Hey man, I don't know what Betty looks like, but you gotta save me on this one."

We rolled up in the van and picked them up. There was no questions asked because we all knew where we were going. And that was the world-Famous Snooty Fox on 41st and Western. (If you don't know what that is, it was a "luxury" motel in the ghetto.)

And why was it famous? Because It had mirrors on the ceiling and a bathroom the size of the bedroom.

We drove up to a drive-through window to check in. Now here's the catch. When the desk clerk looked in the van, he could only see two people, me and Wilma. Big Chuck and Betty were well-hid, sitting right behind us on the floor.

I paid the money, then asked the clerk, "Can we have a room on the end?"

He said, "Yes, my friend," and gave me the key. Then we drove down to the room.

I told Big Chuck, "You guys wait five minutes before you get out."

He answered, "Cool."

So, Wilma and me went into the room and left the door unlocked.

Five minutes later, they came walking in. Next was a big discussion. Who gets the bed, and who gets the bathroom? Guess who volunteered for the bathroom?

(What is the problem with me and these bathrooms?)

There was really no frills and thrills on this night. It was just alright. But here is the killer to the story. As we were about to exit the room, I opened the door.

All of a sudden, this naked girl ran in and stood in front of us.

She said, "He's going to kill me!"

Then she dashed in the bathroom and locked it behind her.

I thought to myself, "Where are her clothes?"

You know what? I better stay out of grown folks' business.

All four of us looked at each other.

Then I said, "Feet, don't fail us now!"

So, we got the h*ll of there! We left the door open and the lights on. I even left the key in the room. That was what you would call a quick rendezvous. But the naked girl don't always come with it.

As we got in the van and pulled off, me and Big Chuck looked at each other and said, "Wow, did that just happen?"

56

Big Chuck said something funny.

He said, "Bro, she did have a nice body."

Then I cut my eyes at him and gave him "that look" as the van headed down the road.

It's December 25, 1983— a normal Christmas day.

I remember a few sad Christmas mornings when my grandmother had to save the day. Her gifts were always new socks and Fruit of the Loom underwear. (That's a grandma gift.)

There were no toys among her gifts. But we appreciated her and the gifts very much. So, of course, this year, she gives me socks and underwear. At this age, I'm too big for toys, LOL.

Now it's December 26.

It was early in the morning, and I was still in bed.

Suddenly, I woke up. I overheard my mother's voice in her room. She was kinda crying on the phone. I got up and went into her room.

Then I asked her, "What's going on?"

Nervously, she said, "Your grandmother is on the phone. She can't talk—but I can hear her breathing in the background..."

She wanted me to get dressed and take her over to Grandma's house, but me, Mr. Bad A**, really didn't want to do it. I'm sorry that I didn't take her.

(I was kinda mad at myself about that. It bothered me for a long time.)

Later, we found out that while my grandmother was on the phone, she was in the middle of having a heart attack. I knew she was a strong woman, but I didn't realize she was that strong.

After calling paramedics, she managed to crawl out of bed, make it all the way to the front door, unlock it, then crawl all the way back to her bed.

Those were a different breed of women back then, 'cause she didn't want the paramedics to break her door down trying to get in.

I don't know if my grandmother passed before my mother got to the hospital or once she got there. I do know this was a great loss to my mother. It had to be so hard on her, first losing her son and now her mother.

We all loved her and missed her very much.

The next day I got a strange phone call, and it was from Queen C. Wow! Really?

My grandmother Luci Winbush (R.I.P.)

That's odd. I don't know why she called me, but I ended up telling her about my grandmother passing.

Cold Gettin' Dumb:1984

It's cold gettin' dumb. In other words, it's time to start getting down to business. First up, Lonzo picks up this 4-track tape recorder so we can make better mixes. A radio DJ named Greg Mack from 1580 K-DAY gave us a call. He wanted me and Dre to do some mixes. They were for his 5:00 show called "Traffic Jams," which aired Monday through Friday. (And to my knowledge, I think we were the first to do mixes in LA on the radio.)

So, I made the first mix. It went very well, and we got very good ratings on his show. After that, me and Dre would alternate every other day making the mixes. We didn't make no money off of it, but we did it for the love of DJing. But there's a couple of issues. Here's the first issue.

Even though they are only 10-minute mixes, it would take us about 2 to 3 hours to make it on a 4-track recorder because we're trying to put so much into it, with all the scratching and mixing, plus they all got to sound good. Now here's the second issue.

The radio station is in Hollywood, but Lonzo's house is near Gardena, California, where we make the mixes. If you don't know the distance, it's about 20 miles and takes 30 minutes to drive there without traffic. So, we have to have the mix there by 5:00 p.m., and we don't usually have the mixes ready until about 3:00 p.m.

That means we have LA traffic to Hollywood, and that's a two-hour drive. And that means I have to drive like a bat out of h*ll just to make it by 5:00! We did this crazy drive five days a week. You know that got old real fast. So, that lasted just a few months.

Next up is the world-famous mixtapes at the Roadium Open Air Market in Torrance, California. (It's like a flea market, or nowadays it's called a farmer's market.)

Now Steve Yano (R.I.P.), who was the owner of a little record shop in the Roadium, contacted Lonzo. He wanted me to make some 60-minute mixed tapes for his store. (Money changed hands this time.) I made the first mix, and if I'm not mistaken, it might have been two.

The mixes took a while to make because these were 60-minute mixes, not like the 10-minute ones we did at the radio station.

Now I heard through the grapevine that the mixtapes were selling out at the swap meet. But you know me (being young and dumb), I didn't do that very long.

After I stopped doing them, Steve asked Dre to make the mixes. I don't remember how many he did, but he did quite a few. And both our skills started to grow.

You know, it looks like people are really starting to catch on to this scratching and mixing game. It seems like the Wreckin' Cru is beginning to get a cool reputation—at least locally. We're taking off and it feels like we got something burning inside of us.

There's another rap group on the rise. They're from New York, and their name is Run-DMC. They got a hot new single out called "Sucker M.C.'s."

So, Lonzo made a few calls, and he ended up getting the group to come out to our club. This would be their first appearance in LA.

It's the night of the performance, and me and Dre are kinda anticipating how this show is going to be. After all, these are supposed to be the big boys. We're watching the show. It's going okay. It's cool. We liked their style, but the set was only ten minutes. The last thing they did was fold their arms and drop the microphones.

(You know, Lonzo almost had a heart attack about those microphones, LOL.)

Me and Dre looked at each other and said, "That's it? That's all you gotta do to make a record?"

That burning inside of us was about the music. Later that night, me and their DJ, Jam Master Jay (R.I.P.), hung out on the club turntables. Actually, he was a pretty cool dude.

After watching their show, me and Dre put our thinking caps on. We really felt there was a change coming. First, it was a DJ thing. Now it's this music thing.

So, we put together a little 4-track demo studio out in Lonzo's garage. Next, he went out and bought a MXR, which is a drum machine. If you don't know what that is, it's a machine that you can make beats on. Me and Dre learned it pretty fast. It was kinda limited, but it did the job.

Now I don't know if me or Cli-n-tel came up with this idea, but we decided to make a 12-inch single.

I would produce the song, make the beat, and do the scratching, and he would write and rap the lyrics.

We came up with a title name and called it "Slice."

People don't know this, but I actually bit off "Sucker MC's" beat. (It was called copying.) Also, during this time, Lonzo started up a record company called Kru-Kut records.

Now it's time to record the song, but we need a better studio. And here's the crazy part. There happened to be this guy named Bucky that's running an 8-track studio with his buddy.

(He was one of many that lived in our **infamous garage**.) Lonzo booked the time, and we went in and did our thing, but the MXR didn't do its thing.

Gladly, Bucky and them had another drum machine called a Linn drum, which was top of the line. I made the beat on there, and it sounded just like "Sucker MC's" because it was also recorded with a Linn drum.

60

Slice opened the door. (1984)

We finished the song. Really, we made two songs, a side A, and a side B.

Lonzo had this artist named Darryl D. do the design on our cover, which was a record and a hand with a long fingernail scratching the vinyl. The song was kinda wack to me, but it was the match that started the fire. Nobody knows this, but this was the Wreckin' Cru's first song.

It only sold a handful of copies, but this was the song that opened the door to our music career.

A month later, Dre let me hear his song while we were sitting in the van. It was called "Surgery."

He produced it, did the beat, and all the scratching. Him and Cli-n-tel wrote and rapped the lyrics. This time Lonzo hired a musician named Daniel S. to program the keyboard, and this new drum machine called a DMX for the 12-inch single. Darryl D. came through again, drawing the cover.

This design was of an operating room with a sketch of Dre doing surgery on turntables. "Surgery" became a local hit on K-DAY.

People were starting to catch on to the Techno music.

61

Surgery got us through the door. (1984)

Now the Wreckin' Cru had graduated from DJs to an actual group. "Slice" opened the door, and "Surgery" got us through it.

1985

The days of **The Penthouse** have ended. The owner didn't renew the lease, so we had to move on. We found a new spot called **Dootos** (Later on this would be called Skateland, USA.), which was located just around the corner on Central in Compton. We wanted to show off our DJ skills a little bit. We had a little routine that we practiced on the turntables, with no headphones.

Who was the "we" and what was the routine? Well, the "we" was Me, Dre, and Cli-n-tel. The routine was...

We stood in a line in front of the turntables. The first person steps up and starts scratching on the left turntable and then scratches on the right turntable.

Then he moves out the way. The second one steps up,

scratches on the left, and then scratches on the right. Then he moves out the way. Then the third steps up and repeats the routine.

Now the crowd stood there, amazed. This was the first time we did that routine with no headphones in public. We were trying to stay ahead of the game and still have fun.

In the meantime, I was thinking to myself, "What about my fringe benefits?"

It was the first night of **Dootos**, and Mr. Bad A** don't even have a plan. On top of that, there's no more club nights every weekend. These events were just once a month.

(You know, that's just a d*mn shame...)

So, I started doing my search. I looked around, and my radar stopped on these leather pants. I smiled at her, and she smiled at me. I nodded my head at her, then she nodded hers at me. I winked at her, and she winked back.

Let me think of a name for her...

(I'll call her Young M.)

And, of course, she was over 18. I figured out the plan. In this particular building, there are some old dressing rooms next to the stage. They don't have doors on them, but they had curtains to close them off. I grabbed Young M's hand and led her down the road to frills and thrills.

Right into one of the dressing rooms, that just happened to be the closest one to the stage.

As we were standing there doing our hanky panky, I had to hold the curtains closed because people were walking right past them.

I had to tell her, "Shhhh, be quiet..."

Wow, did I just do that?

And I gotta be on stage in 5 minutes? ☺

Now there was this other girl I met there a month later. Funny thing, I already knew her, but the curious thing was...

Where are we going to do the hanky panky? I don't want to do the dressing room thing again. It needs to be something exotic. So, I have a new plan.

Let me think of a name for her...

(I'll call her Off The Hook J.)

Why did I say that? Because she was "off the hook." Not in the looks department, but you know what I'm talking about.

Wreckin' Cru's second single: "Juice" (1985)

Hee hee...

Here's the plan. On these event nights, I drive our equipment truck to carry all the speakers. But this was not a regular truck. It looked like a big brown UPS truck, only this one was all-white and old. It was parked next to the exit door, Stage Right.

We both started giggling as I showed her the place of our "get down where we got down." (In the back of the truck, LOL.)

Sometimes I just have to laugh at myself and these crazy places. Now let's get back to the music.

We started working on our second 12-inch single called "Juice."

But this time, we did something a little different. Instead of Dre and Cli-n-tel rapping the lyrics, we used an electronic voice called the Vocoder. We stepped up our game and went to a 24-track studio called Audio Achievements, which was located in Torrance, California. The engineer and owner was Donovan S.

Lonzo had the same musician, Daniel S. We watched and studied how he programmed the keyboards and drum machine.

From that experience, me and Dre said, "That's all it takes to produce? You know what? We can start doing this ourselves."

Then Lonzo said, "And we can save money too."

64

All three of us looked at him and said, "Really?"

"Juice" became a local hit on K-DAY. They would have high school students pick the top 10 songs of the day. Juice" made it to their list quite a few times.

(I wonder if it was because we said different high school names at the end of the song?)

A Time for Change: Phase 1

We're back at the demo studio at Lonzo's. Some new changes were being made. Let me think of a list of them...

First up, Lonzo decided to make a name change. As we were becoming more like a group, the name changed a little bit— from Wreckin' Cru to World Class Wreckin' Cru. Why that little change? I have no idea. To me, that didn't make no difference because we were still the same group. But we started to step our game up. Instead of hiring musicians, me and Dre learned to produce, record, and mix the songs all by ourselves. Our goal was to keep it all in house. Next on the list...

Lonzo bought some new music equipment for the group. Let me think about what it was. He bought us this new Oberheim system. It had a keyboard (OB-8) and a drum machine (DMX). It also had another machine called a sequencer (DSX). Now the sequencer was the brains of the system. It controlled the keyboard and the drum machine. You could program it by playing the notes on the keyboard, and it would digitally record it. Then you program the drum machine, and the sequencer unit keeps it all in sync.

Even though me and Dre were not musicians, we played by ear. (We didn't read sheet music, but I played the drums.) It was more by the sound of what we liked because we could only play one finger at a time. Although our keyboard skills were limited, we somehow managed to learn how to play and program the keyboard with the sequencer. We caught on real fast. It took us no time to learn these machines.

But first, let's take a quick commercial break. (Or should I say a fringe benefit break?)

This one is different. I'm back in love again. Well, maybe not in love, but infatuated.

What do I mean by that? Here's the story...

We had a side job where people would rent our speakers. Lonzo had this buddy named Ralph. He would rent speakers every Sunday night from us for a club called **Close Encounters**, located on the corner of Century and Crenshaw Blvd. Of course, I was the one that had to take the speakers, drop them off, and set them up. I had to either wait around for hours or come back later at 2 o'clock and pick them up.

I said, "What am I getting out of all this? A little pay? Okay, that's cool." (But you know me. I wasn't in for the money.)

So, what else is there? *Hmmm...*

Are there any fringe benefits in this building? So far, all I see is cougars in the crowd, and they all was looking at me for some reason. (Like I was a piece of fresh meat.) If you don't know what a cougar is, it's an older woman that likes younger guys. Maybe this might be kinda interesting. You know me...

One Sunday night, I dropped off the speakers, and for some reason, I hung around for a little while. I did a fringe benefit search, just a little one. As I was standing next to Ralph while he was DJing, I spotted one.

I whispered to him, "What's up with her?"

He turned, looked me dead in the eye and said, "She likes them young."

I said, "Really? I don't understand you."

He said again, "SHE LIKES THEM YOUNG."

Then I turned towards her and stared at her, giving her a wink. To my surprise, she gave me a wink. Guess that means, "Come on over here."

So, I came on over there.

Let me think of a name for her...

(I'll call her Cougar C.)

I found out she was 13 years older than me.

This is definitely something different for me. She didn't take me home that night, but the next day, I was there. She was very "business minded." In other words, she was ballin'. She didn't look her age, and she knew how to get her freak on, which was right up my alley! She had all the frills and all the thrills, but she was very neat about it.

What do I mean by that? In her bedroom, there were two queen beds. Stage Left was for hanky panky, and Stage Right was for sleeping. I thought that was kinda odd, but she was a very

66

clean person. Showered before and showered afterwards...

And must I say she had a very nice bathroom?

(What is it with me and these bathrooms? LOL.)

Now let's get to the goodies.

For some reason, after every "live performance," when I woke up the next morning, there was always a gift for me. I mean some really nice ones. Let me think of a few...

There was a phat gold bracelet. She bought me almost every color of leather pant and a real nice gold chain. But she ended up giving the chain to her girlfriend to give to my friend (Don) that I had set her friend up with. (To make it look like the girlfriend was ballin'.) She also bought me an $1100 keyboard (Roland Juno-106). Let me see...

She also took me, Don, and her friend on an all-expenses-paid trip to Lake Tahoe, California.

Now this is the crazy part. She rented me cars every week.

Different cars...All kinda cars...Cadillacs, Lincolns...

Every kinda car...

Did I fail to mention that she bought us front row seats center stage at the Prince "Purple Rain" concert? And can you imagine this?

During the concert, I got picked to be on stage with Sheila E during one of her songs? Wow!

(Cougar C was allowed to take one picture, and the one she took was a horrible one. She cut my head off of it.) ☹

More about her later. Let's get back to the studio.

Now me and Dre had started to produce more demos. If you don't know what demos are, they're like rough or raw songs that are not completed. Other words, this is where we created the songs. We did it this way because it would save money. At Lonzo's, it was free, but at Audio Achievements, it would cost us by the hour. That way, we would cut studio costs. It's time to get started on our first album.

Me and Dre have our producing hats on. We are both working hard on the music. I'm on the mixing board, and he's on the drum machines and keyboard. Him and Cli-n-tel are also working hard on the lyrics.

We started to come up with some of the titles of the songs, such as "The Planet," "Gang Bang You're Dead," and "World Class," which was also the title of the album.

67

Wreckin' Cru at Dootos (1985)

Then there was the remix to "Surgery" and "Juice." Me and Dre was rolling to Lonzo's in my freshly rented Nissan 300 ZX (the anniversary edition). While we was driving, a Prince slow jam was on the radio.

We made it to the studio, and I had started messing around on the drum machine. Then this slow song beat came to mind. I played a base line on top of it. Cli-n-tel came up with a little melody. Once we started getting in the groove of it, we decided right then that this would be something different for the Wreckin' Cru. We also added a female singer named Mona Lisa to sing the hooks on the tracks. The title of the song was "Lovers." We didn't rap it, but all four of us really talked the lyrics, just like the hit "Float On" by The Floaters.

This song was really geared for the women. But the funny thing is, it became a little hit on the radio, both locally and in the south, like Texas, Louisiana, and Mississippi.

(You know me...that's going to be "imported" fringe benefits.)

Hee hee... 😊

We made it to Audio Achievements to finish the album.

It only took us a few weeks to record it because we did most of the pre-production at Lonzo's house. So that saved us a BUNCH of money on studio time. (Not really us, but Lonzo.)

Now it's time for the album cover. But watch out! There's a joker in the deck. For some reason, Lonzo hired this lady manager. I don't know where she came from, but her father was supposed to be someone famous. She reminds me of the girl on the TV show, *What's Happening*. Let me think of a name for her...

(I'll call her Manager X.)

She started to dig our music and stuff. She was giving us some ideas about the album cover. You know, the way we looked on it and the designs of our clothing. The look we had was trying to be sexy for the women. The only thing I liked about it was the purple color I wore. But there's also one thing that I still don't like to this day. What was that? She had us putting that d*mn makeup on our face for the cover.

(We still get talked about that until this day, LOL.)

The album is finished, and the cover is done. Now it's time to take a roller coaster ride. Let's get to the first hill.

Lonzo and Queen C stopped living together. She went out and got her own apartment.

Wreckin' Cru's First Album (1985)

For some reason, she would call me up and say, "Let's go hang out."

We would go to Westwood by UCLA, walk around, and go to the movies. We started doing this somewhat of a rendezvous quite a few times.

In my mind, I was thinking, "What's the reason for all this?"

To me, it was just a platonic friendship. Let's get on to the second hill.

We're starting to do a few shows around town. And what is the pay? $125.00, which is not bad for less than 30 minutes of work. But keep that number in the back of your head.

Now here's where the joker pops out.

The Big Caper

One day, Manager X had a little meeting with me, Dre, and Cli-n-tel. She had been giving us a heads-up about the record sales. We had told her we hadn't made any money yet from the records being sold. She told us that the album was moving a lot of units and that there should be plenty of mechanicals, royalties, and publishing.

Then we looked at each other and said, "Mechanicals and publishing? What is that?"

This is the part where being young and dumb comes in. Now listen up. There are many ways to get paid off every song that is produced.

For example:

1. **Mechanical royalties** are a kind of royalty that's paid to a songwriter whenever a copy of one of their songs is made.

2. **Songwriters** are the people who write both the music (100% pay) and lyrics (100% pay) for a song. Songwriters receive a total of 200 % pay.

3. **Music producers** usually get a percentage of what the artist's percentage will be.

4. **Artists** perform a songwriter's original work and receive music royalties.

Nowadays, there's digital sales, satellite radio, downloads, streaming, sync licensing fees, and the list goes on and on.

(My advice to all up and coming artists: Make sure you have your paperwork and a d*mn lawyer.)

When we said that, she had a funny look on her face.

She looked at us and said, "Really? I didn't know nothing about that. Maybe we should come up with a plan so I can show you what kind of numbers are being sold."

This is where the movie begins. Lights, camera, action!

I don't know which one of us said this, but one of us said, "I know he keeps papers locked inside his desk in the office, which is in the studio."

She said, "We have to wait for just the right moment to make this plan work. Let's break it down..."

Then she said, "First of all, we have to get his keys from him. Next, we have to wait for the opportunity for him to be out of the office. Then we have to do all this without him even knowing it and we have to wait for the perfect time."

So, we waited...

And waited...

Then we waited some more...

Amazingly, the right time popped up. Lonzo wanted me to DJ this little function on a Saturday afternoon. I usually do these by myself. I didn't know where Dre was, so this time I dragged Cli-n-tel with me.

While I was setting the equipment up, me and him thought of a plan. I came up with this excuse to tell Lonzo.

I told him, "I left some records at the studio. Can I use your car to get there? It's much faster than the van."

He said, "Go ahead."

Boo-ya! We got the keys!

We drove to the studio, got inside, and said...

"Boo-ya! His office is empty!"

Then I told Cli-n-tel, "We don't have much time. So, let's go search each drawer and look at everything. Leave it just like it was. And don't mess up nothing."

We got to the last drawer, and...Boo-ya! We found the papers! (Man, I wished we had an iPhone 11 Pro right now for some pics. LOL.) But we had to do it the old school way. We had to remember what we saw.

We went back to the function, and I handed Lonzo his keys like nothing happened. Then, later on, we reported our findings back to Manager X.

Now things were about to get very interesting. Back on the home front, me and Queen M are doing our what you would call play date. Remember, we are still platonic. 🙂

Now the Wreckin' Cru is on what you would call a small tour. (We even had a tour bus, more like a Greyhound.) But we would call it bulls**t.

Why do I say that? The groups on it were cool. Let me see who was on tour with us...

The Force MD's that made the hit, "Tears," the group that made the song "The Roof Is On Fire," Rock Master Scott, and the guy that made the funny cowboy rap song called "Rappin' Duke."

Now the shows were okay until the one at the Long Beach Arena in California. This is where the bulls**t business of the tour came in.

We was in San Francisco doing a show. Afterwards, it was time to leave, but the bus driver wasn't going anywhere. Why? Because no money changed hands. (Other words, he was still waiting to get PAID.) Somehow somebody talked him into driving us to the last show in Long Beach.

When we got there, we found out that the bus company had told the driver...

"You're fired!"

You see, he was not supposed to drive us from San Francisco without getting paid. Wow! Did he just get fired because of us?

Did I fail to mention the fringe benefits here? Well, there was one. It was on the bus trip back home from San Francisco. Nobody on the bus knows this because it was dark, the lights were out, and Manager X was sitting next to me.

Must I say her fingers "did the walking" through the whole trip from San Francisco? (I just have to laugh at myself again, LOL.)

Let's talk about the show at the Long Beach arena.

We was really excited about this show tonight. This was a 15,000-seat arena!

We said, "This is the biggest show we've ever done!"

Now it's showtime. They announce our name.

"Ladies and gentlemen, The World Class Wreckin'..."

Then we walk out on stage, and all we hear is...

Crickets, crickets, crickets... 🙁

Why? First of all, bad promotions. They didn't have their business together. The arena was way too big. And I don't see how it was just 300 people there. (Somebody lost a bunch of money.)

And what was our pay? $125.00 per show. Now let's move on to the next tour.

Lonzo had ordered a private tour bus for this one. But here's where it gets really interesting. We're kinda upset because we haven't received any royalties from the record sales.

So, we got a plan in place. It's called a BOYCOTT.

When the time came for us to leave on the bus, we were what you would call M.I.A., or in other words, "Missing in Action." Lonzo had been calling each of our houses all day.

(Remember, back in those days, there was no cell phones.)

(L-R) Lonzo, Dre, me, and Cli-n-tel, Wreckin' Cru (1985)

The next day, we found ourselves sitting on my mother's couch, looking dazed and confused.

My oldest brother Corky walked by and said to me, "Lonzo's been trying to call you all day. Seems like there's an issue. What's the problem?"

We told him about the situation.

Then he said, "So what you gonna do?"

We looked at each other and said, "We don't know."

Later that day, I get a call from Queen C.

She said, "Why don't you come over?"

I got a little excited.

I said to myself, "Is this frills and thrills for the first time?"

I thought to myself, "Would I be a dirty rat to go over there?"

NAW... (After all, this could be some back pay.)

I gave her my answer. I said, "I'll be right over." 😊

When I got there, I walked up the stairs and knocked on the door. She opened it and let me in.

I sat down on the couch, thinking to myself about this song by Marvin Gaye, called "Got To Give It Up."

A few minutes later, I heard somebody walking up the stairs. As soon as the doorknob turned, I looked her dead in the eye.

Then I thought to myself, "This 'You know what' done set me up." Wow.

The door opened up. It was Lonzo. He came in, talking all kinds of trash.

He said, "Where you guys been? I been trying to catch you guys..."

I was silent. I got up, headed towards the door, looked him dead in the eye, and said...

"We want our money." Then I walked out.

Now, if you are wondering if me and Queen C ever "did the Hanky Panky..."

Well...I'll just leave that to your imagination.

CHAPTER 4: THE CRU 1986

There's a time of destiny and change in the air.

First thing: We didn't leave. After all this, for some reason, me and Dre decided to stay. Why? Because we had nowhere else to go. We was both broke. He didn't have a car, but I still had my Granada, and we both was living with our parents.

So, what we gonna do now? I guess you're wondering what's going on with Cli-n-tel.

Well...We didn't take it that seriously, but Cli-n-tel did. Me and Dre kinda brushed it off. (I didn't know whether that was a good thing or a bad thing.) At that time, Cli-n-tel was thinking about not coming back. About 24 hours later, we hooked back up with Lonzo. (That boycott sure wasn't that f**kin' long, LOL.)

The tour bus was still waiting at Lonzo's house. But we had a little problem. We needed another member like yesterday. There was a group that Dre knew of called C.I.A. (This group had three members.) One of the members of the group just happened to live next door to Dre's auntie, just off Van Wick Avenue in LA. His name was Ice Cube, but I'll call him Cube. The second member of the group was Sir Jinx, who was Dre's cousin. He lived in the house next to Cube. Now here's the solution to our problem. The third and oldest member of the group was named Shakespeare. This worked out perfectly for us because he was really too old for C.I.A. So, we had to get him up to speed, then learn the songs and get on the tour bus.

Now we're on the road. It was just a small tour. I only remember one date of it, and it was in Pittsburgh, California, a city that I had never heard of. We get back from the road, but we have to deal with a new set of problems.

Problem 1: Shakespeare fits right in.

Problem 2: What do we do about Cli-n-tel?

Me, Dre, Lonzo, and Cli-n-tel had a meeting. Me and Dre wanted him back. We were willing to have five members in the group. But Cli-n-tel didn't want to come back. Like I told you earlier, he took this a little harder than us.

The meeting was over, and he had made his decision. He decided to leave the group.

We hated to see him go, but this was just the beginning of a new chapter for me and Dre. There's a weird thing about this situation. Once Cli-n-tel decided to leave, for some reason, everything seemed to move real fast.

He had good writing and rapping skills, but his season with us was short-lived. His destiny was someplace else. (Later on, he became a high school and college teacher.) Other words let's compare this to a train on a train track. The train we was on first went to point A. Then me and Dre had to get on the next train to get to point B. But our ultimate goal is point C. We had no idea where our destiny was taking us. Let's shake this sadness off and get to some happy stuff—our first trip on an airplane...

Destination—Texas.

(L-R) Me, Mona Lisa, Lonzo, and Dre.

I don't know if it's in the south, but I do know it's just big ol' Texas! Here we are on the plane for the first time. (But not me. I flew to Oakland in the 6th grade.)

After the plane landed, the doors opened, and then—BAM!

As soon as we got off the plane, that Texas heat knocked us to our knees! Remember, we're from California.

So, we said, "Man, we need to get back on this plane and go back home."

But that would be a mistake, 'cause this is good ol' Texas. And they say everything grows big here. If that's true, I want to see what it is—and that means my fringe benefits. 😊

Now here's the crazy part. The guy that I replaced during the **Eve After Dark** days (Dr. Rock) lives here in Texas and DJs on the radio. Me and Dre made a couple of mixes for his show, and the concerts out here—pretty good. When I say pretty good, I mean really good.

(Hint! Fringe benefits. That's what I really mean.)

When we got back to LA, I found out two things. First thing, Dre had met this talented rapper and writer. His name was The D.O.C. He was a member of a group called the Fila Fresh Crew.

Here's the second thing. We find out later that Manager X had created her own shows. They were going on at the same time and the same night as our shows were. While we was doing Texas, they was in Louisiana.

How did we find out about this? Well, the promoter of our show kinda said something funny.

He handed us a flyer and said, "Hey, who is this Wreckin' Cru doing shows in Louisiana?"

We looked at the flyer and said, "Well, that's us, but that ain't us."

So, we just laughed it off. Later I just happened to talk to Cli-n-tel. He told me that Manager X had set up them shows. It was him and my old buddy Don. (I guess he was portraying me.) Then there was this guy that used to be a DJ at the **Eve** who portrayed Dre, and the last guy portrayed Lonzo. (I don't remember his name.)

There was two things Cli-n-tel told me he learned after going on the road for the first time. Keep your money in your pocket and definitely don't leave it in your suitcase back at the hotel. Because once the promoter for their show found out something fishy was going on, he ended up somehow getting in his room and stealing his money. (I guess he went to the front desk and got a key.)

Me and Cli-n-tel didn't talk again until years later. That was the end of Manager X and her shenanigans.

The Wreckin' Cru is starting to do a bunch of shows. We was going down south quite a bit and the shows are getting bigger and better.

We even did two shows with Morris Day in El Paso, Texas. That was off the hook!

77

Now I bet you're wondering if there was any fringe benefits. Oh, h*ll yea. She was very cute, very, very sexy, and must I say a big freak? She was so cute to look at and so much of a freak.

I had to step back and say, "D*mn!" That made me want to book a return flight— instantly!

(And yes, I did return to El Paso.)

The Wreckin' Cru is back in Texas again. We flew over time to Shreveport, LA, then to Mississippi. Maybe I'll stop right there. Let me think about what's in Mississippi...

One night after a show, I was sitting in a tub, having my back rubbed. Well...You guessed it. I found me a good old country girl. Now, these are the southern-style fringe benefits.

(I really just have to laugh at myself, LOL.)

I bet you're wondering whatever happened to Cougar C. Let me get you up to speed. But first, there's a joker in the deck.

She had just rented me this fresh white Lincoln town car, 4-door. We got some shows up north, so I decided to drive the Lincoln. Me, Dre, and Shakespeare are standing in the driveway in front of Lonzo's garage.

Ahhhh... this is where the joker pops out. The LA County sheriffs roll up on us. (These are the ones you don't f*ck with.) This was my third encounter with the police.

They step out the car and say, "Who's driving this town car?"

I raised my hand and said, "Officer, I'm driving it."

One officer said, "Well since you're driving that car, you come over here and sit in the back seat of this car." (Is this pre-BLM?)

I sat in the back seat of their car wearing no handcuffs.

RING, RING! Just then, a call came in over their radio.

"We have a 2-11 in progress..."

They sped off, with me still in the back seat. The crime scene was just a few blocks away.

I'm sitting here wondering, "What the h*ll are they going to do with me?"

They get out the car and start doing whatever police do.

Then a different cop opens the door and says, "You come with me."

Now I'm in his car, and he drives me back to Lonzo's house. I get out, and he drives off.

Watching the car as it left, I was thinking to myself, "They didn't ask me one question. Not even to see my ID. Wow!"

I need to make a t-shirt with 3 letters on it. (F.T.P.) 😊

After we got back from the shows up north, I told Cougar C what happened, and she was p*ssed.

Wreckin' Cru soundcheck

She had a letter drawn up and notarized so I could show it to the cops if this ever happened again. But let's get back to Cougar C. How can I say this without looking guilty?

It's a Sunday night. I'm dropping off the speakers at **Close Encounters**.

But this time, I have Big Chuck with me. (You know this is going to be a problem.) Cougar C is there with her same old friend. I did a "mini-search" and saw a couple of cute girls sitting a few tables behind her. Big Chuck wants to go over there and talk to them. And me being— Let me think of a few words...

"Dumb..."

"Stupid..."

"What are you doing?"

"Don't follow him!"

Of course, I followed him. We only talked for a few minutes. This is not the problem. After the club was closed, me and Chuck went to a gas station next door. Guess who was there? It was those same two cute girls. Let me think of a name for Me and Chuck...

(I don't know who's dumb, and I d*mn sure don't know who's dumber.)

We went over there talking to them at the gas pump. (We was not trying to be gentlemen. So, we didn't pump their gas.)

While we were talking to them, I look out the corner of my eye and see a car pull up. It's Cougar C. I played it off and kinda moseyed my way towards her car. As I'm walking, I turn my head backwards. I see the two girls are pulling off. I make it to Cougar C's car. I turn my head towards her, and then I see it...

She has a Chrome .25 automatic in her hand! Then she said something that I never heard her say.

"Be home by 3." After that, she drove off.

Big Chuck came to me and said, "I got her number! Let's go over there!"

I looked him dead in the eye and said, "I ain't going NOWHERE."

But as I'm driving over to the house, I'm still saying, "I ain't going NOWHERE."

We get to their house. All four of us sit down on the couch and I'm still thinking, "I ain't going NOWHERE."

All of a sudden, Big Chuck was trying to take his girl to her room.

I told him, "Hold up— Chuck, we gotta go!"

He tells me, "I ain't gonna be that long," then goes into the room.

He left me sitting in there on the couch with this girl.

I'm thinking, "I ain't interested in you, not one bit."

I need to be home by 3. My mind was only on that Chrome .25. I look at my watch...

20 minutes go by. I look at my watch again...

Now it's 22 minutes. Is the time going backwards?

When it got to 30 minutes, that was enough. I walked over and bammed on the door.

I said, "Hey Chuck, I'm leaving. I've got to go."

I finally got him out of the room. We're back in the car.

As I was driving, he said, "You better be glad I didn't drive. I would have been staying all night."

I looked at him and gave him that evil eye.

And after all this, I get back to the house at 3:05. Cougar C acted like nothing happened. Things was never the same. (Of course, because of me. It may be that **"Black Curtain"** again.) At that moment, I went from the penthouse to the cellar.

What do I mean by that? Reality set in. I went from freshly rented cars back to the old dusty Granada. (Being young and dumb, why didn't I just have her buy me a d*mn car?)

How could I let this one get away? Bought me almost everything I wanted. Had all the frills and thrills. But you know me. I just got bored. I learned a lot from her.

Don't you like the smell of new cars? If I ever start making money, the first thing I'm going to get is a new car.

She taught me the rich side of life. Because growing up as a kid we was poor. I never really had new things except for that grandma underwear and t-shirts for Christmas. A life lesson was learned here and never forgotten.

So, that three-month "Fantasy Island" was over.

I thought to myself (in my "Old Man" voice...), "You big dummy!"

Back To The Grind

Big things are about to happen. It's time to work on the Wreckin' Cru's second album. But this time, we landed a major deal on a major label. Epic Records picked us up. Money changed hands, but it was a little lopsided. What do I mean by the word "lopsided"? Well, let me go back to the sharecropper days...

No, let's not go back that far back, LOL. We'll stay in the present time (1986).

The deal was for $100K. Hold up, let's talk about the lawyers. Well, we didn't have a lawyer, but Lonzo probably did. Here's how the deal broke down. 10% went to the studio, 45% went to Lonzo, and 45% went to me, Dre, and Shakespeare.

That's about $15K each for us and $45,000 for him, which wasn't bad. But it was a little lopsided, don't you think? We didn't think it was that fair, but it was more money than we ever had.

Now, what did I say I would do when I got some money? I went out and bought me a car.

It wasn't a new car, but it was a 1976 Porsche 914. (This is what you would call the lower-end model.) Dre bought Lonzo's old Mazda RX7. And Shakespeare? I think he bought an old Nissan Z. Lonzo, let me see. He bought a house and a BMW 633.

Here we back in Audio Achievements again. Me and Dre are producing everything! We're starting to be like a real team in the studio. Our production skills are starting to grow since the first album. We even updated our equipment. Let me see if I can remember...

We got another keyboard (Yamaha DX-7), we updated our sequencer (Roland MC-500), and the main thing we changed was the drum machine (SP-12). This was the newest thing in drum machines because it was a sampling drum machine. What is sampling? It is taking bits and pieces from records that you can digitally record inside a drum machine.

Our beats are coming out better. We're finding new ways and tricks to record them. We're starting to get our own sound.

On this album, we made a couple of slow songs, like "Love Letter" and "Masters of Romance." The original song, "Lovers" is what kinda helped us get this deal because it had decent radio play.

Then we made a song called "The Fly" that we created a dance for. And Dre made his personal song called "He's Bionic."

Now we also grew up on the album cover. The clothes had gotten way better. Of course, I had on my paisley design and (we don't have that much makeup this time) we even had matching gold Wreckin' Cru medallions. We're on a major label, living large, and about to jump in the fast lane when the car comes to a screeching halt.

Screeeechhh!

Somehow, we got caught up in red tape or whatever it was, but I call it bulls**t.

The album didn't really have no record sales for whatever reason. So, the record company kicked us in the butt and sent us on our way. Other words, the one album deal was over, and all the money was gone.

It's time to fire up the old Kru Kut Records and get back to the grind again. We started working on a new 12-inch single called "Cabbage Patch."

Inside the single's lyrics, we made a small comment about the record company. We also made up a dance for this song.

Now we're working on a second single called "House Calls." I call this one Dre's personal baby 'cause he did all the rapping on the song. That song started getting a little fire on the radio.

Wreckin' Cru on the road. (1986)

One day we was in Lonzo's "new" house in the "new" demo studio in the back. Me and Dre was there working, and Shakespeare walked in with these two girls. One of them was light-skinned, and the other one was dark. The girl he liked was a cousin of this guy from Long Beach. (Just a hint: He will become the biggest and most famous rapper from that city.) They both sat down behind the mixing board.

I was on the couch in front of the board, but the way the layout is set up, I can't see their faces, but I can only see underneath the board.

What do I see? Some light-skinned hairy legs.

(*Hmmm...*That's right up my alley!) ☺

Now let me think of a name for her...

(I'll call her Miss Sexy S.)

She was tall, light-skinned, and a freak. But this one was a little different. We went to all kinds of places together. We went to some amusement parks and to the movies. I would even bring her souvenirs from our shows on the road. And did I fail to mention we did our thang? Let's keep it right there.

I won't go into detail. Let's just say she was an all-around fun girl. She would stay in my life for over 30 years. But something significant would happen in the future. This would also become a part of my destiny.

But here's a little prehistory that you may not know. One day

83

Shakespeare asked me to roll out with him to Rialto, California, which is about 40 minutes outside of LA. We was driving in his Volkswagen bug. (I don't know what happened to the Nissan Z.) The weird thing was it had an automatic clutch. This was the first time I had seen that.

Why am I mentioning this? You will see in a few minutes. What was our reason for the drive? Girls, of course.

We get there, and I see there's a bunch of girls.

I'm thinking to myself, "Which one is for me?"

Well, none of them was for me. It turned out to be some kind of female rap group named JJ Fad. In other words, it was a dry run.

Let's talk about that bug again. On the way home, I was just amazed how he was driving it with no clutch. But it had two gears. I'm wondering why this model wasn't very popular. As we are getting off on El Segundo Blvd, the engine shuts off. We rolled all the way to the light, then stopped.

He turned the key and... "*Click...*"

Nothing.

We both looked at each other, and he said, "What the h*ll..."

That was the last time that car started. I see now why people didn't like the automatic Bugs. I couldn't say nothing. I just held my laugh in while we pushed the car to Lonzo's house. Now getting back to the Wreckin' Cru.

Along comes Lonzo with this new manager. He's older than Manager X, but he has some credit behind him. Let me think of a name for him...

(I'll call him Mr. Manager.)

So, immediately he sets up a big show. Where? London, England. It's called the **UK FRESH '86**.

Here we are on a 10-hour flight to London. (Of course, not in first class.) The flight wasn't too bad. We had "3 hots in a cot." Other words, we had three meals and a reclining seat.

We made it to London, and it's quite different.

There's no heat here, but they have plenty of rain and fog.

Immediately I'm on the international fringe benefits search and I spotted one—the manager of our hotel.

Speaking of hotels, did I say the room was 5'x5' wide? Everything is small in London. You even have to climb up to get in the bathtub to take a shower.

Wreckin' Cru at UK Fresh. (1986)

Now let's talk about rehearsals. For whatever reason, me and Lonzo got into an argument. This is the first time we ever argued. We were having issues with our equipment because London runs 220 volts. The U.S. runs 120. I walked off the stage, hot as fish grease.

I went and sat in one of the seats. Then I hollered out, "You figure it out!" (Of course, he didn't figure it out.) I had to go to our backup mode and play the music from a reel-to-reel tape. We finally finished rehearsals, but I was still hot.

It's July 19, the night of the show. You could feel the excitement in the air. Just then, the lights went black. The crowd started cheering. I remember walking up the stairs to the stage. 20,000 people packed in Wembley Stadium. As I stood there in front of our equipment, suddenly everything went silent.

From the **infamous garage** to the Queen Mary to Wembley Stadium...

As I'm about to push the button on the tape machine to play our music, the energy just grew. The London crowd went crazy.

I pushed "Start," and a new beginning began. Me and Dre's destiny was now set.

85

1987

It's a road trip for me and Dre. During one of our shows in Stockton, California, I met this girl. Let me think of a name for her...

(I'll call her The Girl from Up North.)

One Friday night, she gave me a call and said, "Why don't you come up here and bring a friend?"

I hung up the phone and heard a knock on the door. I answered it. It was Dre.

I told him, "Dre, let's roll up north. I'll tell you the details on the way."

Did I fail to tell him it was a 5-hour drive? (Did I just put him in the hot seat because we're taking his car?) Here's the big problem.

From past experience, I know for a fact that he falls asleep quick while driving. And I d*mn sure know that I fall asleep while I'm driving. (Other words... Why are these two knuckleheads trying to drive up north?)

I told him, "I'll take the first shift."

Me in London. (1986)

Let's hit the road. We're on the 5 Freeway rolling through the Grapevine. All of a sudden, my eyelids are getting heavy. And heavier...

O sh*t, we need to stop the car and switch. So, we switched.

Okay, Dre's behind the wheel rolling down the 5 near Bakersfield. Now his eyelids are getting heavy. Mines are closed. His foot is pushing down more on the pedal, and his eyes are closed.

We rolling down the freeway at 100 miles an hour. Driving just like the cartoon character Mr. Magoo...

I don't know how far we drove or how long. All I know was we drifted off the highway to the side of the road in the dirt. The trees were whipping past us.

All of a sudden, something woke both of us up. Then he slammed on the brakes. We turned and looked at each other in silence. Now all four of our eyes are wide awake.

He drove off and got back on the road. In less than a mile, there was a parked big rig with its flashers on in the exact same dirt path that we was on.

Had our life been cut short, our destiny would have ended that night. Just imagine this history didn't happen.

No Ruthless Records, no Eazy-E, no N.W.A, no JJ Fad, no Michel'le, no D.O.C., no Snoop, no Eminem, no 50 Cent, no West Coast G-Funk sound, and the list goes on and on.

As we drove past the truck, both of us looked at each other again.

(I hear that same bell sound. "Ding"! Miracle!)

The days of the Wreckin' Cru are winding down, and we are working on the group's last song. The title of this one is "Turn Off The Lights." It's a slow jam, and we went back to the style of all four of us talking the lyrics. We had to bring in a new female singer because the original one, Mona Lisa, was M.I.A. We end up using this new singer called Michel'le. When she talked, she had a baby voice. But when she sang, she sounded like a grown woman. Nobody knew it at the time, but this would become the Wreckin' Cru's biggest and best song.

(So that means it probably sold a lot of records.)

Here's a funny note. I knew this girl that worked at a department store that sold Guess jeans. For some reason, she was hooking me up for free. I was the best-dressed Guess wearing person around. And I was real sharp. I had the Guess jean jackets, Guess jeans, and Guess shirts, in every color.

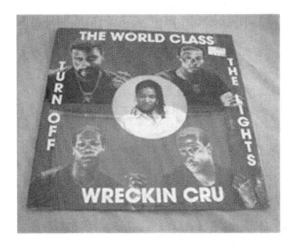

Wreckin' Cru's Final Song (1987)

I also had Guess belts. I had so much Guess, I started to sell some. (I think nowadays, this is what you would call boosting.)

One day Dre brought this guy to Lonzo's house. I would sell him and his pregnant baby mama gear all the time. His name was Eazy-E, but I called him E. He was a little short guy, but he was a baller. I remember he had this custom-painted burgundy Suzuki Samurai jeep.

I don't know if it was because they bought all my Guess gear, but we ended up becoming great friends. I also became the godfather of their son, Derrek.

I don't mean to change the subject, but let's change it.

I met another girl that bought me gifts. But this one is acting a little too much like the cartoon character Richie Rich. Her gifts may not be as extravagant as Cougar's was. But these came attached with a bag of tricks, just like the cartoon character Felix the Cat had.

Let me think of a name for her...

(I'll call her Crazy K.)

She was from the Valley, and she had a friend named Sally. I'll tell you about that later.

88

She was kinda fine, a little cute, and she always wore a headband. I'll get to that later too. Now she had some frills, and she had some thrills. But the girl was really in love or really infatuated. You know what that means. She'll do just about anything for her man. (Did she really think that I was her man? LOL.)

Now back to Crazy K and her gifts. Let me think about this. She bought me some yellow Anvil Road Cases for my Technics 1200 Turntables. But here's one of the bags of tricks. I had to take her to the movies, eat dinner with her, and talk to her in front of her house for hours. (All at her expense, of course. Remember, I'm a struggling artist.)

Anyway, I got through that one. That wasn't too bad.

Here's another gift. This one was more practical because I needed some tires. You guessed it. She bought me some brand-new Pireli tires, low profile series. What was this bag of tricks? Let me set the scene for you.

We were sitting in the Porsche in front of her house, talking for hours again.

I'm bored...I'm getting bored...

I'm thinking to myself, "Here we go again, all this talking. I been sitting here all this time, going around and around, talking about nothing..."

Then I'm thinking, "I took this long drive to the Valley, burning my gas out. And now you want to get out and go in the house? Are you serious? Wow. What about my gift? Am I still getting it?"

Just then, she was about to Exit Stage Right. As I tried to stop her, somehow, my fingers got caught up in her hair.

Remember I told you about the headband? The hair was in my hand, but she was out the door! I looked at "it" then looked at her.

What the h*ll?

In other words, she had a wig on, and this I did not know. All this time, I thought her hair was long and curly— you know that "rich girl" look.

(No wonder she never wanted to get in the shower together.)

Boy, was I hoodwinked... LOL.

A Time For Change: Phase 2

Let's get to the next gift. This one didn't have a bag of tricks. But hopefully, I'm not being evil on this one. Guess what? She's sending me to Hawaii. The evil part was she wasn't going with me. It was just me and Shakespeare. The Wreckin' Cru had done a show in Hawaii a few months ago, and of course, I met a girl. But I didn't talk to her much because I didn't want to run up my mother's phone bill. So Crazy K sent us to Hawaii for seven days. Of course, all expenses paid. ☺

She said, "I will have a big gift for you when you get back."

But my mind wasn't on that gift. It was on the Honolulu girls.

I hooked up with the girl I met a few months ago. She was from LA but lives in Hawaii now. Let me think of a name for her...

(I'll call her Miss Island # 1.)

We did our frills and thrills. It was cool. But you know me, I was bored. (In other words, she had to go back to her boyfriend.)

Now I met another girl. This one was real sexy.

This one had that "Honolulu" shape. Let me think of a name for her...

(I'll call her The Real Miss Island.)

We hung out for the rest of my trip. She was nice and cute to look at. Was there frills? Nope. Was there thrills? H*ll no!

Let me get my mind back to going home and figure out what this big gift is that Crazy K got me. I feel this will be a nice gift, but this bag will have a joker in it.

I made it back home, and WOW! It was a beautiful black convertible Suzuki Samurai jeep! I was overwhelmed and couldn't believe it. A brand-new car!

I was sitting on top of the world. (Just like the character Humpty Dumpty who sat on a wall. But soon, I would have a great fall, LOL.)

While I'm sitting up here, let me tell you about this new record label that's being formed. The name was Ruthless Records, and E started it. In other words, he had the money to get it up and running. Dre produced the first album, which was a compilation. It had a few different artists on there like Eazy-E,

90

Ice Cube, MC Ren, The Fila Fresh Crew featuring The D.O.C., Ron Devu, Rappinstine, Dr. Rock, and Arabian Prince. Really it was just different groups with different songs all smashed together to make an album. We was taking a picture for the album cover, but on this particular day, I had some kinda 24-hour virus, so I couldn't make it on that one.

That was the only one I missed. This was the first record to be sold on Ruthless Records as an independent label distributed by Macola Records. Now, let's get back to this black jeep.

Something weird I heard about it came out. Remember I mentioned her friend Sally from the Valley? (Even though that wasn't her real name.) For some strange reason, something didn't sound right about the jeep. So, I parked it outside my mother's house and left it on the street for about three days. I didn't drive or touch it at all. I was nervous about it for some reason.

I talked to Crazy K on the phone, and she said, "Nothing's wrong with the car. Go ahead and drive it."

I said, "Are you sure?"

She said, "Go ahead."

Since I missed the photo shoot for the album cover, E wanted me to still be in the picture. It was too late for that cover, so he made arrangements for us to take a new photo for a new promo picture. I hop in the fresh jeep and roll on over to Dre's auntie's to pick him up. I get off the freeway at Imperial Highway. I make a left and go toward Van Wick Avenue. All of a sudden, I see red lights behind me. (That was my fourth encounter with the police.) But this time, it's the California Highway Patrol.

The officer pulled me over. He said, "You don't have a seat belt on."

I said, "Excuse me, officer, my bad." He didn't even ask to see my ID.

Then he said, "Have a nice day."

(Why did he pull me over? Was I just profiled?)

I put my seatbelt on, started the car, then went on my way. But that was only about one block. Red lights came on again. (That was my fifth encounter with the police.)

This is where the joker pops out. The same CHP officer pulled me over. But this time, there's a .45 in my face!

I asked the officer, "What happened?"

I looked around, and there was other .45's pointed at me.

All I heard was, "Please step out the f*cking car."

And you know what's funny? I couldn't get the seat belt off.

I'm looking at the officer with my hands in the air, saying, "I can't get it off."

Finally, I'm on the ground with a knee in my back. I guess this is what you would call a G.T.A. (Grand Theft Auto). I was arrested and booked. ☹ (This would be my first and only time in jail.) Are you kidding me?

I made a collect call to Dre's auntie's house.

I told them, "I won't be making it to the photo shoot today. See if you can call E and have him help my mother bail me out."

I get bailed out, and I can't wait to talk to Crazy K. I spent a whole whopping five hours in jail listening to the sergeants say...

"Do this..."

"Follow the line..."

"Move left..."

"Face the wall..."

"Don't move..."

Is this some kind of hopscotch game? D*mn.

This is N.W.A's first photo. (1987)
E is the one who wrote our names on this picture.

This is not my style. I made it home, and the next morning, we did the photoshoot. But the crazy thing is, there were only four of us there. Just me, Dre, E, and Ren—and this was the group's first promo photo. (Was this a sign of the times for our future?) Hmmm...

Later that night, I got a call from Crazy K.

When I answered the phone, the operator said, "We have a collect call from Crazy K, calling from Los Angeles County Women's Jail."

Now I could put two and two together. Her friend Sally had good credit, so Crazy K used her birth certificate and social security card to purchase the vehicle. I didn't know that. The dealer said all she had to do was bring the deposit back, and they would not have called the police. I find out the rich girl is not so rich after all. But this story is not finished.

One day I was at Mother's when I heard a knock at the door. But it wasn't a regular knock. It was the sound of the police—Internal Affairs. (This is starting to be like the show *CSI*.)

I said, "Excuse me, officer, what do you want with me?"

I found out that Crazy K was a big liar. She had lied about everything. She had even lied and said her arresting officers was taking bribes from her.

I looked at the officer dead in the eye and said, "What's this got to do with me?"

The bottom line...They told me if I would be a witness for them against her, they would drop all charges against me.

I said, "H*ll, yea."

I ended up going to court, but I never had to testify against her because they had enough evidence. And a funny note, they showed me a picture of her. I never seen her without her wig and headband on. And with that, the chapter of Crazy K finally came to an end.

THE WORLD'S MOST DANGEROUS GROUP

CHAPTER 5: BOYZ-IN-THE-HOOD

The money was getting funny. In other words, there was no money. Guess what I needed? A J-O-B. I haven't used this word in a while, but Mr. Entrepreneur needed to find a way to make some money. So, I asked Shakespeare a question.

I said, "Man, can you hook me up with a job?"

To me, I didn't care what the job was. He hooked me up with his manager, and I got hired. But let me explain what this job is. First of all, it was in a high-class place. What was the job description? Let me see...

I stand there at attention with a pink shirt on, beige pants, and a pink bowtie. When a car pulls up, I say, "May I help you?"

What am I? A valet. Where am I working? At a brand-new hotel in Beverly Hills.

Now, this is the crazy part. Our song, "Turn Off The Lights" is starting to get a lot of airplay and here I am, chasing and moving cars all around with a pink bowtie on. Was I embarrassed? Yes. Did I need the money? H*ll yes. I ain't stupid. I needed this job.

While I was working, Dre produced this song called "Boyz-N-The-Hood." Cube wrote the words, and E rapped the lyrics.

Now E was not a natural rapper. But to tell you the truth, he wasn't a rapper at all. The song was originally written for these rappers out of New York. For some reason, they thought the words was just too harsh or too street. Other words, it wasn't their style. So, Dre convinced E to do the lyrics. It took a while and many takes to lay his vocals down. The key item was the sound of his voice and that young gangster look. This would be the ground-breaking song that would really launch Ruthless Records. This was a totally different sound from the Wreckin' Cru. This was more like street music, but eventually, this would be called "Gangsta Rap."

Now Dre produced another 12-inch single. This time Cube was the lead vocals on a song called "Dope Man," which was on side A. On the flip side, E had his second single called "8-Ball."

Both of these songs were equally gaining momentum on the streets—not on the radio, but underground.

I remember after work one time, Dre told me, "You should be

a part of this new movement I'm doing. This Ruthless Record thing. This Wreckin' Cru stuff is getting kinda old, and you know we ain't making no money."

I said, "I don't have to think about it. I'm down."

A couple of weeks later, the idea came up of putting together a supergroup. That means pulling people from these other places like Cube from C.I.A., me and Dre from The Wreckin' Cru, Eazy-E and MC Ren from his old neighborhood, and then pull in Arabian Prince, who was a solo artist. The idea was great, but now it needed a name. I don't know who came up with it, but it wound up being N.W.A, which meant "N*ggaz Wit Attitudes."

We wanted that meaning to be an eye-opener. Really to take away the stereotype from the name they used to call us (n*ggers). Because saying the word, "n*gga" is a normal everyday word to us, just like, "Whut up, homie," or "Whut up, homeboy," or "Whut up, buddy?"

It was more than just a name. It would become part of hip-hop culture and music history. Now I need to get back to the job.

After three months, my career as a valet was over. This was really not my style. It was cool. Nothing was wrong with it, but I don't think this was my destiny.

On my last day at work, I was standing there at attention. I was looking up at the building and thinking to myself...

"I have a feeling that I'm coming back to this hotel one day. I don't know why, but I won't be a valet."

The "Turn Off The Lights" single was still hot on the radio. I'm assuming it was selling a lot of units because unofficially, me and Dre had parted ways with the group. Lonzo just didn't know it—yet. That's why we never did any shows from that record, even though it was the hottest song from the Wreckin' Cru.

Now we was starting to do a few shows off the "Boyz-N-The-Hood" 12-inch single. We stepped our game up. We added a drum machine and two sets of turntables for the live show. One of the sets was from the Wreckin' Cru. (Remember Crazy K bought me a set with the yellow cases.)

So, we borrowed that set for quite a while.

Lonzo kept asking us, "Where's my turntables?"

Me and Dre just brushed it off. Our initial thoughts were not to return them at all. (Maybe we should hold them hostage for some of the backpay. LOL.)

One day we was having a ... Let me think of a name for this... I'll call it a "Sit Down at the Round Table."

We was at Lonzo's house, but he was not there. At the dining room table was me, Dre, E, and Unknown and there might have been one other person, but I don't remember who it was.

While we were sitting there, this strange question came up. I don't know who thought of it, and I don't know who asked it. But the question was...

"Would you sell your soul?"

I remember we all looked around at each other. The room went silent. I gave my answer first. I didn't say no, but I remember saying, "I don't know about all that."

I can only recall one answer...

Nah, let me just stop right there. I will keep that person and that answer private. I'm not putting up a **"Black Curtain,"** but I'm locking a **"Black Door."**

Early Days: Ruthless Records

First things first. The "Boyz-N-The-Hood" single is starting to really pick up on 1580-KDAY. It's starting to be #1 every night on the high school Top 5 list. Record sales are starting to pick up. In the meantime, E was selling records out the trunk of his car. So, that means we make many trips to Hollywood, either going to the radio station or Macola Records to pick up the 12-inch vinyls. Did I fail to mention that me and Dre officially left the Wreckin' Cru? It was just like we left. That was it. And yes, we did give Lonzo his turntables back. Shakespeare also left at the same time. Years later, he would become a preacher.

Now back to some of these trips up to Hollywood. Me, Dre, Ren, and E would be in his Samurai jeep. Now think about this. These were not the days of the cell phone. These were the days of telephone booths. If you don't know what that is, it's that square box on the street corner where you can go in and make a phone call. There was also this little device that's called a pager. A person couldn't text you, but they could contact you. Then their number would show up on the screen. I said all that to say this.

As we were on our journeys to Hollywood, E would get a page from his baby mama. Now hold up, I didn't tell you this. E had a glove compartment full of coins. As he was driving, he got a page. He spotted a phone booth, then pulled over. He went in the phone booth, put a dime in, then made a call. Then we take off. Okay, that's cool. A mile later, he gets another page. He spots another phone booth, pulls over, goes in, puts a dime in, then makes a call. Now, did I say this happened every mile all the way to Hollywood? Which was about 20 miles, up and 20 miles back. Other words, that was a lot of phone booths, LOL.

I don't know whether Dre or E came up with this brilliant idea. But the thought was...

Let's make Eazy-E and N.W.A into two separate groups, even though we was one group. Why? There's more money that can be made by being two separate groups.

I said, "*Hmmm... That is a d* mn good idea.*"

That was the plan.

There was no more Lonzo demo studio, so we made E's mother's garage our demo studio. We upgraded our equipment.

(We really had to buy our own equipment now.)

We bought the latest drum machine, which was an SP-1200. The old SP-12 had 5 seconds of sample time. The new one had 10 seconds. This upgraded our sound for the beats even better. That would be the sound of Ruthless Records for the next 8 years.

We had a little 4-track recorder, and we also used the Juno-106. (The one Cougar C bought me.) We only did a few pre-production songs there. And it was here where we got our name (High Powered Productions). Our course was set; the Dynamic Duo was in full effect. E had pulled Mr. Manager from the Wreckin' Cru. The first goal was to find a label deal, not a record deal. Let me give you the ghetto version of these two terms.

Term One: The Record Deal- You sign to the label and do what they want you to do.

Term Two: The Label Deal- This is where you have full control, and you can put out just about anything you want to. (Plus, there's more money this way.)

Mr. Manager set up a showcase for Island Records. So now we have to get some kind of package together. We got a fortunate break about something. Remember I told you about that group JJ Fad? Well, Arabian Prince had been working with them. They came up with a single called "Supersonic."

It was on the label from a guy named Rudy. (R.I.P.) He was

from a group called LA Dream Team. I didn't like the song at first, but once I kept hearing it over and over on the radio, it finally grew on me. Later on, the group ended up being a part of Ruthless Records.

Me at Audio Achievements

Remember the girl Michel'le from our last Wreckin' Cru song? Well, we had been working on a demo for her, so she would also become part of the showcase.

Now it's the day of the performance. The record company had rented a sound stage in Hollywood, California. The lineup is set.

We got Eazy-E, we got N.W.A, featuring me, Dre, Cube, Ren, and Arabian Prince. We also have JJ Fad and Michel'le. It felt kinda weird because we were doing a live performance, but it wasn't a live crowd. It was just some executives sitting there looking at us kinda strange.

During the performance, when we said, "Ho!" they said...
Nothing.

I think we did our thang. But from the looks of it, I don't

know. Later on, Mr. Manger told us they had offered us $10,000 for a record deal, but not a label deal.

I remember me and Dre telling E, "Let's do it! How much cash do we get?"

E said in his little voice, "Naw, man, I'm not selling out."

Me and Dre said, "Yeah, man. I don't know about selling out, but we need that M-O-N-E-Y." (We all about the love for the music, but in our case, we needed that money.)

E said, "Naw, man. We want a label deal, not a record deal."

Me and Dre looked at each other, then looked at him like he was crazy. But till this day, I was very glad E held out for a label deal (Priority Records) and not a record deal.

1988

1988 is going to be a rough, tough, and rare year. What do I mean by that?

Here it is—a label that is only a few months old. We were the hot new kids on the block. For the next 3 ½ years, everything our hands touched would turn to gold or platinum. We was starting to be like a baby Motown, with hit after hit. Me and Dre produced and mastered everything in the studio— from recording to mixing, all the way to splicing tapes. These days it's all done on the computer.

(I wish I had my iMac back in them days.)

This is going to be one of our hardest working years. And did I fail to mention that Cube had to go to some kind of trade school in Arizona for 365 days?

(I think his parents made him go. But don't quote me on that.) He didn't want to go, but he ended up going anyway. He did come back from time to time to do some shows on the road with us. Plus, he also returned to take photos for different album covers and write on a number of our projects.

Now let's get to the bread and butter.

Donovan from Audio Achievements had made some upgrades to the studio. He had bought a brand-new Trident 24-track mixing board, which had a great analog sound. This would be the board that all original Ruthless songs would be recorded on.

E said, "Mr. Manager got us a record deal with this small

company, called Priority Records."

(Now who the h*ll is Priority Records?) Let me think about this for a minute...

E said, "They have the California Raisins."

We said, "The California Raisins? Who the f*ck are they?"

He said, "Their hit song was, "I Heard It Through The Grapevine."

So, we said, "And—what that got to do with us?"

Then he said, "But they went platinum, and that's their only group."

Then we said. "Okay, shakin' it, Boss. Excuse me—listening, Boss."

E said, "Come on, man, you don't get it? They're real hungry, so they can put all the focus on us."

E liked this deal because he got to put on the label "Ruthless Records" in large print and "Distributed by Priority Records" in small print. (In other words, he got to put his red Ruthless label on the actual vinyl.) That was exactly what he was holding out for—to be the label and not on the label.

Let's get to the first project—E's single. When you walk into the studio, who do you see? "The Dynamic Duo." That's me on the mixing board and Dre on the drum machine and keyboards. This would be the look of High Powered Productions.

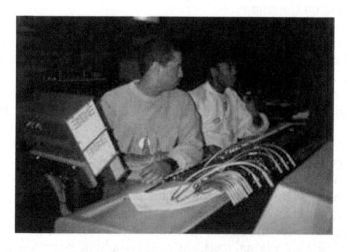

"The Dynamic Duo" ... Me and Dre.

Now we did something out of the norm. Side A of the vinyl, we called the street side. Why? Because all the cussing was on that side. Side B was called the radio side, which had no cussing at all. On the street side, the first title was called "Eazy Duz It," which was the follow-up song to "Boyz-N-The-Hood."

We also did another song on the same side called "Ruthless Villain," featuring Ren. The radio side had E's next title called "Radio," which featured Greg Mack from K-DAY and Nasty Nes.

The last song was called "Compton's N The House." This was the first time Dre and Ren rapped together. (Out of all the songs, this one was my favorite.)

E took the cover photos, but the crazy thing was the back of the cover only had four of us again. Cube was still in school at the time. (That *"Hmmm"* is coming back again—only four of us.)

In the spring of 1988, Ruthless Records released Eazy E's very first single called "Radio."

Now, remember the girl group JJ Fad? Well, the single that Arabian Prince made (Supersonic) was starting to catch a little fire on the radio. I don't know what happened, but JJ Fad ended up signing with Ruthless. But there was a twist to it.

E at Audio Achievements

102

Rudy from the LA Dream Team was supposed to bring us the master of the single (the final mix on ¼ inch tape) for the song, "Supersonic." Me, Dre, and Arabian was waiting in the studio.

And waiting...

And still waiting...

He never showed up.

Dre said, "Let's just remake the song from scratch. That way, Ruthless will own the masters."

We produced the song and landed another label deal (Atco Records). On April 18,1988, Ruthless Records released JJ Fad's first single called "Supersonic." Since the single caught on real fast, h*ll it's time to work on an album. It was like clockwork.

We was knocking out songs back-to-back. Their music was a little different. It was kinda like...electronic- dancey- girl-e-ish style. The girls were really easy to work with.

Remember the guy The D.O.C. from Dallas? He also wrote one of the titles on the album. (And this was just the beginning for The D.O.C.) It took me and Dre about a month to produce all the songs, then mix and finish the album. Arabian was also a co-producer.

On June 15, 1988, Ruthless Records released its first album, "Supersonic." Okay, back to the studio. It's time to work on N.W.A's first single for Priority Records.

(L-R) Dre, Cube, me, Baby D and MC JB of JJ Fad.

Cube was on break from school. Me and Dre produced Cube's single, which featured E, and it was called "Gangsta Gangsta."

This was the follow-up song to "Dope Man." Cube's voice was quite unique and different from E's voice. It was more suave-like but really gangsta style. He also had great writing skills.

Me and Dre started working on the second song, which was called "Quiet on the Set." This was another single from Ren. Did I fail to mention, he had great writing skills also? But Ren had the strongest voice in the group.

The next song, called "Something Like That," would feature Ren and Dre rapping again and the last song for the single we produced was for Arabian. It was called "Something 2 Dance 2."

He also co-produced on this one. (This would be the last of the electronic sound—the old Wreckin' Cru style.) We were somewhere downtown in LA, getting ready for a photoshoot for the cover. But let's talk about this.

One of us said, "What do you think about when you hear the saying of someone shining shoes? 99.9% percent of the time, you picture "us" shining "their" shoes." I don't know who came up with the idea, but it was a good one.

Somebody said, "What would it look like for "us" to have "them" shining "our" shoes? And to top it off, instead of wearing dress shoes, we wear tennis shoes?"

So, what did we end up with? A black and white cover with six guys getting their shoes shined. (Now that might ruffle some feathers!) Since we're on the subject of album covers, we also took quite a few photos from that same photo shoot.

Sometimes I would just roll up to Priority Records and walk in their offices and check on things. While I was there, they would show me what covers they were currently working on. On this day, they happened to show me this one particular photo. I remember this one because the photographer was lying on his back on the ground. He was pointing the lens up while we was looking down at the camera.

I said, "*Hmmm,* this would be a nice shot for an album cover."

But Priority had their mind set on this other photo of us walking in an alley. I was trying to give them a, you know, a "hint, hint" about the photo I was looking at. A crazy thing about it was there was only 5 or 6 photos of this shot taken.

This was quite a unique photo in two ways:
—It would be Arabian's last photo with the group, and:
—This photo would become N.W. A's first album cover.
On September 5, 1988, Ruthless Records released N.W.A's first maxi-single called "Gangsta Gangsta."

Back On The Road Again

It's time to get down and dirty. We're back on the road again. But now there's more work than fun because we were trying to promote ourselves.

Remember the movie *The Five Heartbeats,* where they drove around on their promo tour in a station wagon? Well....

We rented a white station wagon and drove around on our promo tour. We were on what you would call "The Chitlin' Circuit." Did I say that somebody was still at school— still? LOL.

I know it's been a while, but I haven't mentioned any fringe benefits. What happened? Did I fall off the earth? Well, let me see...

There was another Marsha Marsha Marsha in Seattle. (That would bring a smile to my face.)

There's also a saying that people in Oakland would say, "You want to 'G'?"

"What the h*ll is "G"?

I figured it out. It's another saying for fringe benefits.

Well...I would go around and ask all the girls, "You wanna G?" ☺

There was so many girls, I don't even remember one name, LOL. Now let's get back on the road.

Technically we're starting to get off "The Chitlin' Circuit." That means we doing big shows in big arenas. We was sharing the stage with hot groups like Salt-N-Pepa. (Who didn't have a crush on Salt? I d*mn sure did.) Then there was the guys that made the hit song, "A Fly Girl," The Boogie Boys, Eric B & Rakim, and our boy Ice T with his song "Colors."

Then there was Sir Mix-a-Lot, with his hit single, "Posse on Broadway." Now we was doing a show in Texas with a group that had a hot song out.

Guess what the name of the song was? "Turn Off The Lights."

105

Me and Dre wanted to be a little devious. 😐 We wanted to see who these new members of the Wreckin' Cru was. In other words, we wanted to see who was doing our vocals.

We ended up telling the promoter, "Let us perform before the Wreckin' Cru."

We told him, "It's kinda like an inside joke to us." We wanted them to be the bigger group tonight.

We took the stage and did our set. Afterwards, we went up into the stands. We had found some seats on the side of the stage. Basically, we just wanted to see Lonzo and them perform "Turn Off The Lights." It was kinda strange to see somebody actually singing our parts.

We wondered to ourselves, "How do they feel being us?"

Me and Dre looked at each other, chuckled, and said, "Ah, it's just Lonzo and whoever they are." LOL.

You know me— we're back in Texas.

Ain't no sense in wasting time here. Fringe benefits are calling me. I-AM-OUT.

Supersonic #1 12-inch sales

Let me switch the timeline. Here's some breaking news for you. On September 30, 1988, JJ Fad became Ruthless Record's first gold album. This would be the first album me and Dre produced that went certified gold. (This was just the beginning.) If you don't know what gold is, it's 500,000 units (records) sold. And I must say, WOW! "We did what?"

From the **infamous garage** to gold? Really?

We were just some young kids from Compton starting out on the road to our destiny.

A—MAZING...

The Making Of Eazy's Album

Now we can get back into the studio. Guess what?

We got a brand-new toy—an overpriced keyboard. (E-MU Systems Emulator III) What do I mean by overpriced? It was $10,000. Was it worth the price? I say "h*ll yea," because it had almost unlimited sample time. That's with the use of a floppy disk.

If you don't know what that is, this is what you would call a flash drive nowadays. Let's talk about the studio and us.

Me and Dre practically lived in the studio. That means when you walk in, who do you see? Me on the mixing board, and Dre on the drum machine and keyboards.

But hold up. Let's get this straight. Well, technically— Monday through Friday. From 12 to 8, but never on the weekends. That was my "me" time. (You know—my fringe benefit search.) But let's move on.

Remember, I told you—We're one group, but we're split into two entities. As the Wayans Brothers would say, "Mo Money, Mo Money... ☺."

What's next on the list? It's time for me and Dre to produce E's album. Let me think about this for a moment...

That means me and Dre are going to have to sit there and take turns doing E's vocals. That means we gotta do line by line, almost word by word. LOL.

That's about— let me think— about 100 takes per song. Okay, this, we know. So, what do we do? Let me take a deep breath.

We put a piece of tape across the whole board, and we make marks on it every time he makes a mistake. Other words, there are a bunch of marks across the whole board. And did I say I'm still holding my breath?

I step back, take a look at all the marks, let that breath out and think to myself...

"D*mnnnnnnnnnnnn!!!"

Because remember, HE-IS-NOT-A-NAT-U-RAL- rapper.

That's Ren in the background laughing, and guess who that is after a loooonng session...

Let's talk about the cover. If you take a real deep look at the cover, you would swear it was an N.W.A cover. Let me see who's in the photo...

There's E, Ren, Cube, Dre, me, DJ Speed, and there's two more guys in the photo.

(I know they're gonna talk about me, but I forgot their names.)

There's one more thing out front on the cover. It's a little box that says... "THESE SONGS CONTAIN EXPLICIT LYRICS."

And to my knowledge, we was one of the first groups to have that label on an album cover. (I guess that's something else we started. LOL.)

Okay, let's get started. Everybody's on board, everybody's ready. Dre called The D.O.C. up. He packed his bags, then got on the plane. Once he landed in LA, he was ready to get to work.

The first song we worked on was called "Still Talkin.'" This was one of my favorites on the album. The D.O.C. wrote the lyrics. People may not know this, but at the beginning of the song, the two old men's voices was actually Dre and Cube. I like the way E's delivery was on this song.

The next song was "Nobody Move," written by Ren. Then there's "Ruthless Villain," "Eazy Duz It," "Radio," and "Boyz-N-

108

The-Hood," which were pulled from the earlier singles. "Eazy-er Said Than Dunn" was new and written by The D.O.C. This song would also become E's second video.

Let's talk a little bit about this video. This one was shot at a big park in LA. It was a two-day shoot and was made to look like we drove up to a nightclub in E's Aerostar van. When we opened the door to the club, it went outside to the park. At the end of the video, we would walk back on the same path through the same door. While back in front of the nightclub, we would jump in the van and roll off. (Boy, that cost some big bucks to make.)

Now here's a piece of info for you that people really didn't recognize. The song "We Want Eazy" featured Ren and Dre. Did you miss it? Did you get it? I give you one more hint.

This was E's first video. You still don't get it? Think about it. I didn't mention Cube because he was still at school. However, he did make it for the video shoot. Now let's talk about his "We Want Eazy" video.

Was it expensive? H*ll yea ($100K) because it had a lot of special effects in it. But it was actually cool because it was our first time making a video. The main part of the video was me, Ren, and Dre performing live on a concert stage. E was performing his part from a video screen above the stage to make it look like he was rapping from jail.

Me, Arabian, and Dre DJing

109

Towards the end of the video, he would jump through the screen and land on the stage. Bootsy Collins also made a cameo appearance because this was one of his old songs that we remade. We got three songs left. Here you go.

The song "I'mma Break It Down" was written by Ren and Cube wrote "No More?'s" and "Eazy-Chapter 8 Verse 10."

Now, on the final song, Dre wanted me to actually play live drums. This one would be called "2 Hard Mutha's," featuring Ren and E. Wow! Think about it.

From the **infamous garage** to the Queen Mary to Wembley Stadium to now playing live drums in a studio. (On an album that that would become double platinum in the future.)

It's a wrap. All the tracks are completed, and all the songs are mixed. On November 23, 1988, Ruthless Records released Eazy-E's first album, called "Eazy Duz It."

Before I end the chapter, let me share with you a couple of untold stories. (You won't find these in the magazines.) One should have made me happy, and one would be a life lesson for us in the future.

Let's talk about the one that was a life lesson first. This one took place in Seattle, Washington. We were doing a show with LL Cool J. It was me, Dre, Cube, Ren, and E kicking back in the dressing room before we hit the stage.

Just then, one of the strangest things happened. A guy just walked right into our dressing room. Let me think of a name for him...

(I'll call him The Mystery Man.)

He looked around at everybody and stopped at one of us. The Mystery Man started talking sh*t to him, then socked him!

In my mind, I said, "Wow! Did that just happen?"

As the one who got socked picked himself off the floor, he stared back at The Mystery Man and looked him dead in the eye. The Mystery Man talked more and more sh*t to him, then socked him again! And again, he got himself up off the floor. We stood there in shock. Everybody started looking at The Mystery Man kinda crazy.

While I'm standing there, I'm feeling behind me for something to grab so I can crack this dude. I noticed across from me somebody else was doing the exact same thing.

Now, this was the life lesson for us. We had nobody watching our backs—nobody protecting us. We got exposed.

We were vulnerable. That was the first and last time that ever happened. From that day on, we had plenty of security.

(Bodyguards—I mean BIG Bodyguards!)

Now here's the one that should have made me happy. Do you remember E's burgundy Samurai jeep? He hadn't been driving it lately because he bought a new vehicle. It was a blue Ford Aerostar minivan that had chrome rims on it. You might have noticed it at the beginning of the "Eazier Said Than Done" video.

I don't want to throw him under the bus, but I have to talk about him— just a little bit.

One day he let me drive the jeep.

But he said, "If you drive it, you gotta clean it."

Okay, I cleaned it. Now here comes the part when I talk about E. I'm not going to call him a hoarder, but he sure was holding on to trash in the car. Did I say old food in the back of the car? Piled up clothes? Let's just say he's a clean person but just a little junky. After cleaning it up, I ended up driving it for a few days.

It reminded me of the jeep Crazy K had bought me. (Remember the one I got arrested for?) So, E gave me some good news.

He said, "You want that car?"

I said, "Yea."

Then he said, "After Dre uses it for a couple of days, you can have it."

I dropped it off to Dre while he was over at his auntie's house on Van Wick.

I waited a day to get the Jeep back...

I waited two days...

And I'm still f*ckin waiting.

I finally get a call, and can you believe this? Somebody had the nerve to steal the jeep out in front of his auntie's house. Are you kidding me? Really?

Suddenly I went from being happy like a kid, "I'm about to get the jeep," to being sad like Sally ran off with your girlfriend, "The car was stolen."

I almost had the keys in my hand...

Dreeeeeeeee!

Why did you park it on the street and not up–in–the–driveway? Whyyyyyyy? LOL.

111

I am so glad 1988— is —over.

But before we end this year, I have one more untold story. Now E had a bad habit of picking people up to ride with him.

The key was if you rode with him, you're gonna be stuck in the car waiting for him for hours.

(That's when he was doing his "hint." You know, LOL.)

One day, he asked me to ride with him in his new minivan. Of course, I said yes. We drove down to South Central LA.

He pulled up to this house, jumped out, and said, "I'll be right back."

I said, "Hold up! Where you going?"

E said, "Maaannn, I'll be right back." (That was one of his favorite f*ckin lines.)

I looked at him and thought to myself, "I know that trick. That's a 2-3 hour, 'I'll be right back' game."

He dashed into the house. I sat there for about 5-10 minutes, looking stupid. I glanced at this little duplex that was next door.

I thought to myself, "I know this place."

I got out the car and walked a little closer.

I was still thinking, "I—know—this—place..."

I knocked on the door, and a girl opened it.

"The Great Escape, LOL..."

112

I said, "Yep, I know this place because I know you."

Let me think of a name for her...

(I'll call her Ms. G.S.T.D.)

Why did I call her that? Well, after our frills and thrills session...

The next day would remind me of this song by Kool Moe Dee called "Go See The Doctor."

Hello? Doctor? Do you get it?

Her name was G.S.T.D...

In other words, STD, gonorrhea, "the clap," VD ...

That was a h*ll of a joy ride.

This would be the last time I ride with E on one of his little trips.

I paid the price. I had to take one for the team...

What did it take to get cured? Two shots in the a**. ☹

Now 1988 is officially OVER.

CHAPTER 6: STRAIGHT OUTTA COMPTON (1989)

Strap on your helmet. Tighten up your seatbelt —because 1989 is about to be one h*ll of a ride.

"You're now about to witness the strength of street knowledge..."

Once again, we're back at Audio Achievements. But first, let's take a quick commercial break. Guess what me and Dre are up to? We are looking for an apartment together. I'm not going to say he was having issues where he was staying, but he wanted to move out real bad, and I wanted to move out real bad too. I have a difficult choice. I have to be Mr. Entrepreneur or Mr. Bad A**.

Being Mr. Entrepreneur meant I needed good credit. (Remember I f*cked my credit up earlier.) Now being Mr. Bad A** meant I had to figure out another way. We found an apartment we wanted in a city called Paramount, CA. I have to see who I'm gonna be. I guess I'll be my brother René. What do I mean by that?

I'll just give him a call and ask him, "Can I be you to get us an apartment in Paramount?"

Gladly we kinda look alike. (You know how they say we all look alike... 😑)

So, my brother went to the manager's office and filled out the application. He got approved for the apartment in his name. Later on, he brought me the keys.

Wow! I can't believe it! A two-bedroom, two-bath APARTMENT! My very first time moving out of my mama's house! Are you f*cking kidding me? Oh sh*t, how do I tell Dre I want the master bedroom? Because it's bigger and has a bathroom in it. (He should understand, I did get it in my brother's name, LOL.)

Here I am, Mr. Bad A** walking around the complex with my head up, chest out, and I got my stroll on— knowing if I run into the manager, I can't forget who I am.

I have to be my brother René. But who cares? I'm on Cloud 9. No, really, I'm on Cloud 21! You know it's about to be on! But did I fail to mention? We had two extra guests that moved in with us. Our first guest was... Let me think of a name for her...

114

(I'll call her "Mystery Girl.")
Our second guest was The D.O.C. Let me think about this.
Me and Dre bought only four pieces of furniture.
He bought a bed and a refrigerator. I bought a bed and a couch. That was it.
Now I don't want to throw The D.O.C. under the bus, but he slept on my couch. And till this day, I still tease him about it. I would say...
"You slobbered all over my couch, so you owe me one, LOL."
I can't speak for Dre, but I had fun for that whole year we lived together. Me and him was just like brothers. Having our own apartment meant we had responsibilities, so we had to learn on the fly. You know me. I'm about the frills—and—the—thrills!
Before we get back into the studio, here's another untold story. But this one would have a joker in it. Wanna hear it? Here it go...
One morning I remember E giving me a call.
He said, "Come ride with me."
And I said, "Hold up, remember the last time I rode with you? I had to get them two shots in the 'you know what...'"
He said, "Nah, I'm about to go buy me a new car."
I said, "alright, cool..."
So, he picked me up, and we went to a car lot. Matter of fact, it was a Suzuki dealership.
We went in, and I'm just glancing around looking at all the new jeeps. Then the joker popped out. But this one was different.
He turned to me and said, "You want one?"
I had a strange look on my face. My eyes got big.
Then I said, "H*ll-to-the yeah!"
Then he said, "What color do you want?"
I had to pick myself up off the floor.
Then I said, "Are you kidding me?"
I looked at him, and he had that funny smirk on his face.
So, I said, "I want that green one."
The crazy thing was we walked out of there with two brand-new 1989 Suzuki Sidekicks! He got the white one, and I got the green one. They were both paid in full.
A few days later, E took Cube to pick one up. His was dark gray. But Dre had just got a red Benz 190, and Ren didn't want a Sidekick. He got something else.

115

(Now, these would be the jeeps featured in one of our upcoming magazine photoshoots.)

I wonder if this was E's way to make up for that jeep I never got.

Wow! That was one h*ll–of–a— morning! With that being said, let's get back to the studio.

The Making of the World's Most Dangerous Album

Who do you see? Me at the mixing board. Dre on the drum machine and keyboards. Cube's in one corner writing. Ren is writing in the other corner. The D.O.C. is in the back with his pen and paper. And where is E?

On the f*ckin phone, running his mouth like always, LOL. Actually, we started working on the album a few weeks before the end of 1988. It only took us a short period of time to finish and mix all the tracks. All of the songs were produced by me and Dre for High Powered Productions. The five of us is-on-a mission, with the help of a chosen few like The D.O.C., Stan The-Guitar-Man, and LA Dre. (R.I.P.) Nothing can stop us but us. (Remember these words. They might come back to "bite.")

Let's talk about this album. I think I'll start with the old songs first, and then the new ones. But before we get started, I just realized...

Did we put that many old songs on there? No wonder we finished so fast, LOL.

First up, "Gansta Gangsta." That's an old one that was written by Cube, Ren, and The D.O.C. Next up is "8 Ball" and "Dope Man," which we actually remixed. Both were written by Cube. Then we have "Quiet on the Set" and "Something Like That," written by Ren.

Then there's my favorite, "Compton's N The House." That's another remix written by Ren. The last of the old songs was "Something 2 Dance 2," which was written by Arabian.

Okay, let's move on to the new songs. We have "If It Ain't Ruff." This was the follow-up song to "Ruthless Villain."

I think this was the funkiest song on the album. It had that cold guitar lick in it. Ren wrote the lyrics and rapped on this song.

Next up, you have Dre's first solo song, which would be one of

116

the more cleaner songs on the album. What do I mean by that?

It had no cuss words. It was called "Express Yourself" and was written by Cube. This one would also become our second video, with cameos by Tone Loc and our old buddy Shakespeare. You know what's funny? This video shoot had Dre driving down a street (in a 4-door convertible Lincoln) looking like he was the president of the United States of America. There were also shots of him being in the White House. (That's odd because years later, one of us would become president.) Was that predicting what's coming in 17 years (2008)?

Makes you go, "*Hmmm...*"

"I Ain't The One" is another solo song by Cube that he also wrote. I like the funky piano on this one.

"Straight Outta Compton," is probably one of the strongest and most remembered tracks from the album. It was written by Cube, Ren, and The D.O.C.

The opening shot for the video was Dre saying...

"You're now about to witness the strength of street knowledge..." while sitting in front of a burning trash can.

It would take two days to finish the video. Some of the shots were of us being arrested and driving a police paddy wagon through the streets of Compton. This would become our most expensive video. Why? Because it never got any airplay. (It was also banned on MTV.) But the ban was kinda cool. It was a financial loss on the video side, but it would help our album sales to soar in the future.

Now Cube's opening line of the song says...

"Straight Outta Compton..."

That set the tone for the whole song. Ren's vocals were strong, and E's vocals were even stronger. The energy on this song was off the charts. But if you think that song was tough, the next one was even tougher.

As a matter of fact, so tough, it got the FBI to send us a letter. (We'll talk about that later.)

What was this song called? "F*ck The Police." This would become our most controversial song. We didn't try to make it controversial. We were like news reporters from the hood. We simply told the truth of what was going on in the streets.

(You know the crazy thing about it? This song is still relevant to this day.)

117

The last and final song was called "Parental Discretion Iz Advised." It would be the second time Dre would ask me to play live drums. This one was written by The D.O.C., Ren, and Cube. This was a more raw and entertaining song because everybody (The D.O.C., Dre, Ren, Cube, and E) rapped on it—everybody except me, of course. Me and Dre took two days to mix the album.

Now all the I's were dotted, and all the T's were crossed. It was finished, but the work wasn't over. I dropped off the two-track masters at Priority. While I was up there, one of the secretaries just happened to show me the album cover.

Guess what? It was the same d*mn picture I had told them about. You know, the one with all six of us looking down. Later on, people would say that it was an iconic photo.

And the people at Priority wanted to use a different photo— Shame on them, LOL.

Breaking news...

On January 17, 1989, JJ Fad became Ruthless Records' first gold single. Wow! Can you believe that? Another gold record!

From the **infamous garage** to a gold album and now a gold single...

Okay, it's record release party time! Time to be jumping for joy and, of course, time for my fringe benefits search.

Well...That's about all I can say about that party. Why? Let me set the scene for you.

We're at the Beverly Center in LA. The restaurant is packed and off the hook. But here's the key...

We, the group, are outside. The crowd is inside. Did you catch that? We could see all the guests dressed in their casual attire through the windows as the party is going down.

Did you get it yet? I'll give you a few seconds to think about that...

Now here's the answer. They wouldn't let us in our own party that WE paid for. Why? Because we were dressed as usual, in our work attire. (Black hats, black t-shirts, black jeans, and tennis shoes...)

You got to be kidding me. Really? They let all them in but didn't let us in. Ain't that bout' a b*tch! LOL.

No wonder we were labeled, "The World's Most Dangerous Group." We just show up to our events, and we get banned.

118

WOW! But check this out.

Eight days later, on January 25, 1989, Ruthless Records released "Straight Outta Compton," the first album by N.W.A.

Compton's N The House

The boys from Compton did it again. On February 15, 1989, E's album "Eazy Duz It" turned gold in less than three months. Did I just say that right? Our third gold record? Let me pinch myself and check...

Ouch! ... That hurt...(LOL.)

So, this is the real deal. We must be doing something right. Seems like everything we touch is turning into gold! JJ Fad's album, their single, and now E's album...

Wow! From the **infamous garage** to our third gold record!

You know, it's funny. We never even thought about a gold record. We only did it because we loved making music.

And if we could make a few bucks along the way, that's cool too. But the news gets even better. JJ Fad just got nominated for a Grammy for Best Rap Performance! Didn't I just mention the **infamous garage**? Are you serious? A Grammy nomination? For us? Well, not really us. We produced it, but it was still a nomination. But here's the bummer.

On February 22, 1989, we went to the awards ceremony at the **Shrine Auditorium** in LA. Can you believe this? We got suits on. We got our heads up and chests out. We're also wearing our cheesy smile. We feel kinda important today. I thought we was going to be in front of the lights and cameras, but this portion of the show (the rap category) was outside in a little hall. We got hoodwinked.

That part of the show was in the daytime and not aired. And the other bad news? They didn't win. That would be Ruthless Records' only Grammy nomination. But let's get to a happier note.

It's time to promote the album and get ready for the road again. But first, let's take a quick break.

One of the more popular TV shows called *Yo! MTV Raps* featuring Fab 5 Freddie called us up and wanted us to host the whole show. During the filming, we would drive all through Compton, standing on the back of a flatbed truck. We went from the Compton swap meet all the way to Venice Beach, California. It was so cool because they were the hottest show on TV. I don't know about the other guys, but I was excited to do it. We did a bunch of interviews and photoshoots, one after another.

We also did quite a few cover shots over the next 2-3 years. Let me think of a few of them...

We did *Yo Magazine* (a few times), *Rap Pages, Rap Masters, Spice, Hits, Rolling Stone, Hip Hop Magazine, Cash Box, Word Up, LA Times,* and *The Source Magazine.* We also made the cover of *LA Weekly.* Whew! That was a bunch. I'm almost out of breath, LOL.

Okay, let's talk about the road. We are getting ready for a major tour in the summer of 1989. (You know I was looking forward to that.) This will take some work to prepare and get all the ducks in a row. Me and Dre had to put the show together, which was 55 minutes long, pick all the songs for it, and get the sequence of them just right. We made three different intros. One intro is for when me, Dre, and Ren come out, another one for when Cube comes out, and the last one for when E came out. We broke the show down into three parts. Us, Cube, and E, in that order.

We wanted the stage to look like a street in Compton. I remember sketching out a diagram of the stage on a piece of paper. I mean the exact look of it. It was a Level 2 stage that looked like a street. On the top level, we would have stairs, streetlights, and manhole covers. (Dre and Ren would climb out through the manholes.) Underneath would be two chain length gates. E would open, then walk through them.

Cube would come from the side of the stage, and I would come from the back. Now being us, we would not have dancers but girls that looked like hookers walking on the street on top.

(Did we really do that? LOL.)

We would also take our own stage, lights, and sounds to all of the shows. We must be getting "big time." ☺

After all the rehearsals and getting our sh*t together, we was ready for the test. But hold up...

Where are the girl hookers coming from? Me (Mr. Bad A**) had to get on his job. Not to be throwing nobody under the bus, but someone knew a girl that knew another girl that I ended up meeting. She was fine, I mean that J Lo fine! She was sexy, I mean that Apollonia sexy! The kind that made your heart stop. LOL. Let me think of a name for her...

(I'll call her Super H.)

I know this might get me in trouble, and I say this with a little smirk on my face, but she had all the frills and thrills.

Now it's time to test the show before the tour. On March 23 and 24, 1989, we had two shows in Anaheim, California, at the **Celebrity Theatre**. It was Eazy-E/N.W.A and Ice T on the bill.

I think Ice headlined the first night, and we headlined the second night. Both nights was SOLD OUT. The first night went great, but the second, well— that was a little different.

Why? Because during our performance, all of a sudden, everybody wants to throw up gang signs. Other words, a big fight started. The party was over. (You ain't gotta go home, but you gotta get the h*ll outta here!) That was a scary moment because I had Miss Sexy S there. I didn't want her to get bopped in the head when they started throwing chairs all over the place. Oooh Weee! What a night!

Before we jump on this tour, here's some more breaking news. After MTV banned our video, we had no kind of radio play whatsoever. In just under two months, our "Straight Outta Compton" album went gold on April 13, 1989. Now we are getting a little excited. (Just a little bit.) That's four-in-a-row. I can't believe it! Ruthless is on fire!

From the **infamous garage** to four gold records...

We are on a f*cking roll!

The Eazy-E/N.W.A Summer Tour 1989

This was going to be a big one. What do I mean by that? We're talking about 40 dates, 40 nights, and 40 shows.

You know me...

I'm talking about fringe ben-e-fits. Wow, that's a girl each night, and sometimes two. (If I'm real lucky.) ☺

Did I fail to mention the pay? It was $1000 per show. Man, we're stepping our game up! How do I describe the tour?

Well... Let's start with the groups.

You got us, Salt-N-Pepa and—hold up. They didn't make it to the tour for personal reasons.

(I was looking forward to seeing Salt. You know me—I still had that crush on her, LOL.) So, Kid 'n Play filled their spot.

Next up is our boy Too Short, Kwame', JJ Fad featuring DJ Train (R.I.P.), and the opening act was The D.O.C. But on certain show dates, we would hook up with groups like LL Cool J and Public Enemy. The rest of our crew included LA Dre, our sound man, DJ Speed, our equipment guy, and Atron G., our road manager. Then you have Sir Jinx, K-Dee, Crazy D, and our boy, Lay Law. All we have to do now is get on a plane, fly to Nashville (THAT WAS SOLD OUT) for one rehearsal, and "show up to show out." Well, that didn't work out so great.

We get on the plane, and what do we hear? JJ Fad is talking sh*t to flight attendants. (You know where I'm about to take this.)

Just then, one of the flight attendants, with a small voice, said, "GET— THE— F*CK off…"

Wow…We find ourselves getting escorted off the plane. You got to be kidding me.

So, that next flight, we told everybody to "Shhh! Keep your mouths closed." This is costing us money, and we got two tour buses waiting on us in Nashville. We landed in Tennessee and did a full rehearsal. Now we're ready for the show.

Rehearsal time, Nashville, Tennessee (1989)

I was thinking to myself, "What kind of crowd will be in Nashville?"

It turned out to be one h*ll of a show. The crowd loved us!

There was no problems or fights throughout our whole tour.

Wow, we felt like stars... just a little bit.

The people went nuts. Not just there but in all the cities. Places like Cincinnati, Houston, Kansas City, Chicago, and Seattle, just to name a few. (But we never did LA.)

Let's get to my favorite subject—fringe benefits. Where should I begin? Okay, let's start in Nashville. I haven't said this in a while, but I'm in love again. Maybe just road love, LOL.

But let me think of a name for her...

(I'll call her Memphis Fly Girl.)

She was so fine and bad. Yes, there was frills and thrills, but that came later when I flew back to Memphis. I just have to laugh at myself sometimes.

Okay, here we go again. I fell in love with a different one from Memphis. (Guess there's something in the water.) This one was rich, fine, and bad. Let me think of a name for her...

(I'll call her Rich Girl G.)

Our tour stopped off in Atlanta. That was where I first met her. The story goes a little something like this...

She brought a friend with her for me, then went to see somebody else in the group. But I won't throw him under the bus. Me and her friend did our frills and thrills. Afterwards, Rich Girl G came by me and Dre's room. (Me and Dre always roommate on the road.)

I was struggling to iron my clothes on the floor, so she said, "Let me iron those for you."

I said, "Wow, that's cool."

Then somehow (Hint, hint...), we left together and went to her hotel. It must have been one of those lucky nights. We did our frills and thrills, then she brought me back to my hotel and dropped me off.

(And yes, I flew back a few times to see that one, also.) ☺

I went up to my room and noticed our door was wide open. Dre was asleep, and there was a girl in my bed, sleeping.

I woke Dre up and said, "Who the h*ll is that?"

He wiped his eyes, looked at me, and said, "Man, I don't f*cking know."

123

Really? There's −a −girl− in my bed asleep. HELLO?

These are the kinda things we have to deal with. Not money, not our bills, not our rent, not even the girls...

(Oh sh*t, we gotta worry about them every now and then, LOL.)

Now let's change the d*mn subject. Sometime doing the tour, we went to do a show at the famous **Apollo Theater** (Harlem) in New York. This was the first time any of us had been to New York. The sights were amazing, but let's talk about the show.

Think about this: We were the first West Coast group to come to New York. We were excited to be at the Apollo. Backstage we were getting hyped up and ready to rock the house. We touched the famous rock before going on the stage and, "Lights, cameras, and action..."

What did we get? People looking at us like we were crazy. They did not like our style or anything. So, we had to suck it up and finish the show. Gladly we only did a few songs. I can't imagine doing our whole set there. They probably would have started throwing rocks at us, LOL. They didn't clap for us; they didn't boo us.

But instead of saying, "Boo, boo, boo," on the tip of their lips, there was silence.

Nothing. *Crickets, crickets, crickets*...

Other words, that was one H*LL" of a crowd. Here's some more breaking news for you.

On June 1, 1989, E's album went platinum. If you don't know what platinum is, it's 1,000,000 units sold. Right now, we are unstoppable. I just can't believe all this.

But before we move on with the tour, Ruthless Records had just released another album. This one Dre produced by himself. It was called "No One Can Do It Better" by The D.O.C. I also played live drums on this album, on the song called "The Grand Finale."

A little hint. (This album would also go platinum in the future.) Instead of going show by show, city by city, and girl by girl, I'll just say it was one of the best two months of my life. But I'm not finished with the tour. Four major things happened. One of them would eventually change the look of the group.

No. 1: Let's start with the show in Detroit. Did I fail to mention that before the tour happened, we agreed to a deal that said we would not play the song "F*ck The Police?"

So, we said, "Cool."

Fast forward three months. We're at the **Joe Louis Arena** in Detroit, Michigan. Our show was pretty routine— same place, same time. We did everything the same way, night after night.

Well... This night we got to a certain point in the show. Dre was on the turntables, and I was side stage by the drum machine.

Just then, him and Cube said and did something out the ordinary.

I looked at Ren and thought to myself, "Did they just change the show without telling us?"

All of a sudden, Dre scratched in the song "F*ck The Police." Me and Ren were kind of stunned. The song played less than a minute, when...

OMG! All "H*LL" broke loose!

The police started throwing firecrackers in the crowd. Then they started coming towards the stage.

I said, "Feet, don't fail me now!"

I was out the back door of the arena. I ran through the parking lot all the way to our hotel.

Both buses started their engines up and were ready to drive us over the border into Canada. (Which was only a few miles away.)

We all went upstairs to our rooms and grabbed our gear. Then we met up at the elevator and got on it. There were three guys on the elevator, kind of facing the wall for some strange reason. The door closed, and then...

"BAM!"

They turned around, pulled their badges out, then said...

"Detroit Police!"

Somebody said, "These mother f*ckers caught us!"

They took us downstairs, where more of them were waiting.

The moral of the story was...

They just didn't want us to play the song in their city. What happened then? We got a $150 ticket and had to sign some autographs.

All this going on, jumping, and running and making my blood pressure go up. Then, when it was all over, we didn't even get paid for the show. Man, now I'm really p*ssed off! What a night that was...

No. 2: Halfway through the tour, Mr. Manager wanted to discuss paperwork with us in his room, one by one.

(Think about this. I have not mentioned anything about paperwork or money up until this point.)

I remember walking in his room. The lights were kinda dim, and he was sitting at a little desk. I forgot what he said, only up to the part about contracts and a check.

He said, "It took a while to get it done, but here it is. When you sign it, I have a check for $75,000."

I kept calm. The contract was about 100 pages long. I picked it up, flipped it over, and signed it.

Then I said, "Check, please." ☺

After that, I said to myself (in my "Old Man" voice...), "You big dummy!" Didn't you need a lawyer to even look at the paperwork? Weren't you the one preaching about that a while back?

I just shook my head and said, "Forget that—I just got "P-A-I-D."" LOL.

Before I go on to Number 3, here's some more breaking news.

On July 18, 1989, our "Straight Outta Compton" album went platinum. You really got to be kidding me. Ruthless is still on fire!

From the **infamous garage** to now multiple platinum and gold records...

My mother is really happy for me. WOW!

No. 3: Now here's some sad news I hate to report. It happened during the middle of the tour.

One day while we were traveling on the tour bus, I was in my bunk, sleeping. Suddenly, the bus stopped.

I sat up and looked around. I heard a crying sound coming from the back room of the bus. I walked back there and saw Dre on his knees, crying.

Somebody whispered to me and said, "Dre's middle brother just died."

I said to myself, "Wow, I had just seen Tyree (R.I.P.) before we left on tour."

I was about to touch Dre and say something, but I told myself, "No, I'll let him be."

Later, when we got to the hotel, me and him were talking in the room. He told me how Tyree had died. It happened on

126

Crenshaw Blvd. There was a freak accident or something that caused his brother to die. Dre was really hurting after this. He flew home for a few days for the funeral.

That was a wake-up call for us. We learned that you can be here one minute and gone the next.

I just hope I comforted him and said the right things at that time. I also loved Tyree, just like a brother.

No. 4: This was the nail in the coffin. I found out later that Cube didn't sign the paperwork. I have no idea why he didn't. (I stay out of grown folks' business.)

But I do know that after the last show, Cube was out of the group. (Here's where those words I said earlier bit us in the "you know what.")

But a weird thing happened. We never sat around and talked about why Cube left. Remember when I mentioned something about that first N.W.A picture, which only had the four of us in it?

Makes you go, *"Hmmm..."*

There was some more breaking news. It wasn't a good thing at first, but it turned out to be a great thing.

On Aug. 1, 1989, the Federal Bureau of Investigations sent us a letter. Other words, the d*mn FBI sent it.

If it had been the police, we would've just said, "Ahhhh, whatever." But it was the FBI. They are the ones that come in suits. You don't want to f*ck with them. ☹

It all boiled down to this.

One FBI agency sent us a letter, but another agency sent them a letter saying they were messing with our First Amendment Freedom of Speech rights. With all that being said, our record sales went through the roof.

And to that, we tipped our hats and said, "Thank you, Federal Bureau of Investigations."

Life After The Tour

I wonder how it's going to be since Cube left. He had a strong voice, great style, and energy. He was 1/5 of the group but 1/3 of the rapping. So that's going to be a big test in the future.

We finally made it back to the apartment in Paramount. After being on the road for a couple of months, rocking 40 cities and 40 shows, were we tired? Maybe just a little, but with almost $100,000 in my pocket, I-AM-READY to hit those streets.

(I can rest some other time.)

One night some of us in the group went to hang out at **Club Paradise** in Hollywood, CA. We walked in, everybody's checking us out, but I'm checking out this group of girls that were standing together. I walked over there behind them, then touched this girl's hand and held it. She didn't say anything, so I kept holding it...

And holding it...

Annnndddd, I held it til' I got that number.

Let me think of a name for her...

(I'll call her The Beautiful One.)

Remember that name. You'll hear it again in the future.

The next day, I woke up and jumped in the Sidekick, then hit Crenshaw Blvd., just to try and get back to normal. On this day, I was rolling in downtown LA and passed by this car dealership. I saw a white car on the lot.

(Actually, it happened a second time later on, but in that case, it would be a white truck.)

I made a quick U-turn and went back.

What did I see...? A white Corvette with white seats, white steering wheel, and white rims.

It was a 1988 35th Anniversary Edition.

I said, "How much?"

The salesman said, "$28K out the door."

I said, "You take trades?"

He said, "Yes, sir."

I said, "Here's the check." And I—AM—OUT. So, I burned rubber out the dealership, LOL.

Later on, E got on my case and asked me, "Why did you trade

in the Sidekick?"

I swallowed my pride, returned to the dealership, and bought it back. Did I fail to mention...?

That a week before, Dre had bought him a 1989 Black Convertible Corvette? (They can't stop the "Dynamic Duo" now.) About two weeks after I got my 'Vette, I pulled into this gas station on La Cienega Blvd. I started pumping my gas, and this girl pulled up.

She got out, and I said to myself, "D*mn she thick. Am I in love again?"

So, I walked over there and talked to her for a minute. Then I got the number and gave her mines. Let me think of a name for her...

(I'll call her Singer J.)

Then I got back in the car and drove off. Oops, was I supposed to pump her gas? Naw, ain't happening, not today. No wonder it took her about a week to call me back. But this is the crazy part.

A week later, I met this other girl.

This one was a little tomboyish and thick too. Right up my alley. I'm in love again.

Let me think of a name for her...

(I'll call her Tender Love.)

She was a little freak, but before the frills and thrills, I found out that she was cousins with the one from the gas station. How does Mr. Bad A** figure this one out? Well, I had to make a choice.

Tender Love is talking about something. Singer J ain't really talking about nothing right now. (But later, you would hear her name again.) So, I made my choice. Tender Love was it, and the frills and thrills were on. ☺

Now me and her hung out a great deal. I remember one day, me, Big Chuck, and Tender Love was at her best friend's apartment.

Something strange happened to me that day.

I went to the bathroom. No, me and Tender Love didn't do our thang in there. What happened? I couldn't do the number 1. If you don't know what that is...

It's the "stand up," not the "sit down." LOL.

I came out the bathroom and told everybody, "Hey, I can't use the bathroom. Nothing's coming out."

129

Her friend had me drinking glass after glass of water. I went again to the bathroom—nothing. Okay, what's going on here? All this water and still nothing!

Tender Love said, "That's it, you're going to the emergency room."

We get there, and I said, "Let me try one more time."

And guess what? It finally came out.

I said, "Oh, boy," that was a close one. Hold that thought for a moment. Here's some more breaking news. The D.O.C.'s album just went gold on September 22, 1989. Another Ruthless hit. But wait... One month later, on October 13, 1989, Ruthless Records released Michel'le's self-titled debut album, produced by Dre. Her first single would be called "No More Lies."

Ruthless keeps on going and going and going. Now here's some sad Ruthless news.

In November of 1989, The D.O.C. was involved in a car accident. He fell asleep behind the wheel and was thrown out the car. He was just about to take over the rap world, but unfortunately, his vocal cords were damaged in the crash. After that, he couldn't rap anymore, but he could talk and still had those mean writing skills.

(L-R) My sister Monique, Dre, my mother, and me (1989)
He was like my brother from another mother.

130

Back to Tender Love and my little issue. One night I was over her house, and of course, we did our thang. Guess what happened again? I couldn't go. This time the water trick didn't work.

I called my brother René, and he took me to the emergency room. This time I'm on the operating table.

The doctor said, "We might have to do this and do that..."

My eyes got big. Then I looked up at him and said, "Wait a minute, sir. You have to stick that in where and cut what? Oh, sh*t, I'm outta here."

Then I thought to myself, "Let me approach this from another angle. I need to clear the air in here."

So, I said, "Can I have a bathroom break, boss? It's getting a little too technical in here." (But that didn't work—nope. LOL.)

Let's speed up the timeline.

I'm in a hospital bed with a big tube (which is called a catheter) coming out of my "you know what." YOW! I tell you what— it don't feel so good.

As I was lying there (like I'm going somewhere), Dre and E walked in my room and they wanna have jokes, trying to pull the tube out. Being very f*ckin funny. The problem was my urinary tract had closed. So, they went in and cut it open. I'm not going to tell you where 🙁.

After all this surgery stuff, I got rid of the 'Vette and bought me a brand-new fresh 190 Benz. I think I'll end 1989 on that note.

It was one h*ll of a year.

CHAPTER 7: N.W.A 1990-1992

It's a new year and a brand-new decade. Things were cool. After living together for over a year, Dre moved out to the Valley and brought him a house. I moved from the two-bedroom to a one-bedroom, which just happened to be in the next building.

Word on the streets is that we fell off since Cube left. Yes, he was a big piece of the puzzle, but think about what I just said. It's a piece of the puzzle—but not the whole puzzle.

So, we kind of had something to prove, to our fans, but really to ourselves. We loved Cube, but one rapper don't stop no show. That was not meant to be a diss, it was just a compliment. Now having a place all to myself, I can get used to that real quick.

One day me, Dre, Ren, and E decided to go and buy some guns. If I'm not mistaken, I think DJ Speed also went with us. We met up at a place called the HQ Store inside the Carson Mall. It was like some kind of army surplus store. They had all sorts of guns, and all of them were brand new. Let me see if I can remember some of the ones that we bought...

Dre got a Desert Eagle .44 auto mag, just like the Dirty Harry character Clint Eastwood played. (This one would also be in one of our upcoming videos.), E picked up a 9mm Glock and the H and K (Heckler & Koch) semi-automatic machine gun. I bought like four guns— a 9mm Berretta, a Browning .380, a Colt .357 revolver, and a nickel-plated 2 shot Derringer. (Like those in the *Gunsmoke* days. "Yee-hah!") I think Ren got a 9mm pistol. These were the same guns that we used during many of our interviews.

As we were leaving, you know me. I'm on my routine fringe benefits search. I see this light-skinned girl walking our way. She was kind of cute. I walked right in front of her, so she had to stop. I gave her that look. She gave me a look right back.

I said, "Hey."

She said, "Hey."

Okay, we can't do this all day, so I asked for the number, and it was on and cracking. Let me think of a name for her...

(I'll call her Carson B.)

I must say, she was a freak.

Okay, now I wanna talk about something serious, kind of weird, and real f*cking mysterious. This was the first and last time it happened to me. I'll start off by saying Mr. Manager called me up one day and said he had a check for me. The thing was, he always reminded me to bring a check when I came. (That's the way he got his 20%.) Still being young and dumb, I said, "Cool, I'm on my way to the Valley."

First, let me tell you the problem here. He was the label's manager, but he was also the group's manager. At the time, that was a real problem that we really didn't understand. Why do I say that...?

Well, he was both the label and our manager, which is a conflict of interest. He was getting 20% off both ends. But remember, at the time, we didn't have no idea.

So, let's get back to the story. I made it to the Ruthless office in the Valley.

I walked in, and he said, "Here's your check for $90,000."

I said, "WOW." My eyes got real big.

I said, "Thank you."

I handed him a check for $18,000, which was 20%.

Then he said, "Thank you."

I thought to myself," I'm picking up $90,000, and I'm giving $18,000. And you know what? I can live with that!" (So, it seemed cool at the time.)

Before I left, he said, "Stop at the accountant's office before you leave the Valley."

I said, "Alright."

Well, I stopped there and talked to the accountant.

He said, "You owe some taxes from last year, and the amount was $90,000." (Did he just say I owed $90K?)

"Sir, what the h*ll did you say?"

The figure was $90,000. Now I'm about to have a heart attack. I— was—speech—less.

Remember, I just told you about being young and dumb?

Somehow, he convinced me to sign the check over to him after saying he would pay them. You know what else?

I said, "Ok, cool." (I'm a d*mn fool.)

I wasn't happy about that one. I finally left the Valley.

And I said (in my "Old Man" voice...), "You big F*ckin' Dummy!!!"

Did you just sign over a check for $90K to somebody?

Didn't you also write out a check for $18K? You just can't seem to get out of the Valley with your money...

Since you're acting like Bozo, you might as well let them put a clown suit on you, turn you upside down, and shake all your money out. SMH. So, tell me, Mr. Bad A**...

Isn't that a total of $108,000 that just transferred from your hands to other people's hands?

Wow...If I had a gun in my hand, I—would—have—shot—my—own—self. (And I had four of them to choose from.)

That whole situation there makes you wanna say, "*Hmmm...*"

Let's move on to some better news because I'm still hot about that one. No "LOL" to that one!

This is an uplifting story. I remember we were at an awards show. It might have been **The Soul Train Awards**. Anyway, we were walking through the place, and, as usual, I was on the lookout. I try not to miss anything. (You know what I'm talking about.) There she was, standing with her friend. Sexy, I'm mean real sexy, but looked like a little toughness was in her.

"Is that a fur she's got on?" I said to myself. "I'm going to do the 'touch her hand trick' again."

Guess what? VOILÀ!!! It worked! Let me think of a name for her...

(I'll call her Benzo C.)

Why? A couple of days later, when she came to the apartment, I found out that she had a set of Mercedes car keys like mine. So, they called us "The Benzo Twins," because we both had Benz 190's. But back to her coming over.

Now she was a freak, just how I like them. Sometimes when she came over, she would bring a few movies. Let me think of a name for them...

(I'll call them Nasty/Freaky/Adult Movies.)

In other words, grown folks' stuff. Somehow this grown folks' stuff would eventually become a part of my future. But back to these movies.

She said, "You gotta watch this one."

I said, "Alright, play it."

I'm watching it. Then all of a sudden, I said, "What the h*ll? Did she just turn him around, and—What the f*ck do you got me watching?"

Then Benzo C got a little turned on, but I told her, "What you just saw on that TV? It ain't—happening—in—this—house. LOL, for real, no bullsh*t. Don't play with me like that."

Let's move on and change the subject—please.

On February 20, 1990, Ruthless Records released a hot new group called Above The Law (ATL). It was produced by Dre. The album was called "Livin' Like Hustlers."

But Ruthless was still going. On March 12, 1990, Michel'le's single "No More Lies" went gold. Then on April 25, 1990, Michel'le's album also went gold. We just keep racking them up.

Here's some more news that I almost forgot about. There was two anti-violence message songs made, one from the East Coast ("Self Destruction") and one from the West Coast ("We're All in the Same Gang"). The West Coast single featured many Ruthless acts and other heavy hitters.

Let me see if I can name them all...

Michel'le (singing the hooks), ATL, King Tee, Body & Soul, Def Jef, Tone-Loc, Ice-T, Dre, Ren, E, Young MC, Digital Underground, J.J. Fad, Oaktown's 3.5.7, and MC Hammer. I played live drums on parts of the song. (This would be my fourth time playing drums on an album.) We all performed this song on *The Arsenio Hall Show*. It also got a Grammy nomination in 1990.

On May 22,1990, Warner Bros. Records released the West Coast All Stars' "We're All In The Same Gang" single. (It went gold four months later, on September 19.) Now it's time to get back on the road, but just for a short trip—Only two shows.

Next stop, Brixton, London. This time we flew first-class. I guess we were moving on up in the world, LOL. It was a little different for us. This time we were the headliners.

Plus, we brought one of the hot Ruthless acts, ATL. The concerts were cool; everything went okay. But one of the guys from ATL didn't really know about overseas phone usage. He was just a-talking and talking till we got ready to check out of the hotel.

He had a fat a** phone bill, which was about 1500£ (pounds). Other words, $800-$900. That definitely came out of the f*ckin' budget. But me and Dre both enjoyed being on the road and doing shows. That's where our peace and quiet time was. If we would've gotten back on tour just one more time...

135

The Making of the 100 Miles EP

Now let's get back to the studio. Who do you see? Me at the mixing board. Dre on the drum machine and keyboards. Ren, as usual in the corner writing. The D.O.C., like always, got his pen and paper. And yes, E's there, somewhere in the building on the d*mn phone. (That was his little hobby, LOL.)

But this time in the studio, something different was added for our amusement. When you sit at the mixing board and look up at the speakers, in between them was a large TV screen. On it, you would see some grown folks' movies playing.

Remember when Benzo C used to bring those kinds of movies to my apartment? Well, that gave me an idea. I would take a bunch of grown folks' movies and edit them into one long two-hour film (which I called a mixtape). Let me tell you a little bit about how I came up with that.

First, I started with two VCR tape machines. Then I would rent five movies and edit the best parts into one tape. But I didn't dare go into the store and rent the movies. I would have our boy DJ Speed rent them for me. Here's how it worked...

Me and him would walk into a video store. I would stroll around, walking ahead of him by myself, checking out all the movies. Then I would give him a nod, point at one, and lay it on its side. He would follow behind me, grab the ones I'd picked, then drop em' on the counter and rent them. That was the beginning of my world-famous two-hour mixtapes, Volumes 1-5. (Everybody got an eye-full in the studio.) ☺

Now back to the studio. What do you see? Let me set the scene. Volume 1 of the mixtape is playing on the TV screen in the background. Now it was time for us to prove something.

The EP's new tracks would sound even stronger than the first album. This is where our production skills started to grow even more.

We were down one voice, so Dre stepped in and filled that spot very well. There was a new person chosen that played guitar and bass. His name was Mike Sims. The first song was "100 Miles and Runnin," written by Ren and The D.O.C. The vocals were rapped by Dre, Ren, and E.

136

This would be the only single from the EP. Of course, the video would be very expensive—again.

In this one, the FBI would be chasing us throughout the video shoot. We would be involved in many of the stunts, including running on rooftops, flipping over cars, and car explosions.

People didn't know this, but during the filming, Dre hurt his leg. He was jumping over a tall fence and landed wrong in one of the scenes. But you can actually see the real injury when he was limping before he jumped into the back of a moving truck.

Next up is a solo song for Ren, called "Just Don't Bite It." I don't need to explain that title; it explains itself, LOL. This was the funkiest track on the EP. The third song was a remake of "F*ck The Police," called "Sa Prize." This one was rapped by Dre, Ren, and E, and was also written by The D.O.C. Now this song sounded much stronger than the original, but it wasn't better. Why? Because it was hard to top the first one. Then there was a song called "Real N*ggaz." Ren, E, and Dre rapped on this one. (Hint, hint.) There was one line that kinda mentioned a certain person that had left the group. As a matter of fact, this was the only song that I actually said words on. The writers were Ren and The D.O.C. There was also a short song called "Kamurshol," which was really like an interlude. Dre, Ren, and E only talked on this one. It was more for advertising the upcoming album called "Efil4zaggin." You don't get it? Duh? It's written backwards...

So, me and Dre produced, finished, and mixed all the songs. On August 6, 1990, Ruthless Records released N.W.A's "100 Miles and Runnin" EP.

As 1990 was winding down, there was a few more things left on the calendar. First up was *The Arsenio Hall Show*. We were invited to come and perform our new single, "100 Miles and Runnin." The show was cool. Arsenio interviewed us. We did a little skit and performed the song.

Next up— well, this was a little different. E wanted me to work on this new Ruthless act called Yomo and Maulkie. These were some young guys with plenty of energy inside of them.

(They were part of a young generation and had a lot to say.)

This was the first time I would produce something by myself since the beginning song, "Slice." But this time, it will be a full album. Once I hung out with them for a minute, I got in the groove and started producing their tracks. They was pretty good writers, and their voices sounded great. There was three singles from the album, "Mama Don't," "Mockingbird," and the first single, "Glory." (Which peaked at #7 on the Hot Rap Singles.)

The song "Foe Tha Love of $" was a real sleeper track. So much of a sleeper, I used it on another album just three years later. (Hint, hint.) This would be a multi-platinum group from Cleveland.

There was a couple of problems with this situation. They was very political, and the lyrics was raw. But we didn't let them use cuss words. (That was our first mistake.) They were such a young generation the record company (Atco/Atlantic) just didn't know how to promote them. In other words, they was caught up in red tape. Now let's take another break and get to the last thing of 1990.

There was this hot rap video show on MTV called *Pump It Up*. They had us host the whole thing. When they edited and put the final show together, they inserted a short interview of Cube at the end of it, saying a few things about the group.

(They d*mn sure didn't tell us.)

Well...That didn't sit too kindly. All I'm going to say about that is, some words was said, a song was made, and things happened. I will keep it right there. 1990 is over...

N. W. A's Final Year (1991)

There's some good things, and there's some bad things. I think I'll just mix em' up and start where I am. Let's begin with some good things. But watch out! There's a joker in the deck.

We got word that Gun's N Roses wanted us to do a couple of shows in Florida. These was not baby events. These was 100,000-seater stadiums. Now me and Dre got real excited. Remember—that was our place of peace.

This was the deal they wanted. We, the group, would do two 10-minute sets over two nights. And what was the pay? $25,000 per night. That was cool with us. The money was okay. But the bigger thing was to turn those two shows out and maybe get on their world tour.

We was really anxious now because we wanted to get back on

138

the road real bad. So, a few days passed, and VOILÀ! This was when the joker popped out. We found out later that, well...

Mr. Manager had been negotiating with Gun's N Roses management, or in other words, demanding a deal. This was what he wanted to happen. We would do the two 10-minute sets, not for $25K a show but $50K each night. Man, we would have done the shows for free. It wasn't about the money to us.

What happened next? They stopped the negotiations, and we lost that deal. We were kinda p*ssed off about how that turned out. So, let's turn that into some better news.

Guess what I'm in the market for? A brand-new house! Are you f*cking kidding me? A real house and not an apartment?

You know me, the fringe benefits are about to be OFF—THE—HOOK! I am high right now but hold up...

Nobody told me you had to almost jump through a hoop wearing a tutu while holding your breath to get one. Let me explain. I am what you would consider self-employed. That means a 20% down payment, and they stick a camera up your a** looking for everything, like how much money you have in the bank, your bills, your credit...

Then there's the property taxes, the house insurance and a thing called escrow. (I never heard of that.) What about the escrow closing cost and the HOA's? Never heard of that one, but guess what?

My first house. (1991)

There was no grass in the front yard and no grass in the back, either. It was just plain old dirt. That's another $15K-$20K to put grass in. Then you got to pick out the carpet and tile. Heaven knows if you get upgrades, that's gonna cost. Man, nobody told me about all this, but now I'm thinking on the bright side...

I LOVE the house!

I got me a 2500 square foot brand-new house! It has four bedrooms, three baths, a 3-car garage, vaulted ceilings, and white carpet. I wanted marble (you know that price was triple), so I got the ghetto marble (ceramic) tile instead. I also had the black Jenn-Air built-in appliances. Ooh wee! That was high-class back then. Now it's stainless steel everywhere. Plus, nobody had sat their rear end on the toilets.

That's what I'm talking about, LOL.

How do I feel about the house? When the place closed escrow and I got the keys, was it like the house I grew up in? H*ll no. Did I want to live in a house like we had?

Nahhh...I wanted to live in a house just like the one on the TV show, *The Brady Bunch*. Now I got one.

Oh, did I fail to mention that I had somebody with me when I got the keys? I walked up to the house and opened the door for the first time. Wait a minute. There's no bed in here.

I turned around and looked at her and said, "Where are we gonna go do our thang?"

So, we ended up having our frills and thrill party in the closet—excuse me, walk-in closet 😊.

Now here's some more good news. Remember I talked about the new group Yomo and Maulkie?

I had just finished producing their album. All the tracks were done and mixed. They shot a couple of videos, and now it was time to get P-A-I-D. I met with E in the studio, and he gave me a check for $90,000.

I said, "Oh yea, feet don't fail me now to get to the bank!"

I made it there, stood in line, and waited for the bank clerk to cash the check. Just then, she looked at me like I was crazy.

I said, "What's wrong?"

She showed me the check and said, "Do you know this person?"

I looked down at the check, then thought to myself, "I'm going to kill E..."

The check was made out to Mickey Mouse.

I said (in my "Old Man" voice...), "You big dummy!"

Didn't you even look at the check before you left the studio? I had to just laugh at E; that was a good one. He made me look like a d*mn fool in here. Really? LOL. The next day I did catch him and get my money.

I told him, "Very funny, MUTHAF*CKA." 😊

So how did I celebrate after that bank deposit? I went to a Lexus dealership. I walked in, pointed at one of the vehicles, then asked a salesman, "What kind of car is that?"

He said, "Sir, that is the new Lexus SC 300."

Then I asked him, "How much?"

He said, "Sir, it's $40K."

You know what I said. "Thank you, wrap it up, and I–AM–OUT."

The Making of the N*ggaz4Life Album

It's 11 a.m. I woke up, looked toward the other side of the bed, and noticed—nobody's there. What happened?

Oops, I forgot. She left last night. D*mn! I'm late to the studio! I got up, showered, got dressed, then ran out the door. I jumped in the car, put the pedal to the medal, and burned rubber! I pulled up to the studio, parked, then rushed inside.

Before going in, I wondered, "Did I forget to brush my f*ckin teeth?"

Gladly, I got a pocket full of gum. I always carry gum.

Now it's time to get to work on our second album. Who do you see? Me at the mixing board, Dre on the drum machine and keyboards. Like always, Ren in the corner writing. The person with the pen and paper you know is The D.O.C. And the one with the large phone bill, of course, is E. These days, we have the unlimited plan, but in those days, it was the 40 cents a minute plan.

Let me pick out a few chosen ones this time. Mike Sims is on the guitar again, and the new kid on the block playing bass is Collins. And occasionally, Dre's younger brother Little Warren would come to hang out in the studio. Speaking of Dre's brother, he used to wear glasses with white tape on them. Why do I bring him up?

Because Dre would always leave his a** at the studio, and I'd be the one who had to take his a** home to Long Beach. Hint, hint...

Have you figured it out yet— Long Beach and Warren?

I'll give you some more time...

Okay, it's a young Warren G. before his time, if you didn't catch it. Let's get to the main course of the album—the music. We played way more live instruments this time around.

Track #1: "The "Prelude." This was a strong opening for the album. We used the same track called "Kamurshol" from our last EP. It was written by Ren and performed by ATL and Ren.

Track #2: "Real N*ggaz Don't Die." This one had some heat on it. It was written by Ren and The D.O.C., and performed by Dre, Ren, and E.

Track #3: "N*ggaz 4 Life." One of my favorites of the album. It was written by Ren and The D.O.C., and performed by E, Dre, and Ren.

Track #4: "Protest" was a quick interlude.

Track #5: "Appetite for Destruction." Now, this was a different kind of beat. A little high energy, this would become one of the videos from the album. It was written by Ren, The D.O.C., and Kokane and performed by Dre, Ren, and E.

Track #6: "Don't Drink That Wine" was another interlude.

Track #7: "Always into Something" was one of the funkiest and hardest on the album. It was written by Ren and The D.O.C. and performed by Dre and Ren.

Track #8: "Message to B.A." was an interlude. I guess you would call this a little diss commercial.

Track #9: "Real Niggaz." This was taken off the "100 Miles and Runnin" EP.

Track #10: "To Kill a Hooker," was another interlude.

Track #11: "One Less B*tch." I don't have to talk about this one. Just look at the title. It was written by Ren and The D.O.C. and performed by Dre and Ren.

Track #12: "Findum, F*ckum, & Flee." Another favorite and a funky one. It was written by Ren, The D.O.C., and CPO, and performed by E, Dre, and Ren.

Track #13: "Automobile." This was something quite different and funny. This would be the last time I would play live drums on an album. It was written by E and performed by Dre and E.

Track #14: "She Swallowed It" was the follow-up song to Ren's "Just Don't Bite It." It was written and performed by Ren.

Track #15: "I'd Rather F*ck You." Now, this is my favorite of the whole album. It was written and performed by E.

Track #16: "Approach to Danger." This would become the final video from the album. It was written by Ren and E, and performed by Dre, Ren, and E.

Track #17: "1-900-2-Compton," an interlude.

Track #18: "The Dayz of Wayback." Last song of the album. The sample on here was very funky. It was written by Ren and The D.O.C. and performed by Dre and Ren.

I just caught my breath. That was a lot of tracks!

Now it's time to do the album cover. This one was very unique in two ways— the title and the picture. We actually came up with the title during the 1989 tour on the bus.

I don't know who came up with the name, "N*ggaz4Life," but we knew it was kind of harsh to put on the cover. We knew that it would hurt our sales. So, as we were standing in the back room on the bus, I saw a mirror on the wall.

I grabbed a piece of paper, wrote down "N*ggaz4Life" and told them, "Hey, why don't we do it like this?"

I held it up to the mirror, and it said, "EFIL4ZAGGIN."

Then somebody said, "You finally came up with something."

I just looked at him and gave him that evil eye. Very funny, mother f*ucka.

Now let's go to the picture on the cover. That was actually a complicated scene that was set up in front of somebody's house in LA. The photo was done in two parts on two different days. Day one was the part with the bodies laying on the ground. But check this out. Me and E were actually the only ones laying under sheets. The other two bodies were just actors. Also, if you take a really good look at the picture, sneak a peek at my arm. You can see the bracelet that Cougar C bought me. (I just had to mention that one.) Day two was simpler. It was just the photographer taking a picture of us leaning on a chair or something for those ghost-looking shots.

To me, this cover was better than the first one, but the picture on the "Straight Outta Compton" album was more iconic. Even

143

the song's lyrics and tracks were better on this album. But still, the first album was hard to top.

So, me and Dre finished, produced, and started to mix the album. Notice I said started to mix the album. The process of this one would be a little different.

We mixed Side A like we normally do, which would be almost two days. But for some reason, when we mixed Side B, we rushed it. It took less than a day. Something changed overnight. What's going on?

Things were happening in the background that I didn't see or hear. I didn't even want to know what it was.

(I stay out of grown folks' business.)

We finished mixing. Then I took the two-track masters home. I didn't think nothing about it. Didn't realize this would be the last album.

I woke up the next morning, grabbed the tapes, then took the long drive to Hollywood to Priority Records. I walked in the office, and from that point on, it was never the same. To me, not officially, but technically, the group was over. It was like the heart and soul of the group was gone.

NWA's "N4Life" #1 Billboard (1991)

There's no way to explain it—it was just in the air.
On May 28, 1991, three important things happened:

1.Ruthless Records released N.W.A's second album, "N*ggaz4Life."

2.It was one of the first albums that shipped gold, and:

3.It also hit #1 on the top Billboard 200.

Can you believe that? From the **infamous garage** to #1 on Billboard!

And the Beat Goes On

Even though there was still a weird feeling in the air, there was a positive breeze coming. And what was that? Another tour was in the making. Maybe this could help clear the air about the group. I know me and Dre would love to get back on the road. Let's wait and see what happens.

Now it's video time. We made three different videos for the "N*ggaz4Life" album.

The first one up was the song, "Always into Somethin." This one was a very dark video. Most of the shots were done at night. Remember I told you about that .44 Automag Dre had? Well, it was used in one of the scenes during the verse Dre rapped.

We had fun on the set. It was like being on stage again. We did kind of show off our bodyguards in some of the shots. But there was a pair of them that was brothers. These was the new kids on the block. Oops, the big grown men on the block.

Me and The Twins

These two you would not want to f*ck with. They were known as The Twins. Oh, did I fail to mention? I had a couple of Marsha Marsha Marsha's that dropped by the set. And yes, I did find a way to get my frills and thrills on, which was out in the car in the parking lot, LOL. There was a bodyguard watching out for us. (Sorry, I meant me.) But he wasn't looking IN the car. He was looking AT the car, making sure the perimeter was okay.

Next up is the real expensive video for "Appetite for Destruction." We made two versions of it—a clean short form and a long dirty form. This one, I kind of liked the best out of all our videos.

The look of it was from the Roaring 20s. We wore the old suits and derby hats, carried Tommy guns, and drove the old-time cars. This video shoot was also fun because I remembered the make-up girl. She was tall (taller than me), light-skinned, kind of cute, and a little freaky. So, you know me, I had to pull that one after it was over. 😊

The last one was for the song "Approach to Danger."

This one was more like bits and pieces that I had edited together. The two cameramen on the video?

(L-R) Me, Carmen, and E, "Appetite for Destruction" video (1991)

You might know them as the Hughes Brothers when they was just starting out.

Now let's switch the timeline a little bit. Remember our girls JJ Fad? It was time to work on their second album. Dre didn't want to do it, so E had me make it.

Who did I call to help me out? Our boy Arabian Prince. He was known for the fast techno beats. But there was a problem. It had been almost three years since their last album. (That one went gold.) Usually, when groups have a top hit song, they wanna bounce right back with another one.

But three years had passed. That was going to be a steep hill to climb. So, me and Arabian started on it and finished two months later.

Back to the rumors about a new tour. I guess the negotiations didn't go very well. The arenas wouldn't let us do the show unless we had a certain kind of insurance policy. You know what? Nobody wanted to insure us this time around. We was a little crushed. The road was sounding good. But I think that was the nail in the coffin for the group.

(GAME OVER.)

Okay, on to a different kind of subject. The Make A Wish Foundation gave us a call one day. They wanted to know if we would make a kid's last wish come true. He had been diagnosed with a deadly form of cancer. His wish? He wanted to be in the studio with N.W.A. Yes, of course, we would do this.

Sometime in mid-1991, they brought him to Audio Achievements. Me, Ren, and E were there. The kid had a great time. I would pull out his favorite songs, and me and him would mix them right there. "Straight Outta Compton" was the one he loved. That was an amazing day. It was an honor for us— to know that this kid wanted to see us for his last wish. I don't think we ever heard what became of him, but that moment brought a few tears to my eyes that day.

A couple of months later, on August 8, 1991, N.W.A's "N*ggaz4Life" went platinum. This would be Ruthless Records' third consecutive platinum album.

Guess what? The same people that banned our "Straight Outta Compton" video wanted us to be presenters on their awards show. Did they think we would get on stage and not act a fool?

Well...

E did walk on stage, dressed in his boxers, while he was holding his pants in his hand.

So, I guess you could say we kinda acted a fool, LOL.

Now on October 29, 1991, there was a song that Cube made about the group. I guess this is what you would call a diss song. (Even though we never made one about him.)

We did a couple of lines, but not even a full verse of a song. I listened to it at the time.

But it took me 25 years until we got on the set of the movie *Straight Outta Compton* for me to tell him, "You got us."

We just laughed about it, and that comment ended up becoming one of the lines in the movie.

On Dec 7, 1991, Ruthless Records released JJ Fad's last album, "Not Just A Fad." Remember when I told you about the three-year wait between albums? I think that's what ended up hurting their record sales— the time off between the albums killed it.

The Last Dayz

1991 is gone, 1992 is here. There was one last breath left in the group. On January 27, 1992, we had just got nominated for an AMA (American Music Award). This is the first time we ever got a nomination. That was cool.

Someone came up with the idea to wear the "Appetite for Destruction" clothes from the video, which was that Roaring 20s look. Plus, we also rented a couple of Model T automobiles to be chauffeured in for the event.

Everything looks great—the clothes and the cars. But we arrived late—about 30 minutes after the red-carpet event. In other f*cking words, nobody seen us drive up in the d*mn place. That was a waste of money. And to top everything off, we lost to MC Hammer in the Favorite Rap/Hip-Hop artist category. ☹

The next morning, I was asleep in my bed. The phone woke me up.

I turned over to my left and said, "I'm looking at you."

Let me think of a name for her...

(Well, I don't remember her name, so I'll call her Hard 2 Get T.)

I answered the phone. It was Dre— this early in the morning. I said, "What's up...?"

This was one of the shortest, never forgotten phone calls I ever had.

He said, "I'm gone. You coming?"

I was kind of lost and didn't know what to say to him.

My response at the time was, "I'll let you know."

Then he hung up. What was he talking about? I had no idea. Later on, I found out he had left the group. I wasn't caught between a rock and a hard place. I was caught between Dre on my left and E on my right.

Should I go, or should I stay? Dre asked me to be in this group, but I also had nothing against E. Where did my loyalty lie...?

Do I tell Dre, "Yea, I'm leaving E also," or tell E, "I'm not going with Dre?"

I did the only thing I thought at the time was right. I made no decision. I was caught right in the middle. I was "d*mned if I do and d*mned if I don't.

I thought about that question for years. As a matter of fact, that question came up 27 years later, in late 2019. I will talk about that again when we get to that year.

If we could have just did one more tour—just a few shows, maybe the outsiders would not have gotten in to disrupt the group. We would have been on the road with our peace and our fun. Remember, for us, it was always about the music and not the money. But maybe that's what ended up happening—maybe too much money came in. The vultures got off the branches and started flying around us, searching to destroy. Other words, they were searching to profit.

What is wrong with this world? Why can't we just have peace? But in reality, there's vultures, and there's nosey people. So, watch yourself.

Why did the group break up? After all the fun times, great and happy moments, all the shows —even all the songs...

We didn't have a single argument, not even disagreements— just brotherhood. So why did we break up? Because of the outsiders. That includes money. It wasn't because of the inner circle, but the ones on the outside. It's amazing.

How does a group break up at #1?

Most groups break up because of internal problems, the management, or they just fell off.

But how do you break up as the number one rap group in the world? Everything was going great. Everything was fine. How do you break up like that? We was meant to break up. In the future, I would know why.

So, I'll drop the mic and end the chapter— right here.

CHAPTER 8: A NEW ERA

I was kicking back at the house one day and had my mind on a few things. What is this new era going to be like? The group is done, dismantled, and dissolved. We kind of starting all over again—that is me and E. Directly from the bottom. So, where do we begin? 1992 is going to be quite different. What do I mean by that? Usually, a new era is when something exciting, or something great, or just things altogether happen. We are starting from scratch, and I don't have a clue...

What do we do next?

There is some good news. On March 27, 1992, our "Straight Outta Compton" album went double platinum. Wow!

N.W.A's S.O.C. double platinum (1992)

From the **infamous garage** to now going double platinum!

I guess that's a pretty good accomplishment. Now back to the story. One day E wanted me to come over. (He was living in Norwalk at the time.)

He handed me a box of videotapes and said, "Can you look through these, then find and mark the best parts of them?"

I said, "What we gonna do with this footage?"

He said, "We are going to make a N.W.A home videotape for sale."

I said, "Cool, what's the title?"

He said, "I guess, "N.W.A: The Only Home Video."

It took me about a week to go through all the footage. We went to a studio in Hollywood to edit the tape. I remember like it was yesterday. It was April 29, 1992. It was the same day the Rodney King verdict and the LA Riots happened. They had the TV on while I was working in the studio. I just couldn't believe what I had seen. It was craziness everywhere—even near my mother's house. And the old dairy I used to work at? They had even burnt it down to the ground. Wow, it was some serious sh*t going on around town. E wanted to go and loot.

I said, "You must be crazy! What are you thinking about?"

After a week, we finished the tape and turned it in to Priority Records. It was the Summer of '92. Me and E was at Audio Achievements. One of his buddies came up there named Big Man. He had this female rap group from Compton. They was young, cute, and a little sexy. (You know I had to take a second look at them, LOL.) They did some rapping right there on the spot. Sounded pretty good, not bad. We might have something here.

So, E said, "I got to have them, just like the TV show *Let's Make A Deal*. Right now."

A few days later, I was in the studio working with the girls. They wrote their own lyrics, and their delivery was smooth. Now the words... Well, let's say a little nasty, I mean straight nasty. They was real hardcore to be girls. Even the name was bold and hardcore. What was the name?

Think of it like this—three people doing something freaky together. What do you call it...?

It was called Menajahtwa (mə•naj´•Ah•twä´)! Wow! That was the name of the group, and yes, that's how it was written.

Hopefully, that won't hurt them in the future because they was years ahead of themselves. (They was the pre-Nicki "you know her name" back then.) This album took a few months to work on. 1992 was like a blur. It went by kind of fast. But there was still some more good news.

On September 1, 1992, Ruthless Records had another double-platinum album. It was E's "Eazy Duz It."

Two weeks later, on September 16, 1992, our "100 Miles and Runnin" EP went platinum. Man! We STILL racking them up.

Eazy-E double platinum (1992)

On November 2, 1992, Priority Records released N.W.A's home video. That's when things started to change. What do I mean by change?

E released a new EP. Technically, I didn't know anything about it. As a matter of fact, I had nothing to do with it. I didn't even know it was being recorded. Things have really changed around here. Even though we racking up the platinum and double-platinum albums, the foundation is getting a little shaky. But I'm committed to the cause, so I'm here for the long haul.

On December 10, 1992, E released his last EP for Priority Records called "5150 Home 4 Tha Sick."

In the end, 1992 was a year that you can just throw away. Remember, we had to start from scratch. There was a lot of good stuff that happened. Stuff like "Straight Outta Compton" went double platinum, "Eazy Duz It" went double platinum, and "100 Miles and Runnin'" also went platinum. But that was the old stuff. We gotta do some new stuff. We gotta generate some new money here. Maybe 93' could be the year.

Or this new Menajahtwa project I'm working on might be the one. It sure felt funny around here. Remember, there was no Dre, no Ren, no group, no nothing...

It was just me and E on a lonely island.

1993

Now back to the Menajahtwa album. Everything was going good. There was two other producers on the project, Rhythm D and DJ U-Neek. This album had a lot of controversy behind it. Sometimes me and E wasn't on the same page. He wanted this certain song to be a video, and I wanted a different song to be a video. He wanted no cuss words; I wanted the cuss words.

Sometimes I would look at him and say, "What u talkin' 'bout E?"

So, there was some disagreements. It wasn't a knockdown, bloody nose event, but just creative differences. After all that, the album was finally done.

Then there was the controversial title, "Cha-Licious." I'm not gonna explain that one because I told you—they were nasty.

Like I said... Hopefully, this won't hurt them in the future.

Okay, let's talk about getting paid for this project. Remember, I told you about a conflict of interest? This is where it showed up again.

I finished the album and told Mr. Manager, "It's time to get paid."

I'm thinking like that Yomo album, about $90K. I can live with that. So, he gave me an answer. Do you wanna know what it was?

He said, "Ask E."

Then I thought to myself, "Are you serious? Isn't he the one that's supposed to be doing the negotiating?"

That's where the issue comes in. Mr. Manager was supposed to negotiate with the company on how much I got. But since technically he is both managers, now I have to do this on my own. Remember when I told you about the foundation being shaky? I was feeling it again. Why? Well, I was a little upset with the results. It wasn't even HALF of what I expected to get.

I said to myself (in my "Old Man" voice...), "You Big Dummy!" Didn't you go through this conflict of interest before? Won't you ever learn?

Anyway, let's move on to some more news. E's "5150 Home 4 Tha Sick" went gold on February 9, 1993. Now here's some personal news.

Like I told you, the foundation is shaky. Just d*mn outright, not the same. Especially with that Mr. Manager thing that just happened. I don't know where the money's gonna come from, but Mr. Bad A** had a plan. (Remember, I had nobody to talk things over with.) Let me see...

I think I'll downsize. I'll sell my house and buy me a condo. That'll work. I'll sell the house and buy the condo. Whew, I feel better already! That issue is done, and yes, there's another issue. D*mn. What's with these issues?

I hate to speak about this, but...

Sometime in mid-1993, there was another diss song made. This one was about E. This time, it came from Dre. Out of respect for both friends, I just cannot talk about this subject. Let's move on.

Eazy-E "It's On" Visionary Award

It's time to work on E's new EP. Now I'm in another pickle because E wants to make a diss song about Dre. Okay, you killing me now. E knew I would not be a part of the diss song or video. He just knew not to ask me. I will not touch any of that. I produced two of the tracks from the new EP.

One was called "Still a N*gga," and the other one, "Gimmie

That N*tt." (This is a crazy title.) I mixed all the songs from the EP but mixing the diss song about Dre was a little hard to do.

E made a video, and the EP "It's On 187um Killa" was released on October 6, 1993. This EP featured artists that would later be called the New Ruthless Records. In other words, the new "Rappers in the Hood."

Who were they? BG Knocc Out, Dresta, and Dirty Red. Also featured was Cold 187um and Kokane. Ruthless now had a distribution deal with Relativity Records. It sold over 100,000 units the first week, went #1 on the R&B chart, and #5 on the Billboard chart. This EP will end up topping his first album, "Eazy Duz It." But I was still in kind of a hot seat. A couple of TV shows wanted E to perform the diss song, "Real Compton City G's." I just wasn't feeling performing the song. But I went on *The Arsenio Hall* Show and *In Living Color* with him.

Me and E (1993)

He knew I didn't like it, but I did it anyway. I couldn't leave him hanging.

Now it's time to get back on the road again. Not like our 1989 tour, but the bubble gum version of it. What do I mean by that? I said we had to start over, but d*mn. Now we doing shows in front of small crowds.

In other words, "We—are—going—backwards."

Don't mind me. It's called frustration.

On December 28, 1993, E's "It's On 187um Killa" went gold and platinum. At least we ended 1993 on a good note.

1994: Me & E's Last Year Together

Okay, let's start this year off right. I'm all settled in my new condo in Paramount. Funny thing, it's right next door to the apartment I used to stay in.

Hmmm... That means the fringe benefits are going to work out just fine. ☺ One day E asked me to work on another new female rap group. This time they were from Chicago, a little different style, but again, nasty, and also freaky.

I said, "What's the name of them?"

E said, "HWA."

"What the h*ll does that mean?"

He said," Man, you don't get it? "

"NAW! I know it don't mean what I think it means."

E said, "H*ez With Attitudes."

Then he said, "They have some songs already, just tightened up what they got."

I said, "What they look like?"

"You'll see when they get to the studio."

Time went by. Then, one day, they came by the studio.

I thought to myself, "They d*mn sure look the part.

Two of them was sisters. Well...

The third was right up my alley. Let me calm down and keep it professional. At least for the first couple of days, LOL.

I worked on the tracks, had them fix some of their vocals, and mixed all the songs. Hold up, I just thought about something. After the fringe benefits and stuff...Shazaam!

I done been bamboozled! I don't even remember getting paid for this project. F*ck, I—DONE—TRIPPED.

(Well, you can tell by my actions I wasn't about the money.)

Here's another news flash. E's "It's On 187um Killa" EP just went double platinum on February 7, 1994. Also, on February 22, 1994, Ruthless Records released HWA's "Az Much A** Azz U Want" EP. It did okay by hitting #71 on the Top R&B/Hip-Hop chart and #33 on the Top Heatseekers Songs Chart.

Now, this next idea was right up my alley. I give you a little

157

hint. Remember my adult mixtape videos I use to edit?

Well... I was sitting in the studio at the mixing board.

Big Man walked in and asked me a question.

He said, "I just asked E about this idea, and now I'm asking you. Do you want to make some adult movies? Not saying you'd be in them. Weed would be the star in them. You can just film them."

I looked him dead in the eye and said, "H*ll, yea, why not!"

Then I said to him, "Okay, you got to go out and do your homework. Find out who we talk to and how—do—we—get—paid."

Alright, back to the road. This time we got the new guys with us. The shows are starting to get a little better. There was still a few hiccups on the road. Then BAM!!!

Finally! A real show in Chicago! A sold-out 12,000-seater arena. There we was—backstage and feeling the energy in the building. But...

Let me give you some facts about E and what we used to work on before each show. I'm not talking about my buddy, but this was reality. I had to go over the words of the songs with him before each show. For some reason, he didn't like to remember the lyrics. (SMH)

I used to sit and tell him, "Come on, man, let me hear the words to "Boyz N Tha Hood."

LOL. Every f*cking time! We walked out on the stage. The crowd went nuts.

Then I looked at him and said, "That's what I'm talking 'bout." Since we on the road, let's keep going.

There was a show in Cleveland, Ohio. Me and E was backstage going over his words as usual. All of a sudden, he said, "Hold up, I be right back."

I said, "Man, where you going?"

He said, "I be right back."

Then these five young guys walked in.

I said, "What's up?"

They said, "What's up?"

(How the h*ll did they get back here? Security must be slipping.) Then they introduced themselves.

"I'm Krayzie Bone, he's Wish Bone, that's Layzie Bone, the other one is Flesh-n-Bone, and you have Bizzy Bone."

I thought to myself, "That's a lot of f*cking Bones. All you guys related?"

They said, "Just two of us."

Then all of a sudden, they started rapping—rapping and singing some kind of harmony. I had never heard that kind of style before. It sounded pretty good.

What was the name of the group? Bone Thugs-N-Harmony.

Afterwards, E walked back in, and I told him, "You should listen to these guys."

So, I left backstage and went to go soundcheck. The show was cool. There was two more on this trip, then back to LA. Guess who was in LA before us? Bone Thugs-N-Harmony.

Wow! They beat us home after riding on the Greyhound bus for two days. What did they have to eat? One big bag of chips between the five. That's what you call being dedicated.

I don't mean to switch the subject, but Big Man came back with some answers about the adult movies.

He said, "It's easy, just like selling records. Do the project, then sell it to the companies."

Alright, I can go about it two ways—one way the girls, another way the money. Well...

This time it's about the money. But I will treat it like producing a song. I'll just do everything—the filming, take all the photos, and then do the editing. Big Man will do the casting and directing, and our buddy Weed will be the main star. I want to keep it all in-house, so we won't need no outside help.

I went out and bought video cameras, still cameras, and lights. All we need is "action," and we ready to roll.

Now let's get back to the guys from Cleveland. A few days later, me and E was in the studio working with Bone Thugs on their new EP. They were a little different, a little wild, but very talented.

Remember the song I made for Yomo and Maulkie called "Foe tha Love of $?" They loved the track, so they made a new version of the song, with the same title and also featuring E on a verse. I also used the instrumental track of it and called the song "Moe Cheese," which means "Mo money, Mo money." This was the second video from the EP. DJ U-Neek produced the first video and song called "Thuggish Ruggish Bone."

When I said they was different, let me explain why. During

159

one of the studio sessions, I'm not going to say who, but one of them locked theyself in the bathroom for five hours.

The way out of it? All they had to do was cut the light on and turn the doorknob. (Somebody must have been on something that day, LOL.) I'm not going to say anything else about that one. I stay out of grown folks' business. WOW!

Now in the future, this EP would do quite well. Let me think of some of the things it accomplished. It hit #12 on the Billboard 200, #2 on Top R&B/Hip-Hop albums, and was also nominated for a Soul Train Music Award. This group would become the future of Ruthless Records for the next couple of years. They kind of reminded me of us, just in a different way.

On June 21, 1994, Ruthless released Bone Thugs-N-Harmony's "Creepin On Ah Come Up" EP.

Here's some more interesting news. E had a radio show on 92.3 The Beat called *The Ruthless Radio Show*. I did all the mixes, and E hosted it. That went on for most of that year.

On August 14,1994, 92.3 The Beat gave a big concert in LA, called the **Summer Jam**. It was the biggest concert of that year.

This was me and E's plan. We would go on stage at the prime-time slot and bring out Bone Thugs before our set. Then me and him would rock the house. Remember, that was the plan. Okay, here's what really happened that day.

I forgot to tell you that E was a really nice guy at times. (Sometimes a little too nice.) The place is sold out, and we just hanging around waiting to do our set.

So, we waiting... and waiting... and we still f*cking waiting. I'm mad as "you know what", and E knew I was.

He told The Twins, "Don't let him leave the building," because he knew I was packing my stuff, getting ready to roll out.

This was the problem. E kept letting group after group go on before us. Other words, we were getting hoodwinked by the radio station. Because the concert was live on the air, they knew that we would be cussing on our set. So, they secretly kept pushing us back... and back... and back...

Then the rap group Public Enemy went on.

I said to myself, "We got to be going on after Chuck D and them."

But nooooo...

They let Roger Troutman (R.I.P.) go on next, and nobody

goes on after him because he gets down! After he finished, half the crowd left. I'm looking at E like he's crazy.

He said, "Come on, man, there's still a crowd there."

I said, "Are you f*cking kidding me?"

I was HOT!!!

So, we did the show. This was Bone's first time. It was alright. But I was still hot! No LOL.

Here's some hidden facts...

For the past six months, me and E have been working on his new album. We made quite a few tracks. Ren was on one song with him, then we had a lot of the "New Ruthless" artists, like B.G. Knocc Out, Menajahtwa, and Sylk-E Fyne. One song also featured Roger Troutman. But we kept that album a secret. I feel just like a news reporter here.

On August 23, 1994, Ruthless Records released Menajahtwa's album called "Cha-Licious."

Remember, I told you they were ahead of their time. They was so far ahead of their time that the record sales got lost in the shuffle.

Me and Menajahtwa (1994)

Other words, they got caught up in too much red tape or bad promotions.

This next story was no laughing matter.

I found out after the fact that some people was following me around town. They wanted to do me in. If you don't know what that means, they wanted to kill me.

And over what? Let's just say it was about a member of the opposite sex. They was very serious about it, and these people was no joke. But in the end, that plan got squashed.

(There's that bell sound again. "Ding!" Miracle!)

That's all I'm going to say about that.

Now there's some good news and some not so good news. First, here's the good news.

In September 1994, Bone Thugs "Creepin' On Ah Come Up" turned gold and platinum.

Now the not so good news.

Some of the Ruthless distribution deals are starting to fall off. That means some bad negotiations are going down.

Remember the Guns N Rose's negotiation? I will just stay out of grown folks' business.

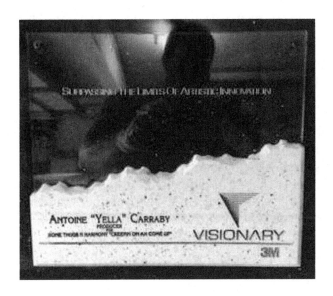

Bone's Visionary Award

Around November of 1994, for some strange reason, me and E did a photoshoot together. To this day, I don't know why we was taking the pictures. They wasn't for no album or anything that I can think of. We just took a bunch of shots. The sad part is, this would be me and E's last photo shoot.

**(L-R) E, my brother Corky, me, and Marvin.
This is E's last photo. (1994)**

Final news flash...

On December 2, 1994, Bone Thugs-N-Harmony's EP went double platinum.

Before I close out this year, let's end on a happy note. It's my birthday, and E gave me a dinner party. A few things happened there. I'll call them, The Good, The Sad, and the Ugly.

Let's start with the good:

Remember that girl I met when I grabbed her hand and didn't let it go? (The Beautiful One) She was there, and we took this picture. If you look at it, we both had funny expressions on our faces. (She would become my future one day.)

Okay, the sad:

During the party, Me and E took this photo. I had no idea that this would be the last one he would ever take.

And the ugly: Where do I start?

People was ordering steak and lobster dinners and not eating them. They ordered all kinds of drinks, four and five at a time, but didn't even drink half of them. Then they would turn around and order more. People was out of f*cking control. They ordered

163

sh*t, but they didn't eat sh*t.

What's was left? A fat $5,500 food and drink bill for E to pay. (These days, that would be about $20,000.)

I said to the people, "You ain't got to go home, but you got to get the h*ll out of here.

This year is finally OVER.

1995

I'm glad to finally get through with 1994. That was an up and down year. Let's hope this one turns out right because I have a good feeling about this year.

Me and Big Man started to learn more about the adult industry. We learned that there is a big convention in Las Vegas every January, called the **CES Show** (Consumer Electronics Show). Don't get it twisted. They're in a whole separate building down the street from the CES Show. This is where all the adult companies come together to sell their new products.

It's January, and me, Big Man, our buddy Weed, and The Twins are on our way to Vegas. E is coming along also. He's working with a company that wants to make a new video game with his character in it. This trip would be a little special.

Me and E flew, sitting together for the very first time. Usually, me and Dre used to do that. We stayed in a room together for the first (and last) time ever because all the places in Vegas was sold out.

I found out a couple of things on this trip. During the flight up and back, all me and E talked about was business. He was showing me how much debt Ruthless was in. E had it all wrote out on a piece of paper, and the numbers was staggering. I won't say the amount, but it was in the seven figures.

The last thing I found out; he was a slob in the hotel room. His side of the room had clothes everywhere. My side was neat.

My clothes was folded up. The place looked like the TV show *The Odd Couple*. We was totally different. I had on my pajamas with the long-sleeved top and pants. (They was blue with polar bears on them.) E had on boxers with a white tank top.

We was as different as night and day. (SMH)

I didn't know it then, but this would be the last time I would see my friend. Maybe I should have talked about more important things at that moment. I just didn't know.

A month later, in February 1995, me and Big Man was filming a scene at E's Norwalk house.

He wanted to watch us film one. So, he's sitting behind me looking at it. I'm shooting all my shots and angles.

The only thing I hear is this sound...

Crunch, Crunch, Crunch!

E is eating on a big bag of chips.

I looked at him and said, "Really?"

He just laughed.

A month passed. Now it's March. This time we filmed at his house, but he wasn't there. One of the girls was getting ready for her scene. She had a little crush on me because I filmed her before. She gave me a wink; I gave her a wink back. She smiled at me. Yea, I'm smiling back at you.

Okay, enough of this back-and-forth stuff. Let me think of a name for her...

(I'll call her Diva D.)

She invited me into the room. Of course, it was the bathroom.

When I was closing the door, I said, "Ohhh Yeaaahhh!"

(I just have to laugh at myself sometimes.)

Later, when I was coming out of the bathroom with her, E called me on my phone from the hospital. (Yes, we had cell phones back then.)

I said, "What's up?"

He said, "Man, you better watch yourself."

I said, "Huh, what you talking about?"

He said it again.

"Man, you better watch yourself."

Then we got off the phone.

I didn't know it, but that would be the last time we would talk to each other.

I said to myself, "That was a strange kind of call."

I didn't think nothing else about it.

Later on, during the week, I started to hear rumors about E having AIDS. A couple of days passed, and I hear more rumors. I can remember like it was yesterday. Big Man finally broke down and told me.

He said, "E has AIDS."

I said, "What?"

Big Man said, "Yea, he didn't want me to tell you he had it. I was going to the hospital every day to see him. He has to have surgery, and hopefully, he can make it through."

So, the next day I went up to Cedars-Sinai hospital. I went in and met E's wife.

(I'll call her Lady T.)

She told me that Dre was up there earlier that day. We went upstairs to E's room.

She said, "He had the surgery yesterday. You can go on in."

I walked in and seen him hooked up to all these machines, all this beeping, and stuff. I stood there, looked at him, and held his hand. He was in an induced coma, so I just talked to him.

The weird thing was when he heard my voice, his hand moved a couple of times. A person is not supposed to be able to move when in a coma, but he did. I held back my tears and walked out. I said a few words to Lady T, and I was gone.

A few days later (it was a Saturday night), E's lawyer gave me a call. I cannot forget what he told me.

He said, "E passed away."

I didn't have very many words to say. I just got off the phone. The next day (March 26), I told myself I didn't want to sleep alone that night because I knew E was coming to visit me. I called up Singer J and asked her to come over.

She said, "Okay." But it took a long time for her to come over. I thought she wasn't coming.

Remember Queen C? She wanted to come over, so I said, "Cool."

She got there about 7ish. I was sitting on the corner of my bed, looking at the news.

The news lady said, "Tonight, Eazy-E died..."

That just hit me like a ton of bricks. Queen C was rubbing my back, but I wasn't paying her no attention. Then all of a sudden, my phone rang.

I said, "Hello?"

It was Singer J. She was downstairs driving up in the parking lot of the building. Oh sh*t, I need to think of something real fast.

I turned around and said to Queen C, "Here's $200. Can you leave, please?"

So, she left without a problem. Then Singer J came up the

stairs and knocked on the door. I opened it.

She said, "Who was that parked in your extra parking space?"

(I got to be quick on the draw with an answer.)

"I don't know, probably somebody parked there by accident."

I let out a sigh of relief and said, "Whew!"

Later on, that night, after our little play date, I fell asleep.

I don't know if it was a dream or some kind of vision. It felt very real. E came and visited me that night. We was flying through the air, and we was talking to each other in the dream, no plane or nothing.

Just us flying, side by side, touching at the fingertips. I forgot most of what we was talking about, but I remember the last thing he said.

"I gotta go."

I turned my head to the left and then back to him. By then, he was gone. I woke up sweating. That scared me for the rest of the night.

E's Funeral

The next morning, I got a call from E's lawyer. He wanted me to come up to Cedars-Sinai Hospital for a press conference. I made it there, went in, and seen E's mother. I wasn't really feeling this press conference stuff, but Lady T kind of talked me into doing it. We went outside in front of the hospital and had the press conference. The lawyer read a speech that E was supposed to have written, but in my opinion, it didn't sound like something he would have said. (Don't quote me, just my opinion.) Afterwards, I said my goodbyes and headed back to the house.

A couple of days later, I got a call from Cube. The last time I seen him was when we got off the tour bus back in '89. I don't remember what we talked about, but it was kind of short. Then we hung up.

Later that week, I met up with Lady T to get the info about the services. She also gave me a gold pin so I could get inside the funeral.

A week had passed. Now it was April 7, 1995—the day of the funeral. I pulled up in front of E's mom's house in Compton. Seems like everybody in town was there. I seen two of E's kids there— my godson Little Derrek, and his oldest son, Eric Jr. Funny thing, I would end up doing shows with both Little Derrek and Eric Jr. in the future.

The limos arrived, and E's mother and family got in. I had security ride with me. We caravanned all the way to a church in LA. Now, this is when the circus started. There was people everywhere—all the big TV news stations, cops, and even undercover cops. It was a straight madhouse.

We walked up to the door. They checked to make sure everybody had the pins on. Then I walked in, and reality hit me in the chest.

The church was filled wall to wall with people. And sitting there was something I was not ready to see. A gold casket, front and center...

It shocked me for a few seconds. This all looked like a Hollywood movie. Too much was going on. Everybody was peeking around to see who was in there.

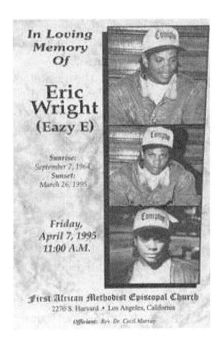

Eric "Eazy-E" Wright...Love you, man. (R.I.P.)

So, I walked down the aisle and sat on the front row. I was just stunned. I didn't even hear what the preacher was saying.

Then it was that time I did not want to see—the viewing of the body. I got up and started to walk out of the church but noticed they didn't open the casket.

I said to myself, "Thank you."

I did not want to see E like that. When I think of him, all I can think of is...

"Say, man..."

"I be right back, man..."

"What color do you want, man?"

That's how I wanted to remember him.

As they was about to roll the casket outside, somebody said, "You get in front and lead us out."

We came to some double doors. As they start opening them, everything slowed down, like it was in slow motion. It went silent; all the cameras was flashing. I just stood there, frozen. All eyes was on me in front of the casket. It was about a thousand people outside.

I thought to myself, "They all loved him."

They put him inside the hearse, then we headed out to the cemetery, located in Whittier, California.

After we arrived, they pulled the casket out, and somebody said again, "You get in front and lead us to the gravesite."

As I walked forward, I looked around, thinking there was drama at the church, but it was even more here. On top of the hill towards the back was at least ten undercover cop and sheriff cars and news helicopters.

Then the part came when people sprinkled dirt over the grave. A couple of shovels were passed from one person to another. They all took turns shoveling dirt over the grave. Then the strangest thing happened. In the movies, the priest sprinkles the dirt, and everybody leaves. But not here. They all stayed.

Later on, a bulldozer came and filled in the rest of the dirt. That was crazy to see.

Everybody left except me, Big Man, my sister Sherreé, and The Twins. While she was standing there, me and the guys stood in a circle together and stacked our hands, one on top of the other.

I said right then, "I—am—done with music."

169

The love of music left right out of my body at that point. I didn't have anything thing else to say.

Oh, did I fail to mention? On my way out, I just so happened to "borrow" his grave marker.

Later that night, I was sitting around, thinking, "That was kinda crazy today."

If only I would have said more to him when I seen him last January in Vegas than just talking about business.

I would have said, "Thank you for buying that first pair of Guess clothes."

That's how our relationship started.

I would have said, "Thank you for just giving me the thought of giving me that Samurai Jeep. (The one that I never got, LOL.)"

I would have said, "Thank you for being a part of me, Dre, Ren, and Cube's life."

Thank you for just being a friend.

THESE FLOWERS WILL BE REMOVED

APR 1 0 1995

This is E's actual grave marker.

If I had only known...

I would have stopped filming in that Norwalk house and just sat there and talked all that day. But a person doesn't know when it's gonna be the last time.

If only I would have thought more about what to say when we talked in March while you was in the hospital.

As a matter of fact, I really didn't say much of anything.

If I had known, I would have just told him, "I love you."

CHAPTER 9: LIFE AFTER MUSIC

Time had passed. All that funeral stuff was over. My music career was done. I had no intention of ever producing again. I wanted to just kick back and relax for a few months and put my mind on making the adult movies.

Having fun on Lake Perris (CA)

Sometimes, me and my childhood friends would go out and have fun, doing stuff like riding quads (a 4-wheeled motorcycle) in the dirt. I bought some jet skis and had a cool little 18-foot boat. So, I just enjoyed life.

Never really thought about, "How—the—h*ll—am—I—going to make money these days?"

You know, like pay the bills—house, boat, jet skis, quad, lights, water, and on and on...

Guess it will happen when it happens. (Wow, did I think like that?)

Now me and Big Man started to get into the movies kind of deep. But I didn't use my real name. I had an alias. I called myself "Tha Kidd."

(Do you know who else called theyself that in a movie?)

Hmmm... I'll give you a hint...
He was a singer that wore purple all the time.
Did you get it?

(L-R) Big Chuck with his head down and me, Azusa Canyon (CA)

Let's move on. I'm really getting into this adult movie stuff. I hooked up with two different movie companies. Let me break it down for you. I would film, edit, add hip-hop music, and take all the photos for each movie. Big Man would write all the scripts and direct them. And of course, Weed would do all the scenes—almost. So, we were like a little team. Oh, I forgot The Twins was security. Nobody got out of line on the set, trust me, LOL.

We was starting to get a little reputation around the industry known as "They don't pay much, but you don't work all day."

(In other words, that was a good thing.) Okay, let's switch the timeline.

It was mid-1995. I got a strange call from Mr. Manager. I wondered what he wanted from me. I answered, and he said that he wanted to meet with me at his house in the Valley.

I said, "Alright, cool."

The next day me, Big Man, and The Twins headed to his house.

We made it there, and as we went in, I said under my breath, "This is a big f*cking house."

I don't remember what we talked about, except for one

question he asked me. He said something about E's last album.

I don't think I gave him a clear answer about it. We said our goodbyes and left.

On the ride home, me and Big Man was talking.

I said, "Did he just try to get E's last album from me?"

He said, "Yep."

I said, "That's what I thought."

Man, I forgot all about that album. It had been sitting at the studio in Torrance since late last year (1994). Ain't nothing I can do with it. That's why I hadn't even thought about it. But a few years later, somebody asked me why I didn't hold E's album hostage for a million dollars.

A few weeks passed, and I got another strange call—this time from a lady that used to do some of our paperwork during the N.W.A days.

Let me think of a name for her...

(I'll call her Ms. Paperwork.)

She told me an independent record company wanted to give me a solo album deal. I told her I was done with music. Plus, I wasn't really feeling it right now. I'm not an artist, and I don't rap. All I do is produce. But after a lengthy phone conversation, and with the right numbers being mentioned—Mr. Entrepreneur was back!!!

Did she just tell me almost a quarter of a million dollars?

I had to say, "What! D*mn-it, where do I sign?"

Okay, I have to put the movies on the back burner for right now.

Wow! from the **infamous garage** to me doing a solo album! Are you kidding me? This is going to be a tuff one, though.

Why do I say that? I don't f*cking rap, LOL. Didn't I just name this chapter "Life After Music?" Now here I am, back in this same sh*t again.

One week later, I walk into Audio Achievements. It's time to work on my solo album. Who do you see?

The Twins in the lobby, Big Man sometimes, and I'm on the mixing board, drum machine, turntables, and keyboards.

Whew! I got to do it all by myself this time, but I had some key players with me on this project. Singer J did lead and background vocals. Mike Sims played guitar, bass, and keyboards. I also used something different—a muted trumpet by

Stan M.

Then there was some of the new Ruthless artists, like B.G. Knocc Out, Dirty Red, Dresta, Kokane, Leicy Loc, and my favorites, Menajahtwa.

I started working on the tracks; everything was coming out cool. Then Ms. Paperwork gave me another call. This time she told me some company wanted to give me a publishing deal.

I said, "Really?"

She said, "$50,000."

I said, "Bring it."

Mr. Entrepreneur is up to something here. Wow, it can't get no better than this. Now back to the studio.

I'm knocking songs out left and right, and I'm about halfway finished. Then I get another strange call. Priority Records wanted to meet with me.

I'm thinking, "What's on their mind?"

A few days later, I'm sitting in their offices with the owner. He wanted me to put together an N.W.A Greatest Hits album.

I told him, "I'm in the middle of my project, but I can take a week off to do this album."

Alright, I'm working on two albums now. The Greatest Hits was kind of easy to do. All our original masters were still in Audio Achievements. I had some rare old recordings from our 900 number vocal tapes. These days, it would be like the psychic hotlines. Right when I get halfway through that project, I get one more strange call. I keep getting these strange calls. But I d*mn sure like them! ☺

I think it was an administrator from the court for Ruthless Records. The company was going through some kind of legal battle about ownership. I have no idea. I stay out of grown folks' business. The reason for the call? There was questions about E's last album. This time it was legit because it was from the court. The administrator also asked me if I would put E's last album together. (Remember I had forgot all about this album.)

I said, "Of course, that was my buddy."

If you notice, I did not even mention anything about money. I would have done it for free.

Well... Not exactly free, LOL.

But I still didn't ask about money.

Now I get one more strange call. It was from Lady T.

She wanted to meet up and talk about the songs on the album. But technically, we had to do it unofficially because of the court stuff. So, we met and discussed the album—unofficially, remember. 😊

Back to the studio...

I am now in the middle of three projects. How do I handle this? First, let me finish up with the Greatest Hits.

I put the sequence of the songs together, then added never heard before inserts.

Alright, time to head back to Priority and meet with the owner. I walked in his office and sat down.

He said, "I'm not going to play; here's a check for five figures."

I said, "What you say? Thank you."

And I—am—out. (Now that was easy.)

But I was a little upset when the album came out. Why do I say that? I didn't get any kind of credits on it. At least it should have said, "Put together by Dog," "Executive producer, Dog," or just "Thank you, Dog." I was a little hot about that. Let's move on.

Now it's time for E's project. All these tracks was finished except for one. I will talk about that later. There was 14 songs, and I produced eight of them.

Other producers was Naughty By Nature, Bobcat, Tony G, and Roger Troutman. Ren also co-produced with me the song "Tha Muthaph*kkin Real." He was also a guest artist on that song. It was one of my favorites.

The intro called "First Power" was a little scary for me because E talked about his death on the track. That was creepy. (Remember this song was made in 1994.)

Other songs on the album were "Ole School Sh*t," "Just tah Let U Know," "Sippin On A 40," "Lickin, S*ckin, Ph*kkin," "Creep N Crawl," "Gangsta Beat 4 Tha Street," and Eternal E featuring Roger Troutman. This was the unfinished one. I found some rare lost vocals from E. I said a few words on it and completed the song.

Okay, I'm all done with the tracks, and everything is mixed. The last thing to do was to turn in the album.

While I was in the studio, somebody said, "Do you trust those courts? It's not the real Ruthless Records. Them people don't know you."

I said, "You're right, I'll just call and tell them to pay me for the eight new tracks, the same price E would pay me. Then look and see if Ruthless owes me anything. That way, I'm good." So, I did.

They said, "No problem."

Let's get back to my album. I'm finished with all the songs except the last two.

Here's a list of the ones that are done:

1. **"Dose of Reality,"** which is an opening intro.

2. **"Westside Story,"** featuring Dirty Red.

3. **"Streets Won't Let Me Go,"** featuring Dresta.

4. **"Neva Had a Chance."** On this song, I actually talked the verses and had Singer J sing the chorus. (Like the old slow songs when I was in the Wreckin' Cru.) I incorporated a muted trumpet on this track.

5. **"Dat's How I'm Livin,"** featuring B.G. Knocc Out.

6. **"Send 4 Me,"** is a remake of Atlantic Star's "Send For Me," featuring Singer J. (This would become the last single for the album.)

7. **"2 Two Face,"** featuring Leicy Loc (Dresta and Knocc Out's sister).

8. **"Ain't No Luv,"** featuring Dirty Red.

9. **"So in Luv,"** featuring my girls Menajahtwa.

Now with the last two, I got a little more into them. I put more feelings in them because they was both about E. The first one was **"4 Tha E,"** featuring Kokane. This was the funkiest song on the album and would be the first video.

The second one was called **"Not Long Ago."** I talked the vocals, and Singer J sang the chorus parts. On this one, I really talked about how I felt towards E. I mentioned my last time seeing him in Vegas and talking to him while I was at his Norwalk house. Singer J really poured her heart out in the singing parts. Whether it was a hit or not, it was how I felt about him. Those two songs was not about the money; they was a tribute to my late friend.

Here's some more breaking news that happened before the year's end. On December 4, 1995, seven days before my birthday, Bone Thug's "Creepin on Ah Come Up" EP went 4x Multi-Platinum.

While Ruthless is still in the middle of court stuff, it's selling records. Before I say what the courts said, Mr. Entrepreneur is in the market for something once again. Now, I finally heard back from the administrator and accountants for Ruthless Records. It was some good news.

Hold Up! It was some good f*cking news. But I won't talk about it till the new year comes.

1996: How Do I...?

The new year has arrived, and the first order of business is...

Breaking news: On January 1, 1996, Relativity Records released E's last album, "Str8 off tha Streetz of Muthaph*kkin Compton."

I don't like to bring attention to myself that much. (Really, not at all.) But right now, I do want to talk about some exciting things. Where do I start...?

Wow! My second house. (Corona, CA)

I just purchased another house! "Are U f*cking kidding me?" A brand-new 4-bedroom, with 3 baths, a dining room, a living room, a 3-car garage, and family room. You know I'm going to Ikea every day, eating meatballs and shopping for furniture 😊.

I also had to go through the hoops in a tutu again, but I didn't care. So, Mr. Entrepreneur did some adding on the numbers from those three projects.

I'm counting...

Still counting...

Now I got the results. Mr. Bad A** has a pocket full of money. How much? Well...

Let's just say, "How do I spend a—half—a—million—bucks?" You know me, I am about to be a d*mn fool. And I got A-1 credit too? From Z-1 credit back to A-1. (In my mind, I'm out of credit jail.)

Where do I start? How many do I need? What color do I want? I got to take a deep breath.

Whoo Wee! Let's begin the adventure!

First of many toys. (1996)

First stop, I want another Benz, this time, "The Big Papa." The S Class, white, with grey interior. Did I fail to mention the payment was $1,100 a month? That's a long way from the dairy when I was getting paid a dollar an hour. It is niiiiiccce! All the hard work is done; now it's time for Jack to act a fool!

Okay, fringe benefits, here I come! Where do I begin? *Hmmm...*

I will begin with a tall, thick, light-skinned, and cute girl. Do I have to say she was a freak? Let me think of a name for her...

(I'll call her Ms. T.T.L.)

Tall, Thick, and Light-Skinned. She will be part of the 4-G's

178

map. What do I mean by the 4-G's?

Well, the 4-G's are for four different girls. The map is five square miles around my new house. (Don't need no GPS for that.)

By the time I finish with the story, you will say to yourself, "What the h*ll is his problem?" LOL.

Back to Ms. T.T.L. She ended up living west of my house, about five miles away. That's one; let's move on.

I met another girl. She was tall, light-skinned, sexy, and kind of thick. This one was bad but a little sophisticated. Let me think of a name for her...

(I'll call her Ms. Tall R.)

Of course, she was a freak also. Now she ended up living south of me, about 3-4 miles away. That's two; I need a break for now. Here's some more breaking news.

On March 26, 1996, Street Life Records released my solo album called "One Mo N*gga Ta Go." It started out cool, peaked on Billboard 200 at #82, then at #23 on the R & B/Hip-Hop chart. But the album got caught up in red tape because me and the label really didn't see eye to eye on the project. So, that killed the sales. Let me get back to something happier—Part 3 and 4 of the 4-G's.

Now I had this friend that also lived close to me. Let me think of a name for her...

(I will name her The Mail Lady.)

There was nothing between us, but she hooked me up with the last two girls. The first one, let's just say she was her friend. And very cute, very sexy, and Bad A**. Let me think of a name for her...

(I'll call her Ms. Special P.)

She was freaky, but just a little different. She lived east from my house, about three miles. And number four...

Me and The Mail Lady was shopping at a grocery store. We was walking down an aisle, and I seen this sexy light-skinned girl in there.

I told The Mail Lady, "Hey, see if you can hook me up with that over there."

She walked over, and a few minutes later, came back with the number.

I said," D*mn, you good." LOL.

Let me think of a name for her...

(I'll call her Ms. Q.)

This one lived right around the corner from me, so that completes the 4-G's.

Am I going crazy? That's four within a hop-skip-and-a-jump of each other. That might get crazy one day.

Okay, some more breaking news.

Eazy-E's last album gold (1996)

On May 20, 1996, E's last album, "Str8 off Tha Streetz," went gold. WOW, still going.

Let's get back to buying things. Where shall I start? Car dealer, the mall, jet ski shop, or boat dealer? Before I pick a place, I have to admit something.

Me being a self-employed producer and filmmaker means I don't have a regular job. So, at times I get bored. I just go buy stuff. Everybody I know has a real 9-5 job. Now don't say I didn't warn you. Let's get back to buying.

One day I went to the mall to look at some watches. Well, I wasn't looking. I knew what I wanted.

(A Rolex Stainless Steel Submariner, No-Date.)

It was the kind of store where they put on gloves to show you a watch.

I said to the salesman, "How much?"

He said, "$3,800 with taxes."

You know what I said...

"Don't wrap it; I'll just put it on my arm." (That was easy.)

I forgot to tell you—I still have the condo in Paramount. But I'm letting someone rent it, you know how that goes. I really need to get back to work on the movies, but not right now.

Here's something kind of funny. My friend, The Mail Lady, hooked me up with another girl. This one wore a badge and had a gun— that's was a little weird but fun. I can't talk about her too much. I don't want those suits knocking on the door.

Now I'll speed up the timeline. I bought two new jet skis and another 18-foot boat. Then I was driving down Lakewood Blvd. and saw a sky blue 1967 Mustang sitting on a car lot.

It was in mint condition, with no dents and no scratches.

I asked the salesman, "How much?"

He said, "$5,500, sir."

I said, "Wrap it up, and thank you."

You know something? I didn't even test drive it. I drove the car once and left it parked at my mother's house.

I said to myself (in my "Old Man" voice...), "You Big Dummy!"

Another toy I bought... (What a waste of money!)

Did I just buy an almost 30-year-old car? Really? What am I going to do with this? No air, no CD player, no power seats, and no electric windows. D*mn sure don't have airbags. WOW.

The car was clean, but that was a waste of money. I never drove it again. It sat there in the same place for three months.

Moving on...

I wanted something a little different, so I pulled up to this boat dealership. (Watch out, there's a HUGE joker in this deck.)

I walked in, and a saleslady said, (with a beautiful smile), "How may I help you?"

Wow! This is a big A boat!**

Before I go on with the story, just a little hint. When you are making large purchases, buy what you came for, not what they want you to buy. I learned my lesson that day. On with the story...

She had that cute smile, but I was very business about it. Let me think of a name for her...

(I'll call her The Boat Lady.)

I said, "I'm looking at the 28-footers."

She said, "I have a few models in that range."

(This is when the f*cking joker pops out.)

She said, "Follow me, sir."

I followed, saw a few boats, then said, "They alright."

182

She said, "Come, take a look at this last model."

I said, "Naww... I like the 28-footer."

The Boat Lady said with those eyes, "Just take a look; it's like a condo on the water."

Alright, so I walked on it and went downstairs. Noticed I said down—stairs. My eyes got big as Krispy Kreme donuts. It was beautiful, luxurious, and extravagant. It even had a marble table and a queen-sized bed! ☺

Other words, it was OFF—THE—HOOK!

You know, when you play poker, you don't want to show your opponent your true emotions. You keep a straight face.

So, I said to myself under my breath, "What the h*ll...This is a big a** boat. Excuse em wa—yacht."

(See? I just learned a little French, LOL.)

I said, "What's the size?"

The look on my face says, "Did I just buy this?"

(Knowing I'm not buying nothing this big.)

She said, "41-footer— 13 feet wide, and 45 feet from bow to stern. There's two sleeping quarters, a living room, a kitchen with a refrigerator, and a full bathroom with a shower. You may also notice there's a microwave."

I said, "How much?" (Kind of joking around.)

She said, "$180,000 plus tax and licenses. You also need a boat slip to park it in and insurance."

I think I have a problem...

Did I just walk out of there with a $2,500 a month payment?

I said to myself, "Have you gone nuts?"

I think I have, but I can use it for my movies, LOL. You know how many I filmed on that boat? Just one.

I said to myself, "Was this a waste of money?"

I'll tell you in a little over a year from now.

Here's some more breaking news...

On July 2, 1996, N.W.A's Greatest Hits album (the one I didn't get credit for) was released by Priority Records. Before we end 1996, let's finish the year on another high note.

(Back row: L-R) my brother René, Dedrick, Allen, Big Chuck (Front row: L-R) Me, my cousin Nichole, my brother Joseph, and my cousin's roommate, Lora.

One day I went to my mother's and picked her up. We went to my favorite Chevy dealership in Lakewood, CA. I had talked to the GM earlier and told him what I wanted to do.

So, me and my mother walked on the lot. We looked at a whole row of brand-new Chevy Cavaliers.

I asked her, "Which color do you want?"

She chose a white one, and if you could have seen her smile... Priceless.

1997: Why Did I...?

1996 is gone, and so is some of the money. Okay, let's get back to the movies. I'm starting to film a little more. I'm doing two and sometimes three lines a month. (Lines–AKA movies.) That's about 10-15 scenes each month, one girl per scene, with about fifteen different attitudes. That's what me and Big Man have to deal with. Let's take a commercial break.

Sometime during this year, I had two small issues with two different 4-G's. But one of them was in both of the issues. I told you it might get crazy. Well... It got crazy.

This was the first issue.

After I hooked up with Ms. Q, we rolled out to Vegas and did our frills and thrills. We stayed at a five-star hotel. (The bathrooms was real nice there.) This was not the issue; I'm just setting up a pattern.

A few weeks later, I took this other girl to Vegas. She was BAD, SEXY, PRETTY, and FINE! Let me think of a name for her...

(I'll call her Ms. Fine C.)

We did our thang, but it was at the same five-star hotel. Are you catching on yet? The next issue came up a week later.

Me and one of the 4-G's, Ms. Tall R...Guess where we went?

To the same Bat place, and same Bat time—Vegas.

The same five-star hotel, in nearly the same room...

Frills and thrills happened; that was great. I was about to go downstairs and gamble some. Before I left out the room, I called the front desk and told them to block my calls. (Like somebody would really call me in Vegas?)

When I got back to the room, Ms. Tall R had a funny look on her face.

She told me she unblocked the phone, and some girl kept calling the room. Why did she do that? Why did she unblock the phone that I just had blocked? You look for sh*t, and you find sh*t. So, a piece of advice—Don't go noseying around for it because it will slap you in the face.

I'm thinking, "Who the h*ll would call me in Vegas?"

I found out later it was Ms. Fine C that I had just took to

Vegas the week before. She had time to call a hotel in Vegas looking for me? You got to be kidding me?

Ms. Tall R also told me that both of them was plotting something crazy. She said that as soon as me and her landed at LAX, Ms. Fine C would show up and show out. WOW...

Glad it wasn't a pot of hot grits. That's what the old school women used to do when they got p***ed off at their men.

(That's just what I heard.) Here is the second issue.

This one took place at my house, not inside the house, but outside of it. One of the 4-G's, Ms. Special P, came over wearing a leather trench coat with nothing on underneath it. (You know it's going down.)

Here's the issue. Little did I know that Ms. Tall R was behind my house, in her car parked on the street. In my bedroom window upstairs, she could see through the blinds. I didn't have them closed all the way. (I —am— slipping.)

A couple of days later, she said, "I was gonna ring your doorbell the other night when you had that gurrrl over."

I said, "You was gonna do what?"

She said, "Yea, I was gonna ring your doorbell."

I told her, "You woulda just got embarrassed. I would have just opened it, heard your mouth, and closed it."

I got to watch myself these days. (SMH.)

Let's get back to what I like best—buying cars. Cougar C's the one that got me hooked on this s**t. Don't you just like the smell of new cars? Where can I start?

I shall move the clock back, then forward. Since Cougar C rented me all those cars back in 85', I've been having an issue with them. (I like new cars.)

How many have I had so far? The first one you know was the Sidekick. There was a Corvette (only one year old), a Benz 190, a Lexus SC300, a Honda Accord, a Toyota Land Cruiser, two 4-Runners, and three different Acuras (a 2 and a 4-door Legend, and a Vigor). Then I had a Nissan Hardbody truck, a Maxima, a 2-door Camry, a Land Rover, a Ford Explorer, a Thunderbird (had only three days), a Chevy 2 and 4-door Tahoe, a 4-door Trailblazer (only had for one hour—the GM said I wasn't going to like it), 3-4 different Silverado trucks (I really don't remember), a Suburban, and a Volvo 850 Turbo Wagon.

Oh, I forgot about the white Jeep Wrangler (E said it looked like a mail truck) and a Benz S Class. That's 28 cars from 89' to mid- 97'. Cougar C sure had me sprung on cars.

Before I talk about some more vehicles, there was a little bad news.

I had the same surgery for the third time. (I couldn't use the bathroom again.)

The doctor told me there's a little growth inside my urinary track, and I would have to go see a doctor every three months for the rest of my life. That was a bummer to hear. If I was to describe the procedure, you might say, "WOW!"

Just imagine a 12" rod with a hook on the end of it and thick as a No.2 pencil. The hook part goes in first. I'm not going to tell you where it goes in. (Ouch!) ☹

During one of my visits to the doctor's office, there was a very cute assistant. Let's just say I did have some fringe benefits there. Was it inside the office? *Hmmm...* ☺

Okay, back to the car buying. I'm rolling around in the big Benz and thinking, "This $1,100 payment is quite large. Plus, I'm getting a little bored with it."

My logic was to reduce the payment and get a cheaper car. Where did I stop at? The Benz dealership. I got out of that one and bought a Benz E class. It had the round lights in the front, pretty cool. Drove that for a little while, then thought...

"I'll get rid of that payment and get something a little cheaper."

Guess where I stopped again? The Benz dealership.

This time I got a C class. It was nice and reminded me of my old 190. But you know me, I got bored again. This time, it wasn't a cheaper car, but a different kind. I called my favorite Benz dealership. (They probably just love me up there.)

I said, "What you got?"

The salesman said, "We have a new model called a CLK. Somebody else ordered it, but if you want it, come get it."

I was on my way! I walked on the lot, and yes, the paperwork was ready for me. I signed all of it, then drove off.

(That was just too easy, LOL.)

As I'm driving, I was thinking to myself, "Why did I SPEND— SO— MUCH— MONEY?" Let's roll into the next year.

1998: What Happened?

This is going to be a very different year for me. It's time to take things a little more serious. I am spending a lot of money these days. As a matter of fact, I'm on my way to the Benz dealership right now. I made a little deal with my brother Arnett. I'll give him the Benz CLK, and I will get the new MLK.

Didn't I just say I'm spending a lot of money? It must be the Cougar C car curse. (I just love cars.)

So, I also picked up another Volvo V70 wagon on lease. Why? Because it was cheap to get in. And I still had my 4-door Tahoe. Let me think about all the stuff I have...

There's the house, the condo (which no rent is coming in from), forgot about the yacht, my mother's car payment, the three cars at home (MLK, Tahoe, and Volvo), dirt bikes, jet skis, and a jet boat. No telling what else I'm paying for. Not to mention, the movies not really bringing no money in.

Let me stop thinking about that right now and concentrate on my fight party this weekend. Why am I talking about that? Well...

I did one of the craziest things ever.

For some reason, Mr. Bad A** invited all the girls I was kind of talking to. Why would I do that? I musta wanted to go out with a "BANG!"

Let me think of some of the girls I invited...

There was three of the 4 G's, and my favorite female cousin that usually sets me up with girls brought three of her friends along. That's six so far. I also had another one (I'm not going to name her), then there was The Beautiful One.

How did I escape death? There was a lot of other people at the party. Let's just say I didn't stay in one place too long. I wasn't hugged up with nooooo body! I'm not that crazy. That evening ended with no fireworks going off, LOL.

Now back to the M-O-N-E-Y issues. I was trying to figure out my monthly payments. They got to be well north of $5,500, maybe almost near $10,000 a month. That is a lot of money.

Mr. Bad A** don't have a plan right now—and don't have one in the future, either.

A few weeks later, I got a strange call. (Another strange call.) But this time, it was from Dre, who I have not talked to in years.

It was great to hear from him, so we decided to meet up.

I drove out to his house. And wow! This was a big f*ckin house! I walked in and when I saw him, I said, "D*mn boy, you doing mighty good these days!"

Did I say a butler, or somebody answered the door? Must be nice. Did I fail to mention that several maids served me during dinner?

He had a smile on his face, just like the old days, the happy days, the beginning days. We talked to each other like no time had passed. We had a great conversation, but there was one thing I remember him saying that stuck with me for a long time—that took me years to understand. As he was about to open his mouth to say something...

He glanced around the house, then looked me dead in the eye and said, "If it wasn't for me and you, none of this would be here."

I said, "Really? Okay."

So, we talked some more, and somehow, we ended up having a conversation about my situation.

He said, "Hey, why don't I give you some money to help you out with your bills for about five months?"

I said, "H*ll, yea, thank you."

My visit wasn't about the money; it was about our friendship. It felt like old times. The sad thing is, we wouldn't talk again until a few years later.

I got back to the house, walked in, and said, "Wooo...I'm baaaccckkkk..."

Now here's some more breaking news. What was it? Here we go. A week had gone by, and I was trying to get my mind on making the movies. But I couldn't focus on them at the time. There was other things to worry about. I can't say it was bad news, and d*mn sure can't say it was news I wanted to hear.

Let's call this little story "The 3 Amigos." It had three parts, and yes, there was a joker in the deck. Where do I start...?

One day I got—can you guess? Another strange call from one of the girls at the fight party. Remember, I didn't give her name earlier.

Anyway, she called and said, "I'm pregnant."

I said, "What you talkin' bout Willis?"

I know she didn't just say she was pregnant...

What happened? Wow, that's a shocker. Okay, I can recover from this.

You want to hear more? I remember it like it was yesterday.

I was driving down Hollywood Blvd., and I got another strange phone call.

I answered it and said, "Hello?"

The person on the other end was The Beautiful One's friend.

She said, "The Beautiful One is having a baby, and she ain't— getting— rid— of— it." (She could have at least said, "Hello dog! How ya' doing, dog?)

I almost went on the wrong side of the street and wrecked my sh*t.

I said, "What?"

Her friend said, "Yea, she keeping it."

I said to myself, "What the h*ll is going on here? How do I recover from this one?"

Things are changing too fast. I don't have time to worry about no bills. I got bigger fish to fry. (Like diapers and milk.)

I don't know if I should tell you this, but this is where the joker pops out.

I get another strange phone call from one of the 4 G's, Ms. Q.

She said, in a very calm voice, "I'm pregnant."

I said, "Huh?"

She said in a medium voice, "I'm pregnant."

I said, "Say what?"

Then she said in a louder voice, "D*MN IT! I SAID I'M PREGNANT."

I know that just didn't come out her mouth!

You telling me I'm about to be a part of the "Three P's?" And what are the "Three P's?" 1-Pregnant 2-Pregnant 3-Pregnant? (All at the same time?)

Ain't no way! This can't be happening! What the h*ll is going on here? Should I fly to London and seek asylum? Do I jump off a building? Is this the end of the f*cking world? 😞

What do I do now? I guess this joker was kinda wild here.

A few weeks later, I find out that Ms. Q was pregnant, but it wasn't MINE. Boy, did I dodge a bullet!

Since I'm into bad news right now (when it rains, it pours), let me just keep it going. A few weeks has passed; now everything is calmed down. I went from being Mr. Bad A** to becoming the future Mr. Mom.

But before that happens, I am on my way downtown to the federal court building in LA. Why am I going there?

Because of all that spending, not giving a d*mn about money and all that buying. Let me see—what did I buy? A house, condo, yacht, clothes, shoes, Vegas trips, and too many cars. (My mother's car gets a pass.) I also bought my buddy a car (twice), plenty of motorcycles, jet skis, even a jacuzzi in the back yard that I got in only two times, LOL.

Did I fail to mention no investments? No guidance, and no one to talk to. That's why I'm here at the BK courts of Los Angeles. If you don't know what BK means, it's the United States Bankruptcy Court.

I walked down the hall. Of course, I had to go through the metal detectors. (This is a federal court building.) All I could hear was my footsteps echoing, my heart beating in almost heart attack mode—and my blood pressure? Feels like I'm about to have a stroke.

I opened the door to this plain-looking room, and I felt relieved. Why? Because there were other debtors on their way to credit jail, too. I didn't feel too bad. Now I am sitting in front of a judge or trustee or whatever you call him.

With all this stuff in my head...all the money, the money, the money. Where did it go? Why did I give it all away? I have no idea. What's going on?

I hope this don't mean credit jail—oops—I mean credit prison. (Again, this is a federal court building.) And to top it off, the judge don't look like he liked me. But I had a sharp lawyer. He laid out a stack of papers (about 500 pages of debts and stuff) on the table.

That judge looked at the lawyer, looked at the stack of papers, and said, "Case discharged."

I got up, raised my head, stuck my chest out, walked out of the courthouse, said "So long!" to my lawyer, and let out a big breath. Oooh Weee! Free at last! Free at last! LOL.

I made it back to the house and thought to myself, "This is crazy! They just allowed me to keep almost everything! Where is the law in this town? All the cars—even the house?"

I told them I didn't want the condo, the yacht, or the Volvo. I figured out the solution to the problem—It's me. I am the problem.

From the **infamous garage** to half a million dollars; from a hero to a zero...

To all you aspiring and upcoming artists...

Don't be a big fool like me! Watch your money.

Let's change the timeline. Now for some good, not so good, and some different kind of news.

Okay, here's the good news.

After all those years of working and providing for our family, my mother finally retired. She had been a nurse, then a phone operator at the hospital for over 30 years. That was a good thing, but here's the not so good news. She had spent all those years working and moving around. Now it seemed like everything was starting to fall apart on her. The doctor said she had hidden diabetes for over five years, plus high blood pressure.

So, I got to think about this.

Not to be funny about the situation, but here it is.

I have two babies, as you would say, in the oven. (They're three months apart.) My mother's starting to go in and out of the hospital. I just got finished with my BK. I'm sitting here in this house all alone and still got those bills coming. I haven't figured out where the money is going to come from. I got the Tahoe, Benz MLK, and the CLK to pay for.

I'm not behind on my house payment. (Only $1,150 a month.) I have some money left, but not enough to last. I need to make a decision. What am I gonna do? But before I try to figure all that out...

Let's switch to a new year.

CHAPTER 10: THE BEGINNING OF THE END

I'm still sitting here in the house, listening to the group, The Police. (They got that reggae feel to them.) Back to my decision. Maybe I should downsize again. Might be able to save some money every month. Should I move to Long Beach in a one-bedroom apartment to be near my mother? That way, I can visit her those times when she goes into the hospital.

I made up my mind. I called a few friends and my brother Beany to help me move. I packed up everything and just moved out of the house; no looking back, no second-guessing. I'll give back the two Benz's and just forget all about it. I walked out and closed the door for the last time, drove to Long Beach, and kept it pushing.

I said to myself (in my "Old Man" voice...), "You Big Dummy!" Did you just walk away from a brand-new house and you wasn't even late on the payments? And the apartment in Long Beach was almost the same payment as YOUR HOUSE? You Big Extra Dummy! You could have put it in your brother's name, or your dog's name (if I had one), or even in an enemy's name.

I need to stop talking to myself, LOL. Now I got to get used to the big change, or maybe the big move, or just being a big dummy.

Six months had passed, and I'm all settled down in my one-bedroom apartment. The movies are starting to pick up, but my mother is getting sicker. That means her diabetes is getting worse. They starting to cut limbs off—toes, feet, and legs.

(Diabetes is a serious disease, so don't take it so lightly.)

I'm going to the hospital almost every other day to feed her. Plus, I'm trying to get adjusted to being a new father. That means two babies, two baby mothers, and two different worlds.

Did I fail to mention, they both did—not—know of each other? I'm living what you would call a double life.

Why? I have no idea.

Now back to the movies. Time to get real serious. What do I mean about serious? I'm putting my face and name on the box covers. Trying to take them to a new level.

On the set... (You know what's going down.)

The first one with my name and face on it was called "Bangin' in LA."

For the next—I would say about a year and a half, I had a juggling routine. (Reminds me of Bozo the Clown.)

I was going to the hospital to see my mother, plus I had two kids, two birthdays, two Chuck E. Cheese's, and of course, there's the movies.

On the movie side, I'm starting to shoot more lines a month. Let me see... that's about five or six movies a month, 30 scenes, 30 different girls, and you know that is 30 different attitudes.

Now it's late 2001, two weeks before 9/11. Me, Big Man, and Weed was on the set in the Valley, finishing up a scene. Of course, there was a girl on the set. (Not with me, but with Weed.)

I got a call from my sister Sherreé. She tells me the ambulance just took our mother to the emergency room. I packed up my gear, then me, Big Man, and Weed headed to Gardena Hospital.

Once we made it there, them two stayed outside for some reason. I walked through the double glass doors. All of a sudden, everything went silent. All I hear is my footsteps.

I walked up to the front desk and asked the nurse on duty,

194

"You know where my mother is—Ms. Carraby?"

She said, "Down the hall, the room on the left."

I took that long silent walk, then made a left through another set of double doors. There she was, lying on the bed motionless, with her eyes wide open. I stood there, stunned. There was no noise, nothing but beeping from the machines. I walked up to her and grabbed her hand. I don't know if I prayed or just talked to her. Just like E, she was unconscious, but her hand moved a few times. I guess she wanted to let me know that she knew I was there. I'm not an emotional person, but I shed a few private tears. I stayed there a little while, then I left her room.

I walked back outside and just sat on the curb. Big Man came over and sat next to me. He knew the feeling because he had lost his mother also.

I said to him, "It's over. I think that was the last time I will ever see her."

A few days later, the hospital took her off the breathing machine.

My niece was there and said, "She stayed alive for a few hours."

My mother, Mary Francis Carraby (1933-2001) (R.I.P)

195

It was hard to believe that she was gone.

It was a sunny day when we had Mama's funeral. It was held at her church, which was a pretty large one, and it was packed out. During the funeral, I remember walking out halfway during the service. I went outside and sat on the steps. A buddy of mines named Big Z came out there and sat with me and talked a while. I didn't view her body or see her in the casket. Just like E, I wanted to remember her with that living smile.

As I write this, tears are falling from my eyes. It's been a long time since I thought about that night.

I'll just say this; she was a strong woman to have and take care of 9 kids. No disrespect to my father, but my mother did the best she could with what little she had.

I just want to say, "I miss her..."

Let's move on. It's 2002, and my Rams are back in the Super Bowl. Even though we lost the game, this was the first time I went to this sports bar called **Yankee Doodles** in Long Beach.

I thought to myself, "Not a bad place."

I'm thinking about coming back here during the football season. (Well, I did, every Sunday for the next nine years, LOL.)

Let's get back to those movies. Money is starting to roll back in again. The scenes are getting...

Let's say a little more wilder, in crazy places like public parks, out at the beach, at the marina in the little rented boats. We was just out of control. Did I fail to mention— on the overpass on the 110 Freeway?

(That was bold, with people driving by and honking.)

And yes, there was some fringe benefits ☺.

There's A Change In The Air: 2002-2006

Since my mother died, time seems to be just passing by. The movies are paying off now—I'm kind of rolling again. You know what that means—it's car-buying season. I brought my father a little Nissan Sentra, and I got me a Black Chevy Tahoe Limited. Sometime later on, in 2002, my father got into a financial jam. (Other words, he was struggling with his rent.)

I wasn't really talking to him much. I was still upset about that gold chain since high school, 22 years ago. But I swallowed my pride and went and talked to him about his money issues.

196

He wanted to sell his Sentra. So, I bought it from him and gave it to Big Man. But a couple of months later, he was back in the same spot. I had to figure out a plan. I'll just let him live in my mother's house. (If she was alive, that would not be happening.)

The time came to move his stuff. I remember like it was yesterday.

I was standing outside by the U-Haul truck. I thought to myself, "I will forgive him about that gold chain I never got."

I been holding that grudge inside me for over 20 years. Tears was in my eyes while I was standing there. I had to let it go. I say to you...

Please don't hold grudges against family and friends over stupid stuff. Just—let—it—go.

My father got to be around his kids and grandkids for about three years. I think he had a little peace and joy during that time.

Joseph Albert Carraby (1928-2005) (R.I.P.)

197

Here's some more breaking news! Me and my first kid's mother just had a baby girl in late December 2003. But remember, The Beautiful One and her still don't know about each other. That secret drama lives on. (But it's coming to an end soon. ☺)

In 2005, I got a strange call in the middle of the night from my brother René. He told me that our father went to the emergency room that night and had passed away. The crazy thing was, he had no diabetes or high blood pressure.

What else was weird about him passing? After my brother told me about it, I didn't shed a tear.

Now it was time for me to grow up. Why do I say that? I had decided to go to the funeral home and make all the arrangements by myself. I think it was something I needed to do on my own.

During the funeral, I stayed outside and didn't view the body, just like I did with my mother and E. I will always remember and miss him. Let me switch to something else.

My mother's house is going through probate. That took about a year.

This next story is what a lot of us have done with our parents' houses (I'm guilty.) that they worked all their lives to get and keep. Here's the story. House. Money. All gone. Did you catch that? I'll break it down for you.

It's 2006, and the housing market is skyrocketing. That means the value of homes is at an all-time high. So, what do most of us do, or what did I do?

Probate is over, so there's no fighting or arguments over the house. I guess Mr. Entrepreneur was left in charge. (The wrong person for that, LOL.) I found a great lender.

The first-round loan was a whopper, six figures. Notice I said the first round. What did I do first? I paid some bills off, gave my brother and sisters some money, and remodeled my mother's house.

Once again, it's car-buying season. But first, I brought a sandrail.

You might ask, "What is that?"

It's what you would call an up-to-date dune buggy. It was a 4-seater with a Subaru Turbo motor.

The price...? $48,000.

How many adventurous rides did I take in it? Just two.

First Hummer (2006)

Another waste of money. (I just HAVE to get rid of the Cougar C curse!)

Back to the car season...

I was itching for something I never had before. Let's take a drive. Where? The car dealership. I get out the car and walk around the lot. I see what I want. That's it right there.

I ask the salesman, "How much?"

He said, "Sir, that's $68,000."

I said, "Sir, that's what I want."

It was a brand-new fully loaded Hummer H2. It had black leather seats, a sunroof, navigation, chrome rims, and a DVD player in the back.

Wow! Did I just spend $68,000 on a truck? Yes, that's a lot of money! But I did, and I LOVE IT!

Remember I told you about that secret life coming to an end? Well... here's how it happened.

Me and my first kid's mother are living at my mother's house in Compton. (Don't forget—it's freshly remodeled.)

One day she said, "My friend told me you have another baby. And the baby's mother's name is the Beautiful One."

I stood there in shock, then thought to myself...

(There's no place like home, there's no place like home...)

You big dummy, you ARE at home.

I said, "You want me to move out?"

199

Hanging out with my babies...

She didn't answer that question. So, I called the Beautiful One and told on myself.

I said, "I have two kids already."

From that moment, the big secret was out in the open. I ain't got to hide that anymore. Whew!

Okay, back to my mother's house. The first batch of money, you know, well...that ran out.

Now for the second-round loan, another six figures. This was just too easy. And that's what it was— way too easy. The easier it came, the quicker it got spent.

Now you may not believe this, but I will tell you. I got tired of the Hummer. It burned too much gas, maybe 10-12 miles a gallon. And the price of gas? Over $4.00 a gallon— that's high.

I went to my favorite Chevy dealership on Lakewood Blvd., sold them the Hummer, and got me a crew cab 4-door Silverado 2500 diesel. That was fun for a minute. Then I sold my sandrail and bought me... A brand-new Funco V8 sandrail.

The price? $67,000. And how many rides in this one? I would say a whopping two times. And yes, that was a waste of f*cking money.

Me and my cousin Nichole at Glamis. (CA)

But hold up—2006 is not over with yet.

One day I was on the set filming a scene. Big Man came up to me and said, "I want to ask you something."

I stopped, turned to him, and said, "Go ahead."

He said, "Do you think we doing the devil's work?"

I looked him dead in the eye and said, "Yes."

Then I turned back around and said, "Action."

Why he asked me that? I have no idea.

About a month later, money was a little tight—again.

Then I got another strange call. This time it was from Ruthless Records. I wonder what they want. They was wondering when I was going to cash the check they had sent me.

I said, "What the h*ll, are you kidding me? A check?"

A few days later, they re-issued me another check. I opened it, and my eyes got big—another six figures!

Instead of making a bank deposit, guess where I was on my way to? My favorite dealership on Lakewood Blvd., trying to buy back my Hummer that I sold them. They broke my heart. It just got sold the day before.

So, where did I go from there? Back to the Hummer dealership.

I walked on the lot and said to the salesman, "I want that right there. How much?"

He said, "Sir, that's $68,000."

Again, I said, "Sir, I'll take it."

It was another brand-new Hummer H2. It looked exactly like the one I bought two months ago.

I said to myself (in my "Old Man" voice...), "You Big Dummy—again!"

Did you just buy another big a** gas guzzler? The same year, the same color, the same price? And what happened to the six-figure check I got?

Had it... spent it... all gone.

That's all, folks. Now on to the next year.

2007: The Downfall

The beginning of the end is coming. I can feel it. I don't know why, but it's near. Before I move on, there was one bright spot from that year. I got a strange call from Lady T. She told me they was doing a tribute show to E in New York, and they wanted me to be a part of it. It was called **The Hip Hop Honors**.

I would be the DJ on the Eazy-E part, and his first son would rap his daddy's lyrics of his songs. (His name is Lil Eazy E, but I call him Lil E.) Plus, Cube was on the same show. That was the first time we seen each other in over 17 years. That was cool to hang out and talk with him for a little while. We joked around a bit with a lot of "Hee hee's" and "Ha ha's." And no, we didn't discuss the diss song he made about us a while back.

Now back to my downfall. Once again, money is getting a little tight. I need to take a big gamble here. After all the movies I filmed, I don't own a single one. I have to make a change, like right now. So, me and Big Man hooked up with this new adult movie company. (Let me warn you—there is a joker in this deck.)

They was filming the latest and hottest movies out there. Between them and us, we could be the biggest film company around. On paper, it looks great. My idea was to pay for two movies out of my pocket. That way, I would own them. They would be the biggest ones I ever done. I'll put about 15 girls in each one. I would also play a role in the movie. (Just acting only, no hanky panky.)

Now I had to come up with a name for them.

Let me see...

I'll call them "Str8 Outta Compton, Volumes 1&2."
Everything went well with the filming, editing, writing, and
music. The box covers looked great.

Now, this is when the joker popped out.

Hold up! Before I say what happened, here's some more car-
buying news. After three months, I got tired of the Hummer. I
sold it and got me a brand-new Benz MLK. (Didn't I buy a car
like this before?) Funny thing is, I sold the first Hummer I
bought after three months also. (What's with this three-month
crap?)

Now back to the joker. Yes, it popped out. Everything about
the new company looked great on paper. But it was having
financial issues. This I sure in the h*ll didn't know.

Does this picture look kinda familiar? (Hint: S.O.C.)
(L-R) Weed, me, Cousin T, and Big Man.

No money was made, so me and Big Man had to go up there
and get a little Comptonish. In other words, we tore some sh*t
up and got all my masters back. (Reminds me of the old Wreckin'
Cru days.)

It's still 2007. I know it can't get no worse. (Or so I thought.)
One day me and Big Man took a drive in the Benz to this little
shop.

What kind of shop? A pawn shop. I parked in the front.

Then I said, "I can't do it. You gonna have to take my Rolex in and pawn it. I just can't do it."

Did I fail to mention, a while back, I had bought me another new Rolex Submariner Two Tone gold watch? The price? $8500.

He said to me, "Let's just wait for something to come in before you do all that." So, we drove off.

Later on, some money did come in. But it wasn't enough to stop this rollercoaster—with no brakes and no wheels. Where's it going? The GPS said, "Str8 2 H*ll." It sure felt like it.

Now that brings me into 2008. Me and my first kid's mother moved from my mother's house to Eastvale, California. My brother Corky, my sister Sherreé, and Big Man stayed in her house after me. I came up with the down payment, then she bought a house. Everything was cool.

It was the same routine for me for the next two years. Being Mr. Mom, taking the kids to school, dropping them off, and picking them up. All their practices, soccer, baseball, football, homework, and of course, housework. The odd thing is, I spent more time with the two kids and not enough time with the one son I had with The Beautiful One. But hopefully, in the future, it will work itself out.

It's January 2010, and everything had shut down for me. The movie business had ended. The internet had started to take over. In other words, there was plenty of free adult movies right at your fingertips. This means the "St8 Outta Compton" DVD sales have hit an all-time high...excuse me, an all-time low. Other words, NO—MORE—MONEY.

In February of 2010, Big Man somehow found Dre's address. Why? I had something to send him. What was it? It was what I would call a care package. What was in it? About 15-20 DVDs of the movies I had made. I also wrote him a letter and put my phone number on it.

About two weeks later, something very strange happened to me. This was the first time in 25 years that Mr. Bad A** didn't have a car. I could not believe that! I had to give back my brand-new Chevy Tahoe. I didn't have a choice. (I couldn't afford the $900 payments anymore.)

When I handed the keys over, it was like handing that person my life. All I knew was cars. Buying them and trading them in.

Remember the new car smell? That's all I did. Never owned any. Wow, after having over 50 new cars, and now I didn't have a vehicle. Mr. Bad A** was hitting rock bottom. That's just the beginning of the Domino Effect. Plus, me and my first kid's mother are not seeing eye to eye. But before those dominoes fell, I got two strange calls. The first one was from Cougar C. I have not talked to her since the 80s.

We talked a bit, and she even asked me if I had talked to Dre. I told her no, and that was about it.

Then a week later, in March of 2010, Dre gave me a call. It's been over nine years since we talked. (The last time was the day of my mother's funeral.)

He laughed and said, "Thanks for the care package."

I said, "No problem, those are my latest movies."

He said, "Why don't you come by the studio and hang out?"

I said, "Cool, but first, I got to see if I can borrow a car."

He said, "What?"

I said, "It's like that right now."

We hung up. I borrowed my friend The Mail Lady's car, made it to the studio, and walked in. Then me and Dre had one of the biggest hugs we ever had. It was the first time we seen each other since 1998.

He said to me, "What's going on? What did you do not to have a car?"

I said, "Nothing. Just ran out of money, plus me and the kid's mother is not on the same page."

Then he told me something that, to this day, I never forgot.

He looked me dead in the eye and said, "Whatever it takes to fix you, money is no problem."

(I hear that same bell sound once again. "Ding"! Miracle!)

"What do you need first? A car or an apartment?"

I said, "H*ll, I need a car."

Now that's a real friend. This was the second time I didn't ask for help but ended up getting it. I was just there to see my old buddy.

The next day he gave me the money, and I bought a brand-new car. Nothing fancy. It was a Nissan Cube. Pink slip in hand.

For the next almost three months, me and Dre was hanging out like old times. Dinner, studio, at his house— and we even went to the Lakers-Boston Game 7 at the Staples Center.

(That was my first time sitting up in a luxury box.)

One night we were at his beach house, hanging out on the balcony.

I told Dre, "God sent you to me."

He said, "God blessed me."

Then I did something that I had never done before. (And till this day, never done again.) I was playing around, then got on my knees and jokingly bowed down to him.

He laughed and said, "Get up from there."

Ever since that day, it seemed like all my dominoes started falling down—one after another.

There was a series of events that led me to...

I would say, "The bottom of the barrel." Where shall I begin?

Remember I told you me and my first kid's mother was not seeing eye to eye. To make it worse, we was on the page of me sleeping in the guest room. You know that won't last too long.

Matter of fact, the next step was already there. She wanted me OUT. That was unexpected. (Must had been my "creative" actions—me being me. All my fault, I guess.) Didn't see that one coming. Okay, Mr. Bad A** don't have a plan. I know I can recover somehow. But since the dominoes are falling, let's see where they fall.

It's mid-July 2010, and I'm talking to Big Man on the phone about my new issues. That included my car.

He said to me, "Why don't you sell your new car and get a used one. That way, you could have some money in your pocket."

My heart dropped right in my shoes. Did he just say what I thought he said? Sell my new car with the pink slip in hand for a used one?

I told him, "Man, I got to think about that one."

Wow. I will get back to that story in a moment. Now my other kid's mother, The Beautiful One, was living in Texas at the time. We was at her house in West Covina, talking about her daughter that was about to get married. I used to buy school clothes for her when she was in high school. So, the daughter wanted me to be in her wedding.

I told The Beautiful One, "Cool, but I can't afford a suit for the wedding."

She said, "I will pay for everything."

Somehow, we ended up talking about one of my issues.

206

(My first kid's mother wanted me out the house.)

The Beautiful One said to me, "I had renters in this house, but for some strange reason, they just unexpectedly moved out."

Then she said, "You can stay here."

(All of a sudden, I hear that bell sound again. Ding! Miracle!)

I said to her, "Thank you."

Life Will Never Be The Same

It's August 2010. Back to the car story. I got the pink slip in my hand, and just a little pride left in me. How do I start this one? Well...

I can't believe I got a car that's paid in full but cannot afford it. How is that so? No job—Like what kind of job can I get? No money coming in, no hopes, and d*mn sure no dreams. I'm about to be stuck in "Wonder Wonderland." Wondering how, wondering where.

So, I find myself driving to a little car lot on Pacific Coast Highway in Long Beach. I swallowed that last bit of pride and walked on the lot. Being used to new cars, I felt a little weird looking at them, but I had no other choice.

I pointed at a car and said to the salesman, "I want to trade this car for that car."

He looked at me strange and said, "Are you sure, sir?"

I said, "I have to do what I have to do."

I sold the new Nissan Cube and got a used car. And what kind was it? A 2004 cream-colored PT Cruiser. It was low on miles—only 63,000. Wow. From 2010 to 2004. Am I going backwards here?

You know something? I didn't actually love cars. I think it was just the process of going and buying them. D*MN that "Cougar C curse! LOL.

It's been a long time since I had a used car. It was an eye-opening experience. I drove home with the radio off to make sure I didn't hear any crazy noises. It can't get no worse than this—can it? (Just a little hint, one of my brothers is still driving that PT Cruiser to this day.)

It's the day of The Beautiful One's daughter's wedding. It was outside on a hill at Palos Verdes near the ocean. Her daughter looked beautiful; everything was nice.

The music for the first dance comes on. All of a sudden, you hear a...*Screeeeecccchhhh*!

That's the sound you would hear of a record scratched on a turntable. This is where the drama begins. What was that? They had me take the first dance with the bride. Did they just ask me to do that?

As I'm dancing with her, I said to myself, "I know they didn't want me to do this..."

And the rest of this story? That's a whole book of drama by itself, so I think I'll just close it. LOL. Alright, let's see how many more dominoes will fall.

Two weeks later, in September 2010...

Well, I was not really prepared for what was coming. It was the end of my journey with my first kid's mother. After about 10 years, our time of living together was up. I packed all my stuff in the car, then made a few trips back and forth to drop things off in West Covina. On the last load, I had to say goodbye to the kids. (Whatever is going on between me and her had nothing to do with them.) I gave my oldest son a hug, then walked by the car and hugged my seven-year-old daughter. Now, this was hard, I mean inside my guts f*cking hard.

I told her, "Daddy have to move out. Me and your moms don't see eye to eye anymore." (Me and my first kid's mother are still on good speaking terms to this day.)

As I walked to my car, I thought to myself...

"I am about to be homeless."

My tears fell to the ground. I sucked it up, got in the car, and drove away.

That was a feeling I never felt before. I was not worried about me, but I just hated to disappoint the kids. Not to change the subject, but reality just hit me.

I am about to be the first one in my family to become "homeless." Wow. Did I just say that? Let me repeat that to myself. I am now "HOMELESS."

I'm not living on the street. (I have a roof over my head, but it's not my roof.) I'm still one step from the curb.

But after about 50 new cars, 3 new houses, blowing hundreds and hundreds of thousands of dollars, after making over 300 hundred adult movies for 15 years, and all the man toys I can think of...

That's right, I —am—homeless. ☹

I said to myself, "You Big Dummy! You blew everything! What was you thinking?"

That's the key. I wasn't thinking. But out of all this misery going on around me, there is a silver lining somewhere.

I make it to The Beautiful One's house in West Covina. Remember, her and my second son live in Texas. Now, this house was vacant, not abandoned. It was a 3-bedroom, 2-bath and in good shape. It had a TV, a couch, and a bed. (Hint, Hint; I should not be thinking like that, LOL.) I am thankful for a roof over my head. It took me a couple of weeks to get adjusted to the shock. It's very different, not having your own place. The funny thing is, I can't blame nobody but myself.

Now I'm settled in. Then I get a strange call. It was a certain female. (One of the 4-G's, Ms. T.T.L.)

I know you're saying, "He should be down in the dumps, crying, and all stressed the h*ll out."

I should be. That's why I must laugh at myself sometimes. I need to be thinking about how to make some money and where my next MEAL IS COMING FROM!

Did I fail to mention it's winter, and I don't have no d*mn heat in THIS house? Forget all that for the moment. That's why I told Ms. T.T.L. to "Come on Down!"

I said (in my "Old Man" voice...), "YOU ARE A BIG DUMMY."

Let's switch the timeline to my mother's house. After 40 years, my mother struggled and worked all her life to provide a home for us. What did Mr. Bad A** do? He lost her house. I couldn't make the payments on it.

So now my oldest brother Corky, Big Man, and my sister Sherreé was out in the cold. My brother Corky became the first one in my family to live in a homeless shelter. Big Man bought him an RV and started "Boom Docking." If you don't know what that means, it's people that live on the street in an RV. And my sister went and lived down the street at her son's grandmother's house.

Times are getting a little rough. But the crazy thing is, I wasn't there sitting in a dark room, thinking about jumping off the cliff or shooting myself, or doing something else stupid.

I just thought to myself, "It is what it is."

Plus, I had a few more free passes from Ms. T.T.L. ☺

As the song would say in the future, "Everything is gonna be alright."

Now back to these issues at hand. Like I said before, it's getting a little rough—but Mr. Entrepreneur had a plan.

You're probably thinking, "What kind of plan can he come up with?"

Let me tell you. I had a nice Star Wars collection just sitting there. They was kind of looking at me, and I was kind of looking at them.

I thought to myself, "How 'bout I just mosey on down to the bookstore and see if I can make a sell of these things.?"

Hold up! I have much more to take with them. Let me see what else I got. Well, there's a bunch of Michael Jordan baseball cards, a signed Scottie Pippen basketball, many signed baseballs, and lots of NBA memorabilia.

I hopped in the PT Cruiser and made it to a little mom- and-pop bookstore.

I walked in and said, "Sir, what do you think these are worth?"

The clerk said, "Well, sir, they're worth about..."

"I'll take it!"

I know I just got beat on this. I wish it was in the future, then I could Offer Up, LOL. I don't have time to haggle with nobody. I'm not attached to nothing. If it gotta go, it gotta go.

Alright, let's change the timeline again.

Two different situations and two life-changing events was going on around the same time. One is about my brother Corky, the other is about Big Man. First up, my brother Corky.

Remember when he moved out of my mother's house and had to go to a homeless shelter? He told me the first night that he was at that place, it was about 40 other men there sleeping.

My brother looked around the room at all those people.

Then he said to himself, "This is either gonna make me or break me."

He made his choice. It was gonna make him. His life would never be the same again. After over 25 years on drugs, in just one night, he was off drugs forever. (Definitely wasn't no 12-step program.) I dropped him off one day at a trucking school, and he hasn't looked back since.

Next up is Big Man. He had been living in that RV on the streets for a little while. One day I got a call from him.

He said, "Can you take me to the hospital?"

I picked him up and dropped him off at the emergency room in Bellflower.

Later on, Big Man told me he had walking pneumonia, and to top it off, he needed to have open-heart surgery.

I said, "What?"

He said that his heart valve was no good. They had him stay in the hospital for at least a month. Wow, really?

Right back to my issues. The situation is not getting no better. A weird thing was happening. My brother Corky was driving trucks now—all of a sudden, he was trying to help me.

He was going upwards, and I was going downwards. All the years, I helped him—now the tables had turned. He's sending money to me every week out his checks. (Do people still help folks like this these days?) I really didn't know how to respond to that kind of help. Plus, he was still getting money on his EBT card. If you don't know what that is, it's the modern-day electronic food stamp card. He kept trying to get me to use it for food, but the last of my little pride was too embarrassed to use it.

But after a few weeks of that grumbling stomach, I finally broke down and used the EBT card. I was smiling that day with a bunch of groceries ☺.

The card was cool for food, but I needed money in my pockets. So, I turned and looked at the safe I had in the house. I wonder what I got in there? I know it ain't no money inside.

I opened it up, and what do I see...?

A Ziplock bag with some rare silver dollars— can't touch that. Those are my brother André's coins. He told me to hold them almost ten years ago. I moved them out the way and VOILÀ!

I forgot all about my guns! I have not thought about them since me, Dre, Ren, and E went to the gun range. They was still in mint condition. Let me look and see what I got in there...

I still had that 9mm Beretta, the nickel-plated Browning .380, the Smith and Wesson 9mm, and the 2 shot .357 Derringer. Did I fail to mention? They had 15 round clips that they don't make anymore.

But you know me. I ran outside and hopped in the Batmobile—Excuse me—I meant the PT Cruiser and burnt

211

rubber to the nearest gun shop. (And yes, all my guns were legally registered.)

I walked in and said to the salesman, "Sir, how much do you think these are worth?"

The man said, "Sir..."

I said, "Sold." (Ain't got no time to be playing around here.)

I had it, they got it, and I needed it. I can't believe I just sold all four of my guns for the original price of that one Beretta. Like I said before—it is what it is.

Now I got gas money for a little while. That means it's football season, and I'm back on track for the sports bar. I still have my Mr. Mom duties, but it's just a little longer drive now. I think I can make it; I think I can, I think I can, LOL.

It's Going Down

It's 2011—a brand-new year. I feel like a good one is coming. But I hear that sound again.

Screeeeecccchhhh! That's how long that feeling lasted.

This is how the year started.

I just got word that The Beautiful One and my son is moving back to California. Matter of fact, they moving to West Covina to this house, which is hers.

I'm kind of thinking, "Is that a good thing or a bad thing?"

Well, she didn't say, "You have to move out."

I guess that's a good thing. Then I got excited for a moment and thought about something else. There's only one bed in the house. *Hmmm...* Looks like it might be going down. Nope, let me stop thinking like that.

They made it back and settled in. She was cool about everything and took the room with the bed in it. (It is her house, no complaints.)

Now, where do I sleep? Let me tell you about that. Mr. Bad A** slept on an air mattress with a time clock. What do I mean by that? I blow it up around 12 midnight, and by 3 a.m., I'm laying flat on the hard floor.

You might say, "How is that possible?"

Let me explain it to you. There is a tiny little hole in the mattress that takes about three hours to deflate. When morning comes, my fat a** is flat on the ground.

Folded up like a pretzel. I'm not complaining, but that was not comfortable at all.

How low can I go? I went from houses, condos, and many beds to an air mattress—with a hole in it.

You probably think life sucks for me, huh?

As I roll off the ground every morning, I think to myself, "Hey, it is what it is."

Now Mr. Mom is in full effect, driving to Eastvale to pick the kids up from school and watch them for a while. Then go back to West Covina to pick my other son up from karate or other activities. This was my routine for the rest of the year. Remember, I don't have no job and no gas. I am what you would call "Riding on hope and a prayer."

One Sunday morning, The Beautiful One asked me a strange question.

She said, "Would you like to go to church with us?"

I looked her dead in the eye and said, "Naw, I'm going to the sports bar to watch my Rams."

The funny thing is, she asked me that twice, and I gave her the same answer twice.

André Carraby (1954-2011) (R.I.P.)

A few days later, I'm on my daily routine, being Mr. Mom. I left Eastvale with the kids and got to West Covina a little early

213

for my son's karate practice. As I'm sitting outside in the car waiting, I get a strange call, this time a little disturbing. It was from my brother Corky.

He tells me that my brother André had passed away. I got out the car and leaned against it, feeling stunned. My brother said he had died over a month ago, and the LA County coroner's office didn't know what to do with his body. At that moment, I felt kind of bad. Here I was homeless, and I couldn't even pay for a funeral for my brother.

He had been in a nursing home for about 10 years. For some reason, the family had lost contact with him over the past few years. So, I'm a little upset with myself that I didn't visit him more. I just hated that my brother died alone.

All I can say is, "I love you, André." Let's move on

It's late November 2011. I'm doing the same dance, on the same song, no new lyrics, no new melody, and the same old beat. In other words, it's the same old sh*t every day; same place, same time.

But one morning, the rhythm changed. I got a heads-up message from The Beautiful One. This is what she told me.

"I am selling the house and moving at the beginning of the year."

Did she just say that...?

That was a h*ll of a wake-up call.

She just ruined my day. It was like having Captain Crunch with no milk. Wow. How do I recover from that?

Thanksgiving rolls around, and the family dinner is at my brother Arnett's house this year. I get a call from Big Man. I told him about the heads-up message from The Beautiful One. I also told him I was not feeling the family dinner this holiday season. After we was on the phone for a while, he finally talked me into going to the dinner.

A few days pass, and I find myself at my brother's house. It was a typical dinner; eat till you get stuffed. I need to lose a couple of pounds after this meal.

Me and my brother René went out on the porch. I told him about my situation. For the first time, Mr. Bad A** breaks down. I can't remember having tears fall like that in a long time. It felt like the weight of the world had crashed down on me all at once. I found myself about to be homeless for the second time.

We talked a while, then went back in the house and sat down with everybody.

All of a sudden, my sister Monique said, "You can stay at my place."

(Then I heard that bell sound again. "Ding!" Miracle!)

How strange. This is the second time I've been offered a place to stay without even asking.

I told her, "Thank you very much."

I went back to West Covina that night and slept pretty good. (Until that air mattress time clock woke me up, LOL.)

Two months passed, and it's 2012. The Beautiful One sold the house, and we said our goodbyes. Then reality hit me in the chest. I thought I was at the bottom, but now I realize I'm about to be at the lowest point of my life. Why would I say that? Well...

I kind of knew my sister was a little ghetto. I didn't know the area where she lived. Where was that? Off Pacific Coast Highway and Western Ave., in—the—projects. Other words, "Tha Hood!"

Wow... I am a little stunned. I have never lived in the "real" ghetto before. But there was a bright side.

My sister gave me my own space. (Better known as the living room.) It had a couch, a love seat, a TV with cable, and its own little closet. (Not too bad.) She also gave me blankets, pillows, and a curtain in the doorway so I can have some privacy. Everything seems cool, but there's a wild and crazy joker in this deck. I didn't get the memo from my sister about her boyfriend that lives with her. Let me think of a name for him...

(I'll call him Raider G.)

The memo says he's a workaholic, nice guy, cool, quiet, and relaxed. But once or twice a month, he...

I can't really explain it. Let me just tell you about one of the events.

It was a Saturday, very early in the morning, and I was asleep on the couch. All of a sudden, I hear Raider G talking real loud, like to hisself. Then the music comes in blasting.

He is having a self-made drunken party all by hisself, singing and rapping (he can't hit a note) Eazy E songs, all day long, and getting on my last f*cking nerves from next door. (Which is really behind the curtain in the kitchen.) And did I say it was 6 in the morning?

You know, my sister had the audacity to say, "Oops, I forgot to tell you about that, my bad."

I can't believe I just witnessed that! He got me once, but he won't get me again.

So, Mr. Bad A** had a plan. On party days—Excuse me, party mornings, I would get up early and head out to Big Man's place.

Did I fail to mention? He's out the hospital and living with his daughter, which happened to be my goddaughter. At his house, we would sit around all day watching TV shows, like *Love & Hip Hop*. I don't know which one was worse, party days or reality TV day. Has it really come down to this? Let me think about that for a second...

Yes, this is what it has come down to. Now I find myself going over to his place every day doing this reality TV thing. I have become a real fat a** couch potato.

I thought to myself (in my "Old Man" voice...), "You big dummy!"

Now let's get to the next chapter!

WITNESS THE POWER OF GOD

CHAPTER 11: A NEW BEGINNING

Time has gone by—now it's late October 2012. Big Man is back in the hospital, having another open-heart surgery. He made it through with no complications. I'm visiting him quite often at the hospital, plus it was only a few miles away from my sister's. (That way, I can escape from Raider G. Excuse me—now Karaoke G.)

One day me and Big Man started talking about church. (I don't know how we got on that subject.) Remember that time when he asked if we was doing the devil's work shooting those adult movies? Now he is asking me about church. Wow, where is this conversation going? Big Man kept telling me I was close to being saved.

He said, "You don't drink, and you don't fire up the blunts."

If you don't know what that is, it's a fat marijuana joint in blunt papers.

Then he said, "And you don't cuss."

He's right. I really don't cuss anymore!

I looked at him and thought to myself, "I have no idea what he's talking about. I wasn't looking for God at all. I didn't know you could."

Funny, him telling me about being saved.

"Man, PLEASE... LOL."

What is this world coming to?

Now it's about a week later. (November 2012.) I remember that day like it was yesterday.

Karaoke G was getting warmed up. (You know it's 6 in the morning.)

I hurried up and got dressed. As I'm walking out the door, I'm telling myself, "I—am—not—going to the hospital today. I'm going by my old neighborhood and hang out there."

But I get in the PT Cruiser and find myself driving to the hospital. Why am I going there? (I am about to find out in just a few moments.)

I walked into Big Man's room and took a seat on his right side, opposite the window. All of a sudden, this tall, light-skinned guy walks in and stands on the left side of the bed.

I've never seen him before.

Big Man said, "It's Pastor Johnson."

Let me tell you the crazy thing. Pastor Johnson didn't plan on coming to the hospital either that day. But we both ended up there about the same time.

(I hear that bell sound again. Ding! "Miracle.")

Now, this is the weird part. He starts telling me about my whole life.

I'm glancing at Big Man and thinking, "Did you tell him about me or something?"

While he is speaking, he is naming stuff on point. About the money, the women, I mean everything. He stops talking and asks me a question...

"What are you going to do now?"

As I'm about to answer him (I was looking very puzzled, plus I didn't have an answer), he told me...

"Let me tell you what you're going to do. God put you on pause, then He's going to restore you. All you have to do is get baptized."

I looked Big Man dead in the eye. I remember what we had just talked about a few days ago—about getting saved.

Then I turned back, looked at Pastor Johnson, and said, "I'm coming to you to get baptized."

(That bell goes off again. Ding! "Miracle.")

I thought to myself, "What just happened?"

Later on, I went back to my sister's. While I was sitting on the couch, I was thinking, "That was kind of weird but different. A stranger just told me about my whole life. Wow."

Now it's three days later—Saturday afternoon. I went to Pastor Johnson's church. The crazy part was it was only about three blocks away from my sister's place. (Is that a coincidence or what?) I hopped in the PT Cruiser and made it over there.

Well... I guess it was a church. It looked more like a storefront with no windows and no name on it, and all the doors looked the same. Now I'm just standing there looking a little crazy.

I called Big Man and told him, "I'm outside and don't know where to go."

He said, "I'll call you right back."

Then all of a sudden, Pastor Johnson walked out to greet me.

He said, "Welcome to Jesus Is The Answer Church."

I thought to myself, "That's a strange name for a church."

(I guess whatever works, works.)

We walked inside, and he had his assistant, Pastor Raymond explain the baptism to me. He read some scriptures, Acts 2:37-41 and Mark 16:15-18. Then he asked me three questions.

#1: Did I believe what I just heard? That Jesus walked the earth?

#2: Did I believe that Jesus died on the cross?

#3: Did I believe that Jesus rose three days later?

**Me and Pastor Johnson just before I got in that *FREEZING* water...
This was when my life changed forever.**

Well... I really didn't understand it all, but I said yes to all three. Next, they handed me a purple choir robe. I got undressed and headed to the baptismal pool. I got in and sat down in the water.

I said, "Oh my gosh, this water is *FREEZING!*"

Did I fail to mention, there's no heat in this mutha... Wait a minute, I can't cuss here, can I?

Pastor Johnson came and prayed over the water, then he asked me the same three questions.

(Did I believe that Jesus walked the earth, died on the cross, and rose three days later?)

I said yes to all three again. Then he asked me if I had repented of all my sins. I said yes. Then he submerged me into the water...

Suddenly I hear that record sound. *Screeeeeecccchhhh!*

Hold up! Everything didn't go under the water.

I'm thinking, "You telling me I have to lay back down in this I can't say, cold (blank) water?"

This time he submerged me fully into the water and baptized me in the name of Jesus Christ for the remission of my sins. All of a sudden, he was pulling me out of the water.

(That bell sound goes off. Ding! Miracle.)

Then, I started talking in some strange language. Other words, I'm thinking in my mind, my mouth is moving and making sounds, but my brain is not controlling it. Plus, I don't even know what I'm saying. That went on and on for about 10 minutes.

WOW. Really?

I don't know what just happened. Later on, they tell me that I was speaking in tongues. (What is that?)

So, after this life-changing experience, I made it back to my sister's and had a great night's sleep. I mean the best sleep I had in a looooong time. When I woke up the next morning, which was Sunday, it felt like the whole world had been lifted off my shoulders. But you know what? I—am—still—homeless. I'm still in the Karaoke G's arena.

What am I going to do today? It's Sunday, so I'm on my way to the sports bar to watch my Rams. 😊

The Transformation

Monday rolls around, and Mr. Mom is back to the same routine. This time the drive is much further than before. I'm going all the way to Eastvale from Harbor City. Don't forget—no job and no gas. But I had a solution. Me and my first kid's mother made an arrangement.

I told her, "I'm not charging you to watch our own kids, and this long drive is killing my gas tank. Can you at least pay for the gas to get up here and back?"

She agreed with no problem.

Okay, it's December 2012, and I get another strange call. It's from a girl that I been knowing for a long, long, long time. Me and her have been playing tag since high school. (We never done anything, but everybody thinks we have.) I went by where she was staying, and we played around just a little bit, like two people fighting, but not real fighting. We looked the part, but we didn't do the part.

We talked about it and decided to do our "thang" on Saturday night. She was ready. I was ready. I went back to my sister's and went to sleep. (I also took a coooold shower that night.) The next day I thought about Saturday night really hard. I didn't feel right about it.

So, I called her up and told her, "I don't feel comfortable about our 'Hump Day' on Saturday."

I told her I'd rather keep our friendship than to mess it up over a few hours of fun. We both agreed, and I got off the phone. (Till this day, me and her are still lifelong friends.) But that day, I made a promise to God...

"The next girl I'm with is IT."

(I hear that bell sound again. Ding! Miracle.)

A week later, I get a strange call from a girl. Guess who it is...?

It's one of the 4-G's, Ms. Tall R. I answered the phone and heard her voice.

Then I said, "You CAN'T be the one."

She said, "What did you say?"

I repeated, "YOU CAN'T BE THE ONE!"

She said, "Hold on."

I waited for her to come back to the phone, but the funny thing was —she never did.

Let's remember what I promised God. It was the next girl I'm with, not the next girl I talked to. She was not the one, NO! LOL.

A couple of days later, my old buddy Unknown gave me a call. It's been a while since we talked. We just had a regular conversation. Nothing out of the ordinary. As I'm about to hang the phone up and before I can push the "end" button...

The word "DJ" popped in my head.

I said to him, "I think I want to get back into DJing."

Now keep in mind, I haven't DJed in over 18 years, since

222

1991. (And I had no thoughts of doing it ever again.)

He said, "Okay, I will work on it," then he hung up.

(Ding! Miracle.)

It's now January 2013, and my path of life is about to be set. So, buckle your seatbelts and strap your helmets on. It's about to be an amazing journey. But where do I start...?

Well, today is Sunday, and I'm at my sports bar. As usual, the Rams is on TV, and this year we suck. No playoffs for us, plus we losing the game. I think it will be the last one for the year.

While I'm sitting there in misery, watching them get their butts kicked, a weird thing happened to me. I've been going there for over 9 years in a row, every football Sunday, just like a job. But all of a sudden, I started noticing all the loud talking, all the cussing, the girls flirting, and of course, all the drinking. I've come to realize this WILL probably be my last time going there.

(That bell got louder. Ding! Miracle.)

Funny thing...I heard that a few months later, the sports bar had closed down for good after being open for more than 20 years. So, what was God telling me?

"I won't be going back there. Period!"

A week went by, and guess what? It's Sunday again, this time with no jersey on. I found myself sitting in Pastor Johnson's church. Yes, the one with the weird name (Jesus Is The Answer).

I'm just sitting there, looking around, trying to be invisible, checking out everything. And you know what? This is not that bad, different, but not that bad.

Then all of a sudden, I see people lining up in the center aisle of the church.

I asked a guy in front of me, "Excuse me, what is that line for?"

He said it was the tithes and offering line.

I said, "What is that?"

He said, "Well, tithes are 10% of your income, and offerings are whatever God lays on your heart to give."

I said, "Okay, thank you."

I thought to myself, "Whenever I get some money, I want to get in THAT line."

Afterwards, I got to talk with Pastor Johnson.

He said, "Brother Antoine, you need to start reading the Bible from Matthew to Revelation."

(Still to this day, I can't get used to that "Brother" stuff, LOL.)

I said, "Okay, no problem."

When I got back to my sister's, I thought to myself, "I don't even own a Bible, let alone ever opened one."

So, I downloaded the app on my computer and started to read a few chapters. Later on, that night, I had a dream, but it was only three words. What was those words...?

The Beautiful One...

I had no clue what the dream meant.

It's now Monday, and I'm back to work—Excuse me, back to being Mr. Mom. While I was sitting there at the kids' house in Eastvale, I got a strange call...

Wow! It's The Beautiful One. Remember the dream last night? Ain't God something? I haven't talked to her in a few months.

I heard her voice and immediately said, "You—are—my—wife."

She said, "Huh?"

I said, "I'm saved now, and you—are—my—wife."

"Hello... (*crickets...crickets...*) Helloooo...? Can you hear me?"

She finally came back to the phone. I guess she had to pick herself up off the floor. She was surprised, I mean really surprised, because I told her I was saved. The funny thing was, she had prayed to God for a saved man. We did something I had never done before. We started what you would call "Dating."

I also told her, "We—can't—be—doing—no—fornication and all that other stuff, either."

We both laughed and agreed. (Did that just come out of my mouth? Woooow.) Since we in this miracle mood, let's keep it going.

A couple of days passed, and I get another strange call. It was from Cube. I haven't talked to him since **The Hip-Hop Honors** show back in 2007 in New York. He told me that Universal Pictures wanted to make a movie about us called *Straight Outta Compton.*

(I hear that bell sound again. Ding! Miracle.)

He also said it would take about a year to get it all together.

I thought to myself, "A year? Antoine need new shoes right

now, LOL."

I told him, "I hope they don't forget about me."

(Chuckle, Chuckle.) But for real, I hope they don't leave me out. At least make me a consultant or something.

Tell them, "I'm shaking it, Boss."

We talked and laughed for a while, then got off the phone.

I said to myself (in my "Old Man" voice...), "You Big Dummy!"

"Did you just put "only a consultant" in the air? Why couldn't you say a producer or something else? You're not just a Dummy, but a Double Dummy!"

Later on, I talked to Unknown. I told him I had been on the internet, searching for DJ equipment all day.

I said, "It's not like the old days anymore. They rarely use turntables and vinyl—it's all digital these days. Boy, am I out of touch? I need to get with the times."

Unknown told me that he heard about this music trade show coming up in late January called the **NAMM** (National Association of Music Merchants) in Anaheim, California.

I said, "Cool, we will roll to that and check it out."

In my mind, I said, "Duh— your pockets have no money in them."

Later that night, I had another dream. This time God told me to call Cube and ask him for my DJ equipment money.

So, I woke up the next morning and thought to myself, "Call Cube? Really?"

I had never asked him for anything in my life. Since I knew it couldn't be no one but God, the old me had to swallow its pride and give him a call. You know what the crazy thing was...?

I called Cube up and told him I was getting back into DJing, and I needed some equipment.

(That bell sound rings again, Ding! Miracle.)

Three days later, a check was in the mail. WOW!

The old saying is... God works in mysterious ways, but I'm gonna say WONDERFUL ways.

The Blessings Keep Coming... And Coming...

Now Sunday rolls by, and I didn't roll out of bed. (Excuse me—I meant I didn't roll off the couch.) So, I missed church that day. The next day I was back to being Mr. Mom, but on off days it's Big Man's place for reality TV.

Late January comes. Me and Unknown went to the **NAMM** show. We walked in, and let me tell you, it's a whole new world out there. I haven't been in the music scene since E's funeral, back in the mid-90s. (Other words... It's been a looong time for me, LOL.)

As me and Unknown are walking around checking out the new gear, we stepped into the Pioneer DJ booth.

I said to him, "Yea, I like their stuff. I like how it looks."

The feel of the faders reminded me of the old school equipment.

"Yep, I can do this, I can get my swag back," I said to him, "But let's not forget why we came to the NAMM show— to get prices on the new DJ controllers."

We met this guy from Pioneer there. He knew who I was, and we talked for a while. The crazy thing was...

He never gave me a price for their unit. This is a miracle in the making that I wasn't even aware of. I think I'm going to ring that bell. ("Ding Dong!") Why...?

Because the Pioneer guy ordered me a unit for free, but he never said anything to me until I called him about pricing.

He told me, "I ordered you one, but it's on backorder. You should have it in three months."

I said, "Thank You, Jesus."

Wow! I never even asked for it. Let me think about this...

Cube sent me a check for equipment (it took 3 days to get here), and Pioneer is sending me a unit for free that I never asked for. (It's gonna take 3 months to get here.) I didn't just fall off a turnip truck— Are you kidding me? What's with all these "3's"? God is amazing!

So, you know, on Sunday, I was in church. Speaking of church, let me tell you about that day...

Wow! All the glory goes to GOD!
What just happened here?
You have just witnessed the power of the HOLY GHOST!

I'm back at Pastor Johnson's church, and I'm sitting in the same seat I had the first time I came. Big Man is with me, and we're listening to him finish his sermon. Then he said something towards the end that I never heard before, but I will never forget.

He was speaking and said, "My hands are on fire."

Then all of a sudden, people started rushing up towards the center aisle. He was laying his hands on them, and they were falling all over the place.

I said to myself, "What the... I know I can't say no cuss words, but, what the blank is going on here?"

I got up and got right in that line. (Big Man stayed in his seat.) I walked up to Pastor Johnson, then everything was like in slow motion. I looked him dead in the eye. Soon as he put his hand on my forehead...*Zappppp*!

The next thing I knew, I was looking up at the ceiling. Some kind of electrical power went through my whole body like a super

227

charged turbo!

I said to myself, "What... just... happened?"

I went back to my seat and tried to tell Big Man what happened, but before I knew it, I was in that line two more times. (I'm gonna get mine, whatever it is!)

And you know what? The same thing happened. I was looking at Pastor, then looking up at the ceiling.

OMG! I am speechless and out of breath. But a funny thing happened after church when I went to Big Man's place. I was standing against the wall. Big Man and a few other people was sitting down. I was telling them about my experience at church, how I got knocked down three times.

I said to them, "That was the most amazing thing I ever felt. It must have been the power of God or that Holy Ghost I been reading about in the Bible. It was just... Off-the-hook. Man, I can't stop talking about it. I'm hooked on church now."

But Big Man said jokingly, "I think you don't have to be all that... Holy and stuff. You can relax."

I said, "What?"

It seemed like everybody was against me because I started really liking church a lot.

I thought to myself, "The devil is a liar in here."

(Maybe I need to rebuke everybody, LOL.)

They was kind of joking, but I was real serious.

I had to "click my heels three times" and get up out of there.

When I got in the car, I called Pastor Johnson and said, "That dirty devil was trying to get me over there at Big Man's."

He said, "Calm down, Brother Antoine." (I still can't get used to that "Brother" stuff.) We both laughed about that one.

Let's go ahead and change the timeline.

Me and The Beautiful One are about to go on this dating escapade, but I have to mention two things before we go there.

First one, I'm going to change her name from The Beautiful One. Let me think of a name for her...

(I'll call her My Future Wife.)

The second one was when I got the check from Cube. It took a few days to cash it. Sunday rolled around again, and My Future Wife said something strange to me.

She said, "If you want to tithe at church from the check, I can give you the cash until it clears."

I said, "Wow!" (Ding, Dong! Another miracle.)

Alright, back to the dating game. You know it's time for me to learn this new way because I have no idea about dating stuff. (Never done it, never wanted to.)

And we both agreed on "No fornication."

Oh, boy... That's going to be a hard one to get through. God never said it was going to be easy. Okay, let's date.

The funny thing is I'm going over there almost every day after Mr. Mom duties. We go out to the movies some days and dinner on others. We sit around and look at TV together. (Look at me, trying to be a gentleman.)

No fornication, but I wonder—Do massages count?

Let me think about that...

I guess long as I'm not thinking nasty, right?

Naaahhh! We will just stick to the movies and dinner—no massages. ☹

A few months pass. My new equipment arrived. I bought a new laptop and an Anvil travel case for the unit from the check I had got. I'm playing around and practicing with the Pioneer DJ controller, and you know what? I'm kind of getting the hang of it. I don't really miss the vinyl records.

My new equipment. Thank you, God...

One day I was over My Future Wife's apartment, and she asked me an odd question. She said that her and her friends were going to have a birthday party and dinner. It was going to be held at a little hall that they were going to rent.

"Now, this is the question," she said with those sad eyes, "Can you please DJ our party?"

I looked her dead in the eye and said, "Okay."

I also told her it's been a long time, and I don't really do private parties. Plus, I might be out of touch, just a little bit.

She said, "Okay, it's going to be an old school party anyway."

I said, "Cool, that's right up my alley."

But of course, there's a joker in the deck.

Oh boy! My first DJ gig...

It's May 4, 2013, and I'm the DJ at their party. It feels a little different, and I'm trying to get the hang of this "New School" DJing.

But this is when the joker pops out.

Here comes the first complaint of the night— excuse me— the first request of the night.

And who has it...?

My Future Wife's younger sister. Let me think of a name for her...

(I'll call her Sister G.)

And what was her request?

"Can we hear some new and up-to-date music, future brother-in-law?"

I said, "But your sister said she only wanted old school music."

Now they got me feeling like a "Big Dummy."

Why? Because all I have is stuff like Cameo and the Ohio Players, not this song called "The Wobble" or whatever Sister G is talking about.

I'm a little nervous. First day on the job and everybody wants to hear new music. (Did I fail to mention this one is a "freebie?") In reality, it's only Sister G and her crew that wanted to hear the new stuff.

Well, it was a long night after about five hours of DJing.

In other words, it was "So Ruff, and So Tuff."

After 20 years of stepping away from the turntables (the last time was on the 1989 N.W.A tour), I made it through. Thank You, God.

My Future Is About To Change

Okay, let's kind of speed through the timeline. But there will be good news, bad news, and some "Oh my gosh, what am I going to do?" news. Then there's some amazing news.

First up, some good news. I get a strange call from Lady T again. (You know the one that owns the record company.) She tells me that they are doing a hologram of E during the middle of the Bone Thugs, and Harmony set. (If you don't know what a hologram is, it's a 3-D image of a person.) She was calling me to see if I was interested in being a part of the show, called "Rock The Bells."

I said, "No problem, I'm down with it."

Next up, the bad news. It's July 5, 2013, and I remember that day very well. Me and My Future Wife are going out to get some fast food. I don't know what went wrong. (Maybe it was something I said? *Hmmm...*)

231

We was on our way back from eating, and all of a sudden, the tires on her car went... *Screeeeecccchhhh!!!*

She stopped right next to my car. It was parked on the street in front of her apartment building.

I turned towards her, and the look on her face was...

"Get—the—blank—out."

I said to myself, "I guess that means, Exit Stage Right."

Soon as I got out and closed her door, she put the pedal to the metal. I'm standing there, looking dumbfounded.

I mumbled to myself, "What happened? WOW!"

Then I get in my car and take off, trying to burn a little rubber myself. How bout' that? (AND with front-wheel drive.)

As I'm driving, I'm telling myself, "I ain't never going back to her place no more. Ain't—no—way. Period." (Now, let me tell you how God works in mysterious ways.) You're not gonna believe this.

I'm rolling down the 605 Freeway, just talking to myself about how I'm not going over there no more. And guess what? I ran over some kind of wood on the freeway, and— What the heck...?

Pssssttt.... FLAP! FLAP! FLAP! FLAP!...

I got a "blank" flat tire!

You know what the "blank" stands for. But I can't say that because God's still working on me.

The sound of a flat tire— It's the worst feeling in the world.

"ARE YOU SERIOUS?" It's dark. Did I say it's pitch black and near the cemetery where I'm parked? And it looks like Jason from *Friday the 13th* is nearby?

Now I have to figure out how to change the tire with this little bitty jack that comes with the car. Should I also mention that I have no flashlight, either? (No, I don't have an iPhone with the light on it.)

After all that, I finally make it back to my sister's place. (Yes, I am still homeless.) I sit down, get on my laptop, and check my emails. I have one from Dubai. They were inquiring if I wanted to come and DJ at a club. That would mean my first paid gig overseas! So, who do you think I called first?

(Ding! Dong! Miracle.)

The same one that just kicked me out the car not two hours ago. I guess dating is back on. I said I wasn't going back over there, but we see God sent me right back.

The devil was trying to mess things up, but God told him, "No way, homeboy. Go sit down somewhere."

I'm like, "Wow." God didn't say this was going to be perfect.

A few days later, I get a call from an old friend. I have not talked to him in years. Let me think of a name for him...

(I'll call him Big Z.)

We talked a while on the phone and started to hang out like the old days. Now, here's the crazy thing. God just happened to have him off work for a month.

Hmmm... We will see where that goes.

Before I go any further, let's get to the "Oh my gosh, what am I gonna do?" news. I get some...

Let me say some disturbing news.

My brother Corky gave me a heads-up message. (Another one. "Really?")

This time it was from my sister, the one whose couch I'm sleeping on. This was the message...

My niece is coming back to my sister's place (which is her mother). And she's bringing her boyfriend and her three kids with her.

So, let me think about this...

Niece is coming back—okay— with boyfriend—alright—and her three kids coming. Now, what do that equal? I think that equals...

I—got—2—go. My sister really didn't want me to move out, but there was just not enough space for all of us.

Everything is about to move fast now. I guess God is showing me the way. Two days later, me and My Future Wife was talking on the phone.

I told her about my situation, and she said, "You can move in here." (Must I say it again? I did not ask.)

It's August 1, 2013. Big Z picks me up, and we roll to my first interview since my N.W.A days. It was cool. They was asking me questions about the group, this and that, nothing new. I was just a little bit rusty. It's been a long time.

But let's keep it going. You got to keep up with me. Put your running shoes on.

It's Friday, August 2, 2013. Now for the amazing news. All my stuff is packed at my sister's, and my buddy Weed helps me move it to West Covina at My Future Wife's apartment.

Hold up— did I just say I moved in with a female? I did, but let me explain.

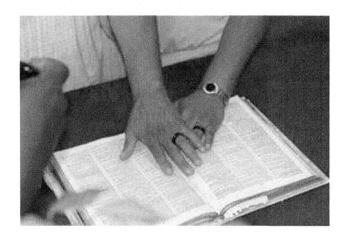

This is the beginning of our future...

I know you're thinking, "Didn't he just get saved?"

Yes, my sister needed me out. My Future Wife said I could live there at her place.

The first thing I told her was, "No fornication."

I can't live like this, no-no-no...The devil is a lie! We agreed, and you know what? Three days later, on a Monday afternoon at about 2 p.m., we both said, "I do." (Pastor Johnson did the ceremony in front of just a few friends.) Let me see who was there. She had her two friends, and I had Big Man and Big Z.

The funny thing is, one month ago, she kicked me out the car. WOW. I just became "Un-Homeless."

Why? Because my wife had a one-bedroom apartment. God is just so amazing. Now let's get this timeline rolling.

First up, it's August 7, 2013, and the event is the **IES Hip Hop Honor Awards** in Los Angeles. Me, Big Man, and Big Z roll up to that. They presented a Hip-Hop Award to me for being a part of The World's Most Dangerous Group, N.W.A.

It's August 14, 2013. Arabian Prince just hooked me up with this DJ gig at the **Red Bull Event** in Hollywood. This is what I like. It's not a house party or nothing like that.

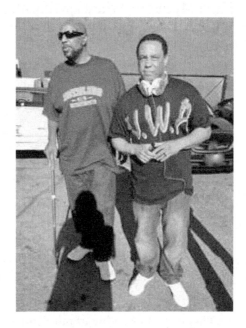

Big Man and me outside at the IES Hip Hop Honor Awards.

This event was like a mini concert with nothing but DJs. I was a little nervous. There was a few hundred people in this outdoor place. The sounds were great, and I was able to get a little loose.

Red Bull Event in Hollywood (2013)

235

But I have not yet perfected my style. That will come later. Right now, God got me on a roll.

It's August 22, 2013. I find myself on a flight heading out the country.

"Where?" you might ask.

Dubai, which takes about 19 straight hours on a plane.

I get there the day of the show, take a quick nap, do a soundcheck, and eat some Mickey D's. (If you don't know what that means, McDonald's. Duh.)

I DJ a few hours later, and it looks like the Dubai people had a great time. I noticed they liked our old school hip-hop. The next morning, I was on the first thing smoking back to LA. My goal was to make it to church on time and tithe, even after another 19-hour flight.

While I was on the flight, I fell asleep and had a dream. What was the dream? God told me to text Dre and tell him how the airport was handling my DJ equipment.

(They was tossing my luggage all over the blanking place.)

I made it back to LA, and did I fail to mention we got in early? I got to church on time and parked in the parking lot.

Me and Dre (2013), our first photo since the 90s.

I texted Dre and wrote what God told me to write–about a new DJ controller, a new laptop, and a new case. Okay, this is the crazy thing.

By the time I sent the text, got out the car, made it inside, and sat in my favorite seat, Dre texted me back and said, "No problem."

Are you kidding me? God is something else.

Three days later, I met Dre at a studio (there go those threes again), and he gave me a check for the second set of DJ equipment. The next day, I went and bought all the stuff.

What can I say about God? He is awesome!

CHAPTER 12: MIRACLES OF GOD

A couple of days later, Lady T gives me a call again. She wanted me to put together some of E's songs so they can be the music bed for his hologram. In other words, it's the music track for the video. It took about two or three days to finish it. I called Big Man up to see if he wanted to hang out while we filmed the hologram. (He gave me a strange answer and said no.) *Hmmm...*

Okay, me and Big Z rolled out. The funny thing was the filming was taking place near Compton, inside an industrial complex with sound stages. We get there, and I see Lady T, Lil E, and his second born son E-3, which is my godson. Let me break down the process. They're using Lil E for the movement of the hologram, which is being videotaped with special cameras.

Next, they're using E-3's voice of his dad. The actual lyrics of the songs are the same. But the talk parts between me and the hologram was me and E3. It was a time-consuming day that took hours to finish and perfect.

Filming of the hologram with Lil E.

It's August 29, 2013. This T-shirt company contacted me a while back on Facebook. It was called Fifty150, and it was located in Oxnard, California.

The owner said, "I would like to do a meet and greet with you at my recording studio. Plus, I'll pay you a fee."

I said, "Okay, that's cool—But what is a meet and greet?"

He said, "People come to see you and take pictures, and also get your autograph."

I told him, "Ohhh... We use to do that back in the group days."

So, me, Big Man, Big Z, and the new guy—Let me think of a name for him...

(I'll call him Bodyguard D.)

We all roll up to Oxnard, which was about an hour and a half away. We get there. It's a nice little setup. People come in one at a time; we talk a bit and take some pics. Actually, that was pretty cool, not bad. Now, let's speed the timeline up.

(L-R) Bodyguard D, me, and Big Man. (Oxnard, CA)

It's September 3, 2013. Me and Big Z are on our way down to San Diego, California, for the "Rock The Bells" hologram rehearsal. We walk in, go through a few doors, and onto this soundstage.

I looked to my left and said, "What the—?"

You know I'm still trying to be saved.

It's E standing on the stage! "Boy, do that thing look real!"

It's E's hologram just standing there. Let me break down how it works. The hologram have to have a special stage that sits on top of a regular stage. It has its own lights, projectors, and all that technical stuff. Too hard to explain. (That would take a whole book by itself.) Other words, it looks very real.

Me and E's hologram.
The head is animated but the body is Lil E's.

But when you stand on the stage with it, you can't see it. You have to look down at the mirror on the floor to see the hologram. Also, you can't walk in front of it. Right now, I'm about to set you up for the joker that will come a little later.

Remember— I put E's tracks together of different songs with me to perform with the ho-lo-gram.

Let me see...

There was" Boyz-n-the-Hood," "Still Talkin'," "Eazy-Duz-It," and "Foe tha Love of $." We rehearsed for three straight days, working on the movements and timing of me interacting with the hologram.

It's now September 7, 2013, the fourth day of rehearsals. This time it switched to where the actual show was going to be held, at Glenn Helen Amphitheater, outside LA. We go through rehearsals again for the lights, sound, and bringing the stage down from the ceiling to get the timing just right. Remember that we rehearsed this for me and the hologram to work in sync.

What do I mean about that? I made the music bed just right for it to look like me and the hologram was talking to each other. Remember that!

Rehearsals ran really late, and I was supposed to be at this birthday tribute for E in Anaheim.

Rock the Bells: Los Angeles, CA (2013)

So, me, Bodyguard D, and Big Z race to the birthday party just before it ended. (They can't say I didn't show up, LOL.)

We make it in, I take a few pics, say "Hee Hee" and "Ha Ha" to everybody, and that's all folks.

It's now September 9, 2013, the day of the "Rock The Bells." My wife and two sons came to the show (not her style with all that Hollywood stuff), but she didn't want to be backstage. They sat out in the crowd. This is when the joker pops out.

I got some upsetting news— the kind that makes you wish you wasn't saved.

After all the rehearsals, hours of getting the timing right for me, and the hologram, they want to have a meeting to discuss changes to the show.

THE DAY OF THE SHOW.

"Are you kidding me?"

They wanna move me from the hologram stage and put me way back in the corner on the turntables. And not interact with

241

the hologram, only talk in between the songs, which made no sense. I looked at them like they was crazy. We went back and forth about it.

I looked at Big Z and said, "I'm out of here. Let's roll."

I got outside and was ready to get in the car. (This is when God used Big Z.)

Somehow, he convinced me to stay and do the show. Let me tell you...

I was not happy about it.

I have no words. Just look at my face. (2013)

It's September 14, 2013, and we're at the second "Rock The Bells" show in San Jose, California.

It's time for that part of the Bone Thugs set with the hologram. Things didn't go as planned. Well, the stage didn't come down. It got stuck. (God don't like ugly.)

This is when God showed up. Everybody was running around like their heads were cut off, trying to figure out why the stage didn't come down.

God kept me cool, calm, and relaxed. I entertained the 10,000 plus fans until they got their "blank" together. The stage finally came down, and the show went well. God is wonderful.

December 2013 rolls around. Me and Lady T are having lunch in the Valley. (Once again, I get a heads-up message.)

Rock the Bells: San Jose, CA (2013)

Unofficially, we are kinda discussing things about the upcoming *Straight Outta Compton* movie. As we're eating and talking, she said something to me kinda under her breath, in a very low tone. What did she say?

"Don't expect what you think you're gonna make off the movie."

I know she didn't just say that to me. Right?

(In my mind, I'm thinking 6, maybe... 7 figures.)

I said, "Wow! Really?"

I thought we was gonna move to Bel-Air, like "The Fresh Prince", but it looks like we are going to be staying right in this one-bedroom apartment. (I guess this is a reverse *Beverly Hillbillies?*)

So, I said, "Thanks for the message." ☹

All I can do is thank God. Let's end this year on a good note. Two things happened.

I got another phone call from the t-shirt guy in Oxnard. (The one I did the meet and greet for.) He wanted me to host a mixtape for his new artist called Kiki Smooth.

I said, "A mixtape? I used to make mixtapes back in the day. But what is hosting a mixtape?"

243

He explained it to me. All I had to do is talk in between the songs. Plus, he's paying a fee.

I said to myself, "Let me think about this..."

It's Christmas time. My wife and kids need gifts.

I told him, "Sounds like a winner. But I'll do it on one condition. If you pay me a deposit before Christmas. It'll have to be before, not after."

He said, "That will work. Can you do it in January?"

I looked at the phone, thought about it, and said, "No problem."

(Thank you, God, for the gifts.)

Now, I get one more call before the year ended. This time it was from Lady T. We talked for a while, and I think God put something on her heart. For some strange reason, she sent me an advance check from future royalties or wherever it came from. It was a blessing that I was not expecting. I know that was nothing but God.

2014

I hear that tire sound again.

"*Screeeeeeccccchhhh*! Whew!"

2013 is over. A whole lot is going on in 2014, so keep your seatbelts tight, and let's get started.

It's January 12. I began working on the mixtape in Oxnard. Everything is going good, but that's not the news I wanted to start off with.

It was not a strange call, but a different kind of call. I thought I was about to jump through the roof, but reality slapped me in the face. Here's how that phone call went.

The lawyer from the company that's making our movie said, "It's time to talk."

But the talking was one-sided. Let's get to the meat of the conversation.

He told me, "They really didn't have to pay you anything."

(I know he didn't just say that.) He also said they would rather keep it clean and pay me a consultant fee.

(Remember I put that in the air a while back— a consultant?) Why didn't I say a producer or something?

I said, "I will think about it and give you a call tomorrow."

So, me and my wife talked about it.

She said, "At least ask them for double the price they're offering." (I'm not mad at her about that.)

How can I describe the fee they offered? Well, if the movie budget was like a large bag of chips—I mean a REAL large bag of chips, like the industrial size...

You know that little salt that's at the bottom of the bag? Well, I got a few grains of it.

"Hello? McFly?"

I was what you would call—Let me think about that...

I was caught between a rock and a real hard place. (Rent got to be paid, wifey needs new shoes, and the kids need some kind of new electronics.)

If I had a pocket full of money at the time, I would not have accepted the deal. I prayed about it, thought about it, and called him back the next day.

I asked him, "Can they double the fee?"

The lawyer said that it just wasn't enough in the budget. (Later, I found out it took almost 25 million dollars to make the movie.) I took a deep breath, swallowed my little pride, kept my cool, and accepted their offer.

I hung up the phone and thought to myself, "Just four months ago, I was homeless and had nothing. Now I have a wife, healthy kids, and a roof over our heads."

It didn't turn out the way I thought, but all I can do is thank God for everything. Now we are really about to WITNESS THE POWER OF GOD.

It's January 25, 2014. Me and Big Z are rolling back up to Oxnard to finish the mixtape for Kiki Smooth. Everything is mixed and done. Now it's time to focus on where God is sending me. First, I get a call from Unknown. He told me this agency wanted to book me some shows in Canada.

I said, "Really? Are they paying for my services?" LOL.

He said, "Of course they are. Let me set it up."

Let's get back to being Mr. Mom, Daddy Daycare, and did I fail to mention, Mr. Husband also? Okay, Unknown booked me a couple of shows with this new agency.

It's February 28, 2014, and I am on a plane flying to Montreal, Canada, for another **Red Bull Event**.

I land, look around, and you know what? This almost looks

like the states, just a little bit colder. No, a whole lot colder. The event was pretty cool, a nice crowd, I would say about 300 people. I still have not perfected my style—at least not yet.

Red Bull Event: Montreal, Canada (2014)

The next day I'm headed back to LA. Afterwards, I go back to my Mr. Mom, Daddy Daycare, and Mr. Husband jobs.

Two weeks later, on March 14, I'm back in Canada. It's Toronto this time. They have a car service to pick me up from the airport, then take me to a five-star hotel. I get out the car and look up at the top of the building.

The name on it says Trump Towers. (I didn't know he had a hotel. Excuse me—I guess he does.) Then I realize something else.

People are looking at me kind of strange. Was it because I was from California? Or was it because I had a t-shirt on, and it's 0 degrees outside.

I thought to myself, "GET—IN—THE—HOTEL! You Big Dummy!

It's *FREEZING*!"

(Funny thing, I don't own a real jacket. I'm from Compton, LOL.) Everything was nice. They treated me like I was some kind of star.

Lil E and me in Paris. (2014)

Now it's showtime. I set up my equipment, they announce me, and...

"Crickets, crickets, crickets..."

There's nobody in the building—well, maybe five people.

WOOOW! They said it was one of the coldest days in a long time. That didn't make me feel no better.

The next day I'm back in LA, but not for long. A few days later, I'm back on a plane.

It's March 19. This time it's a little weird. Me and Lil E are flying to Paris, France. "WeeWee," we doing big things. Now let me tell you the weird part. We on this 11-hour flight, and Lil E is sleep.

I looked at him and said to myself, "He talks like his dad, and he's short like his dad. Plus, we have to go over the words of the songs just like his dad." SMH. Wow.

We land in Paris, and it's beautiful—looks just like in the movies. We stayed at the promoter's house. We slept, we slept some more, and we still slept. After about 16 hours of sleep, we was on another plane going to Norway. That's where our first show was. It was cool, a small venue with about 200 people. The next morning, we on a plane headed back to Paris.

247

Wow! Me in Paris, France. (2014)

The promoter took us around to see the sights, and I do mean "THE SIGHTS."

All these French women...I have to put my blinders on extra dark. Why? Because I am saved and married. (I have to laugh at myself sometimes.)

The Paris show was sold out. There was about 900 people that night. I was on the turntables; Lil E was on the mic doing all his daddy's songs.

For a moment, it took me back in time when me and E were doing shows during his last couple of years of life. I must say we did rock the house.

We made it back to LA, then I was back to my Mr. Mom, Daddy Daycare, and Mr. Husband chores.

Did I fail to mention— the marriage part wasn't perfect? God didn't say it was going to be perfect. That means I'm in a whole new ball game, and I don't have the new uniform yet. This is going to take some time. (But I ain't going NOWHERE.)

Remember—it's two separate people from two different roads made into one.

Don't mean to change the subject, but I haven't talked about church in a while. Doesn't mean I haven't been going. Matter of fact, I'm there every Sunday. I've been reading that Bible and really getting into the word. But let's speed through the timeline.

It's April 2014, and this girl contacted me on Facebook. She wanted to know if I would DJ her family's private company party.

I told her, "I don't really do private parties, but for some reason, I will do yours."

Her and her brother put it together. Let me think of a name for him...

(I'll call him Rich Guy E—or in other words RGE.)

That's a lot of E's in my life; E, Lil E, and now RGE, LOL. The party was very nice and Richie Rich-looking. That means they had it going on.

It's now May 12, 2014. I'm on my way to do a podcast interview called *The B-Side Show*. That was pretty cool, but let's keep it going.

This is the part of my life where it gets a little tricky. Why do I say that? Well...

First of all, my cousin comes into the picture. He came around to take photos and film me DJing. But God really sent him around me to book my shows. That's what he do. He's from Oakland, so he's a fast talker. He can sell you anything. He was also around in the adult movie days, helping me film. His real name is Tyron; he goes by Playboy T, but I will call him Cousin T.

Here's where it gets a little tricky. There's a problem brewing between Big Man and Big Z. I have no idea what it is. There will also be a future problem with Big Z and Cousin T. More about that later.

Big Z wanted to book the shows, but God had Cousin T book them when the time came. It's not my cousin's fault. He just knows how to do his thang. That is booking and negotiating shows. (Like selling ice to the ice man and selling sand to the beach.) He loves everybody. But for me, I-KEEP-GOD-FIRST. I follow no man. That's what the Bible says. Now, back to the timeline.

It's May 28, 2014. Me and Lil E are doing a show in LA. Also with us was Big Z and Cousin T. I think this show was booked by

Big Z. It was just a small one. It was okay, not too bad.

Two days later, I'm on another plane by myself, heading back to Canada. (Unknown hooked this one up.)

Me, Cousin T, Lil E, and E3. (Los Angeles, CA)

Toronto...

OH-NO! It's cold again. You know what happened the last time. "*Crickets, crickets, crickets...*"

This time, I redeemed myself. The club was packed out.

I'm still trying to get my style; it's coming. Breaking news...

God had blessed and moved us on up. (Not on the east side.) Where? To a two-bedroom apartment in Covina, California. Wow, things are looking up. I'm still going to church, reading the Bible, and keeping God FIRST. Let's switch the timeline.

Me and Cousin T are in downtown LA at the S.O.C. movie pre-production offices. (If you don't know what S.O.C. means, that's *Straight Outta Compton*.)

I met the director for the first time, and we had a... Let me see what I am going to call this. I guess this is called a meeting or blowing smoke up my "you know what."

Other words, as I'm sitting there, I'm telling them a little bit about my story. But they don't seem to be paying me much attention—they're not really showing no interest in what I'm saying. You know that meeting wasn't very long.

I'm walking out of their office, and I see this young guy coming towards me. Hold up! I had to pinch myself. It looked like I was looking at myself walking.

I said, "Wow, is that my son or is that an actor looking like me?" It was the actual actor portraying me. (Neil Brown, Jr.) Man, that's some good (got to remember I'm saved now) "blank" casting. (SMH.)

We sat and talked a while. He said he had studied me. I mean, all my movements, the way I chew gum, how I move my hands, and the way I posed in pictures. Now that's a real actor.

It's June 4, 2014. I'm doing another meet and greet— this time at the **Low Rider Fest** in Orange County. If you don't know what a low rider is, it's an old car that's fixed up really nice, and the driver can push a button to make it go up and down, front and back, and side to side.

Let me see who was there with me that day...

There was Lil E, Kiki, Big Z, and Cousin T. It was kind of cool, quite a few people, and some very nice Low Riders.

Low Rider Fest (Orange County, CA)

It's June 8, 2014. Me and Cousin T is back at the S.O.C. pre-production offices. This time around, they actually asked me some questions. The set design people wanted to know all about the equipment we used, like the keyboards, the drum machine, the mixing board, and what the studio looked like. They even had the nerve to ask me about what kind of car I had in the group days. I also met the other cast members, like E's actor Jason Mitchell, Dre's actor Corey Hawkins, and Cube's actor. That was a perfect match— his own son O'Shea Jackson, Jr. He's a little bit taller but looks just like him.

Back to the home front, this new apartment and new "double the price" rent. The one-bedroom was way cheaper, and it's the "First of the Month," and I have "No Rent, No Rent, No Rent." If you don't know that melody, it's Bone Thug's "First of the Month" song, LOL. (That went 4x platinum.) Back to this rent.

I didn't have it, for real. Here's what God did for me.

It's July 4, 2014—three days after the rent is due, but one day before it's late. RGE wanted me to DJ his family's private 4th of July party in Big Bear, California, in the mountains. (That's where the rich folks kick it.) Me and Cousin T rolled up to the event. Everything was first class again. I would DJ in between the live band when they took breaks. It was just so classy, and the food was excellent. Now here's the miracle. At the end of the night...

Let's say my fee was about half of our rent. This is where God showed out. RGE's sister handed me an envelope with the pay. When I opened it, I dropped to my knees.

It was the WHOLE RENT! Are you serious? They tipped me like double my fee! Y'all gonna believe what I say sooner or later. "GOD IS WONDERFUL."

Okay, moving on to July 13, 2014. It's the biggest Low Rider event of the summer. The site? The LA Convention Center. The event? **The Torres Car Show**.

Let me think about it. Who was there? It was me, Lil E, Kiki, Cousin T, Big Z, RGE, and my old Wreckin' Cru buddy, Cli-n-tel. Me and Lil E performed. The show was kind of wild. And the crowd...? I would say a few thousand people— and yes, we did rock the house. Let's keep it going.

One week later, on July 19, 2014, me and Kiki was a part of The DJ Quick Show in the O.C. (For the people that don't know what the O.C. is, it's Orange County, CA.)

August comes around, and I haven't forgotten about my Mr. Mom stuff, the Daddy Daycare, and Mr. Husband chores— and of course, church every Sunday. Now, I have to figure out how to juggle all this. Plus, I got a two-month filming schedule coming up.

Cli-n-tel and me at the Torres Car Show. (Los Angeles, CA)

Torres Car Show (2014)

253

The Making Of The *Straight Outta Compton* Movie

It's August 5, 2014, the first day of filming, and I was doing my regular Mr. Mom thing. I heard about some kind of trouble on the set in Compton. I think it was a shooting or something. (You know me, I stay out of grown folks' business.)

On the S.O.C. movie set

The set was more like on lockdown, very tight, and secured. That means no extra guests, no more open set— after only one day of filming. So, here's the first question. When I go to the set on August 8, should I be packing...?

(Just joking, but for real, should I?)

Oh, I just remembered— I sold all my guns, and I am still saved, LOL. That leads me to this problem.

On August 8, 2014, everybody wants to go to the set on the first day I go. Well...

Really Big Man, Big Z, and my Cousin T automatically roll with me. I wanted me and Cousin T to go first and check out how tight security was. Here's the problem. I told Big Z that the set was closed, and I'm going by myself. I tell Big Man the same thing, so there won't be no mess.

But you know there's a joker lingering around.

Why? Because Big Man had already talked to Dre about coming to the set. So now I'm thinking I'm going to meet Big Man there, but NOOOOO! Somehow, I had to pick him up.

Okay, me, Big Man, and Cousin T make it to the set. I looked around and thought, "Man, this is what you call a big-budget production."

I mean, big rig trucks, trailers, and dressing rooms was everywhere. (But of course, I didn't have a dressing room, LOL.) They got all kinds of cameras and lights, and they filming in 4K, 5K, and 6K.

I said to myself, "They doing all this for our movie? WOW!"

From the **infamous garage** to a full movie set about us.

I—am—speechless. But, back to the drama.

The D.O.C., DJ Speed, Big Man, and me.
S.O.C. movie set (2014)

We meet up with Dre on the set. They was filming the scene where Cube gets jacked by the cops outside his house. I also see The D.O.C. and DJ Speed sitting there watching the action.

We all take a group picture and, VOILÀ! The joker pops out.

How? Because I posted it on Facebook and Instagram, and you know who saw it? Big Z.

I said to myself, "You Big Dummy!"

Big Z got upset because Big Man was on the set. The funny thing is Big Man originally wanted to come to the set only one time. I wish I would have known that in the beginning. (Then I wouldn't've had to go through all that drama.)

In the end, neither Big Man nor Big Z wanted to come to the set anymore. Really? (Remember the words I just spoke.)

OH, MY GOSH!

I couldn't just enjoy my cake and ice cream too? People wanting to come on the set was a daily conflict for me. I had no peace about it. (Sometimes grown folks can act like kids. Ain't that the truth...)

I started going to the set two, maybe three times a week. I still had to do my Eastvale and Covina chores. Me and Cousin T was starting to fly out and do more shows. Now back to the set.

The characters, the locations, the story, and the filming look great. The actors are really getting into their parts.

The saddest part of the movie was the hospital scene. While they was filming, I notice that everybody on the set was quiet, because it was a very intense scene being shot. It was when E was on his deathbed in the hospital.

Neil was really deep into his character. I mean, you couldn't even talk to him. So, I just stayed out the way and kept my mouth shut. He really did his job in portraying me in that scene and Jason played E's character to a tee. In reality, I didn't talk to E in the hospital, but for the movie, it looked great.

Let's take a quick commercial break.

It's August 16, 2014. Me, Lil E, E3, and Cousin T are heading to Seattle, Washington. We are doing the **Hempfest**.

I asked myself, "What is a **Hempfest**?"

Well... If you're old enough, you would remember a thing called Woodstock back in the 60s. It was where the young people, called hippies, had a weeklong concert where they just sat around, listened to music, and got high all day.

It's the same thing. It's three days of music, and everybody just sitting around on the ground with no shoes on, smoking weed. That's the truth.

When we went there, that's all they did—legally smoke pot. The crowd was high for three days, LOL. Now back to the set.

It's time for the concert scenes. The first one was at the old LA Sports Arena. This was a three-day shoot. (Here's some history. S.O.C. was the last movie filmed there before it was torn down.)

E3, me, and Lil E in Seattle. (Hempfest, 2014)

Remember, it was still a closed set, but they had maybe 500-1000 extras for the scene. To the outside world, it looked like we was just having fun on the set. It was very time-consuming. They would film the crowd in one section for a few songs, then repeat the songs and move the group over to another section.

That happened about ten times.

They did that to make it look like it was 20,000 people at the concerts. (That's a little trick of the trade.)

Me, Cube, and Ren was on the side looking at the monitors, saying, "Wow! The actors look and act just like us."

A few days later, the venue changed to the Santa Monica Civic Auditorium. The same thing happened. A whole bunch of extras were there for the concert scenes.

But you know—there is another joker in the deck. I was standing on the side of the stage during the concert shots, and I got a strange call.

257

Me and Ren on the S.O.C. movie set. (2014)

Me and Dre on the S.O.C. movie set (2014)

This was when the joker popped out. It's Big Z.
He said, "Where you at?"
I said, "I'm on the set filming."
While I'm doing all this and getting Big Z inside the set,

258

Cube's looking for me. He wants me to go on stage with him to talk to all the extras over there.

Cube, me, and Dre on the S.O.C. movie set (2014)

He said, "I'm right down the street from the Santa Monica Civic Auditorium."

I was thinking, "Didn't he tell me he wasn't ever coming to the set?"

Wow! On the S.O.C. movie set (2014)

259

I took a deep breath and said to myself, "Okay, two wrongs don't make a right."

I said, "Let me give you directions and get you a parking pass, so you can park where we are and not in the crowds."

(And this was the only time that happened throughout filming.)

But "Noooo..." I'm helping somebody find a parking space to get in. I'm out here shakin' it, boss. I'm out here finding parking spaces, boss. I'm out here getting wristbands, boss.

So, I missed my spot on stage. Really?

October 2014 is finally here, and all the filming, locations, and crowd scenes...everything comes to an end. The movie is finished, and that's a wrap.

Before we go into the next year, God did a remarkable miracle for me and my brother Corky. It was December 2014.

Me and my brother was heading to the Toyota dealership. I had told him I wanted a new car, but my credit was still jacked up. Here's the amazing thing. We walk on the lot, and I see this 2012 Scion XB. It was used but had very low miles on it.

My brother whispered to me, "I don't think I can get this car with my credit. I have never brought a car off the lot."

I said, "Do you have anything bad on your credit?"

He said, "Nope."

I told him, "Then trust God."

We talked to a salesman.

He ran my brother's credit and said, "Sir, you don't have anything bad on it."

That's right. The salesman said he had nothing on his credit.

I mean, not anything. Do you know what his score was? Did you get it? Did you see it? That's it. Zero.

My brother whispered to me again, "They are not going to give us this car."

I said again, "Trust God."

Guess what happened next? I drove off the lot with that white XB. That was my miracle, and the other one was I gave my PT Cruiser to him because somebody had stolen his little Honda a while back. You know I'm going to say it. God is AWESOME!

CHAPTER 13: I'M ON A MISSION FROM GOD

It's a brand-new year. And how do I start it?

Hmmm...

Let's go to the beginning of January 2015. I have been talking to my brother Corky for a while about church. Some people might say I was ministering, but I was just telling him how much I loved God.

I told him I got saved, and he said, "You say what?"

I said, "I just got baptized in Jesus' name."

Now here's something a little funny. He said when he was in the homeless shelter, there was a church around the corner that would pay people $5 to come into the service. The preacher would put oil on his forehead and say a prayer. For a while, he thought he was baptized.

I kind of chuckled and said, "No, No, No. You have to believe in Jesus, get fully in the water, and then receive the Holy Ghost."

He said, "Really?"

I said, "Yes, really."

He came to church one Sunday, and before you know it...

BAM!!!

Pastor Johnson done laid him out on the floor for about 30 minutes. Ever since then, he has been faithful to come to church every Sunday. Since we in the church mood, let's keep it going.

God put something different on my heart, and it was about feeding. So, before church service one Sunday, I went into Pastor's office.

I said to him, "If I buy all the food for some sack lunches, do you think any of the church members would help me prepare them and pass them out?"

Pastor said, "That's a great idea, Brother Antoine. Let the Lord use you." (I still can't get used to that "Brother" stuff.)

The next week, on January 17, 2015, we made 50 sack lunches and headed out to Long Beach, California. Boy, I was in for a real eye-opener. I didn't know how rough people really had it. That almost brought tears to my eyes, and I thought my little homelessness was something.

If you got a roof over your head, you better be VERY thankful.

261

Because some people don't realize how good they have it until they see how hard some people really got it. I thank God for the roof over our heads.

Jesus Is The Answer first food drive (2015)

Now it's late January 2015. Me and Cousin T go to the NAMM Show. It was cool, but let's speed up the timeline.

Valentine's Day rolls around. My wife wants to go to the San Manuel Casino. She had to ask me about ten times because I—did—not—want—to—go. I finally agreed, and off we went. Of course, she had to bring her friend. Let me think of a name for her.

(I'll call her Bingo D.)

While we were having dinner at a steak house, something very odd happened. I asked the waitress for the check. God just put me on a new mission, but I didn't know it at the time. She told me the check was paid.

I said, "Huh? Say that again?"

She said, "Sir, the check is already paid for."

Me and my wife looked at each other and said, "Really, who paid it?"

The waitress said, "The gentleman that was sitting across

262

from you paid for it on his way out. He told me not to tell you who it was."

I said to myself, "*Hmmm... That's strange.*"

You want to hear something else strange?

Two days later, a girl on Facebook contacted me and said her husband was the one that paid for our dinner at the casino.

I said, "Oh, really?"

I hope these people are not like those on *Catfish: The TV Show*. I ain't into all that. Think about it. I mean, some strange man pays for our dinner and don't say nothing? And now the wife contacting me on Facebook? That's kinda weird, don't you think?

(This will be the mission that God put me on— but hold that thought for a moment.)

A week later, on February 21, 2015, I'm doing my second food drive. We moved up a little bit; this time, it's a 100 sack lunches. Me, my son (the one that lives with us), and some members of the church went to pass them out in Compton and Watts.

Pastor Nick and me, second food drive (2015)

Okay, let's get back to the "paid for our dinner guy." Let me think of a name for him...

(I'll call him Money R.)

We talked a couple of times on the phone, then we met and shared our testimonies together. We both had a lot of money, we both blew lots of money, and we both went homeless. I guess we have something in common. (Which was not a good thing, LOL.)

The crazy thing was money just happened to be a little tight for me at that time. Well... Real tight.

Then Money R said something totally off the wall. He offered me a job.

I thought to myself, "When was the last time I had a REAL job?"

Wow... I have to go way back to when I was a valet at the hotel in Beverly Hills.

Money R said, "Not just a job, but a co-owner of my company."

(I knew right then that God had His hand in this.)

I said to him, "I hope it ain't nothing illegal."

He said, "Naw, we just recover money for people that lost their homes."

Oh, okay. I was about to exit Stage Left, LOL. Now, let's speed up the timeline.

It's still February 2015. I'm in my office, and I kind of don't know what I'm doing there. Did I feel out of place...?

Not really— I just do what I do. What is that you might ask? Ministering to people. That's—what—I—do. But here's the mission God had me on.

One day I invited Money R and his wife to church. They both enjoyed the Word. They went up to the altar, and before they knew what happened to them... BAM!

Pastor had laid his hands on them, and they wound up flat on their backs. They was down there a looong time. They both ended up getting baptized in Jesus' name and received the Holy Ghost. My mission was not over just yet.

The next Sunday, I invited all the employees, and 7 out of 10 got baptized. However, there was a joker in the deck. When I say joker, I mean, the devil himself would be the joker. We will get to that in a minute.

It's March 14, 2015. I invited Money R, his wife, and some of the employees to my next food drive. This time Money R chipped in, and we bought 200 sack lunches.

(We really moving on up.)

We went to Downtown LA and Watts again. While downtown, we drove by Skid Row. Maaaan...

I had never seen it before. My heart just dropped. We rode through there, and everybody rolled their windows up in the car like in slow motion because it looked so scary. It was like a war zone to me. That was the worst thing I ever saw in my life.

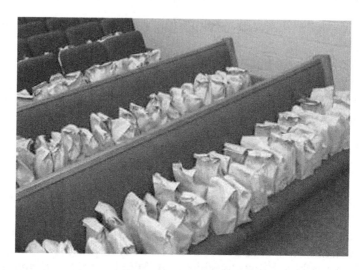

Third food drive (2015)

The families, the kids...If God ever blesses me with millions, I am going to help all the homeless people that I can. Now let's change the subject.

One day I was coming home from the office. As I was driving, something was telling me to turn into the gas station. I slowed down and cut my blinker on.

Then I said, "Nah, I'm going home."

I drove a block and made a right turn. What did I see? Red lights behind me.

I said, "What the blank?"

What did I end up with? A speeding ticket! What did I learn from this? I was disobedient to God. How was I disobedient?

I didn't listen to his voice. How did I know that?

Because I had to pay a three hundred—and—fifty—dollar ticket!

God tried to warn me, and that ticket was my lesson. The Bible says warning comes before destruction.

A few days later, I'm driving down the 71 Freeway, and it's pouring down rain. I'm headed to the office. As I'm going, my car is next to a big rig truck. Now, remember, it's pouring down rain.

Once again, I hear this voice. It said, "SPEED UP!"

This time I'm not going to be disobedient, so I put the pedal to the metal. As I was speeding away, I looked in my rearview mirror, and in slow motion, I saw a black F-150 spinning out of control.

All of a sudden... "BAM!"

It slammed right into the big rig truck.

(It was in the exact place where I was just driving.) They both ended up going towards the wall.

I thought to myself, "Wooowww!"

I just got the answer to that lesson. And what was it?

When God speaks, you better do what He says. Let's move on.

One day, I was at the office. Remember when I was telling you about the devil and the joker? Well...This was when he showed his face. (That dirty dog...)

I always knew one of the young employees had a crush on me. (She was in her early 20s.) I tried to ignore it. Every time I looked around; she was staring at me with those goo-goo eyes. Always laughing with the "Hee hee's" and the "Ha ha's."

(God forgive me, let me repent right now.)

On this particular day, it got a little serious for a split second. What do I mean by that? Somehow, we were in the office alone (during office hours) and joking around. She got a little too close for comfort, and her lips somehow touched mine, BUT NOT A KISS!

I freaked out and said, "The devil is a lie! I gotta get out of here! Feet don't fail me now! Ahhhhhh!!!! Somebody help me!"

So, what did God do? He didn't just get me out of there. I was on the next thing smoking, headed to Australia on March 19, 2015. I guess my days working there are over. My mission was complete but not finished. Not just yet. (That would come four years later in 2019.)

Let's talk about Australia. Written on paper, it was the perfect mini-tour. (Now I know nothing is perfect.)

It was about seven cities, starting in Melbourne, then going across to Perth, and winding up all the way back down to Sydney. It was a few other groups like Lil E, Spice1, and the Alkaholiks. Very simple, right? Wrong! Let's start it off. Another looong flight and 15 hours to be exact. I went by myself on this trip, but Cousin T was supposed to fly with me also. Well, that's a whole story by itself.

The promoter sent me my ticket, but no deposit. Let's say I got a deposit (fake paperwork), but the money never came, just like Cousin T's airline ticket never came. You gotta be kidding me.

My cousin said, "You get on the plane, and I will meet you when the promoter sends me mines." Before I go on, let me think of a name for this story...

(I'll call it the "Janky Promoter Story.")

Cousin T and me (2015)

It started off bad and ended up a bunch of mess. What do I mean by that?

First of all, let me say— Australia is a very beautiful country, kind of reminds me of the states a little bit. But, back to the story.

I land in Melbourne, go through customs with no problem.

Okay, I walked outside the airport and no promoter.

Hmmm, that's a little strange. (Issue #1)

Next, I don't see Lil E coming out. I see his brother E3.

I asked him, "What happened to your brother?"

He said, "That's a long story." (Issue #2)

Then after a little while, I see Dre's son, CY. He said there was a problem with customs, but he made it through.

So, now it's a few of us standing outside the airport, looking stupid.

I couldn't call the promoter because I had no international calling (I had only pre-paid, LOL.) So, CY used his phone and finally got through to the promoter.

He turned to me and said, "The promoter is parked outside the airport and said that he's not allowed inside."

I said, "What the—?" (Issue #3)

Instead of going on and on and on with this story, let's say it was about 99 issues with this tour. From the pay to where we stay. (Wow! Did I just do a rhyme? Remember, I'm not a rapper. LOL.)

Did I fail to mention? I didn't get paid for a couple of shows and got half paid on another show. I wound up staying in not a four-star but a half-star hotel. (Other words, a motel.)

And don't forget— I didn't get my deposit, and Cousin T never made it there for the show. So, the moral of this story is...

"Don't do a show or get on a plane with-no-deposit." Otherwise, you would end up looking like me— a "Big Dummy." LOL.

I finally made it back home, and for the next three months, it was the same routine. Driving from Covina to Eastvale doing the Mr. Mom and Daddy Daycare things, then taking the drive back to Covina doing the husband and father things. I'm in my favorite seat at church every Sunday. Plus, I am really getting into that word. I'm trying to stay 100% — and keeping God first.

Joy And Pain

It's summer 2015, and I get some, let me see...

There's some good news, more good news, some kind of bad news, then some real sad news. It will be a lot going on this summer.

Where do I start? I'll begin with the S.O.C. movie release date, which is just a couple of months away. I forgot about the commercial we shot for the movie in Compton, and of course, on the first day of filming it, there was trouble near the set. I shall not go into that. (Remember I stay outta grown folks' business.) You can always Google it.

The commercial was cool. I got a little cameo spot, but I'm not going to complain about that. Let's move on.

I get a strange call from my kids' mother, the one that lives in Eastvale. She tells me that she is moving to Atlanta with the kids in a month.

I said, "Wow." It didn't really bother me at that particular moment, but it should have.

I told myself that day, "I got to get all the kids together and do something before they leave."

I know it's my fault that the kids didn't get to hang out together that much. I should have put just a little more effort into it. That way, they could've gotten to know each other a little better. So, in June 2015, I took my two boys and daughter to Universal Studios in Hollywood. To make it even to ride the rides, my daughter invited her friend. (For people that didn't catch it, that means two and two on the rides.)

*Schreeechhhhh!!!!!!!!*Wait a minute—hold up...

I have to pay for her friend, too? I didn't know about all that till we got to the ticket booth.

The lady inside said, with a straight face, "Sir, that will be $505."

I almost lost it then. I looked her dead in the eye and said, "They couldn't leave the $5 off?"

Really? Well, I guess we gonna have to split a hamburger five ways and five straws on a bottle of water.

(With my budget? Man, LOL.)

At least the kids had a great time.

There was a bright moment to this day, even though my pockets were depleted.

We was in line for a water ride. I looked to my left and saw a S.O.C. billboard on a building. Now that's what I call going big time. I didn't say the money part, but just the look of it.

I said, "Wow! Hey kids, look at your daddy's movie poster on that building! Matter of fact, look at all these buildings— there's posters everywhere!"

I had forgot Universal made the movie. That was one heck of an experience with my kids. God is so great!

The next day I get a strange call from Cube. He asked me if I wanted to be a part of a reunion show.

I said, "Where?"

He said, "At the Staples Center for the **BET Experience** weekend."

I said, "Cool." This will be the first time N.W.A got back together to do a show in 25 years.

But Dre would not be a part of it, just me, Cube, and Ren.

We had one rehearsal and said, "Yeah—we can do this."

It's June 28, 2015, a little over a month before the release of the S.O.C. movie. The location? The Staples Center. Where are we? Getting ready for the BET reunion show. This day would start out very joyful and end up as one of the saddest days in my life. Let me begin.

We had a soundcheck early in the morning that day. I walked in the Staples Center and said, "Wow, this is where the Lakers play."

Remember, the only time I had been there was for the Game 7 Championship in 2010. I see the huge stage they working on for tonight's show. It was actually round, and it rotated. That's different. Also, there was a LA police car on the side of the stage. That would be used when we did the FTP song. Cube and Ren would drive out in that while I was on the turntables. I walked to the front of the stage and told Cousin T to take a pic. (This would be a pretty historic night.)

From the **infamous garage** to the Staples Center!

Thank you, God.

Now, let's get to some...Let me say sad news, but really heartbreaking news. I was on my way to Eastvale to pick up my son so he could attend the show with his brother later on that night. Remember I told you that they was moving to Atlanta?

Well... It just felt like somebody punched me in the gut. This would be the last time I would see my kids for a while. I never told my wife about how I felt, even to this day. (I already told her she cannot read this book.)

I made it to Eastvale and walked in the house. I see all the moving boxes, and then my daughter came running down the stairs. We had a quiet moment by ourselves in the living room. I remember like it was yesterday. It reminds me of the day I had moved out in late 2010.

I hugged her like never before, as tears fell to the ground.

I kept telling her over and over, "Daddy will miss you, and I love you."

That was the first time I ever had a broken heart. I never felt like that before. (Man, I feel like a piece of crap, even right now as I write this.) I had to wipe my tears and get my composure, so I can take my son back to the house.

We both got in the car, and I'm driving on the 71 Freeway. My son didn't know, but I was tore up inside. The show tonight was the last thing on my mind. I didn't even feel like performing no more. I prayed to God right then and asked him to heal my heart. I'm gonna tell you this, and believe me, it's the truth. I felt Him sewing it back together.

By the time I got to Covina, my heart was completely healed. I was ready for the show now. Nobody really knew about this. It's been inside me all this time.

Now it's showtime, in a sold-out arena of 20,000 people. My wife, my two boys, and her friend Bingo D was in the audience. (Remember, the wife don't like that backstage stuff.)

Let me think. Who else was back there with me...?

There was Cousin T, Money R, and some of the office crew. (No, I did not go back there and work, LOL.)

I walked up the stairs to the turntables, looked out at the crowd, then everything went silent. I thought about the past and all the stuff I went through over my life.

From that little garage to being homeless, getting saved, and now the kids leaving. My mind was racing through everything.

Then all of a sudden, I heard the crowd. Cube announced Ren, then he introduced me. God has brung me a long way.

We did our thing. We turned the show out. Maybe this might be the start of something. I didn't think about it at the time. But God had allowed my kid's mother to move them to Atlanta.

He released me from Mr. Mom and Daddy Daycare chores. Why? Because He was about to open the flood gates to traveling and performing all over the world. We'll talk more about that later.

The Release Of The *Straight Outta Compton* Movie

Now here we are, a few weeks before the S.O.C. movie premiere, and it's guest list time. Okay, you know everybody and their mama wants to come. I'm not about to go through all that. If I can get tickets for my wife and son, brothers and sisters, and a few of her family, I'm good. It was only supposed to be a small gathering, so I was trying to get around 15 to 19 tickets. But this is how God showed out.

The venue changed at the last minute to a much bigger place, next to the Staples Center at LA Live. (How did that happen?) Now, they gave me, Dre, Cube, and Ren, a 50-person guest list each. (I wonder how that happened?)

I had a list, my wife had a list, and I invited all my childhood friends. *Hmmm...* (Guess who's behind this miracle?) The list was almost full. Then, my wife asked me something.

She said, "Are you going to invite Big Z and his wife?"

I thought to myself, "Wait a minute... He hadn't talked to me since last year when he showed up at the movie set in Santa Monica."

I looked her dead in the eye and said, "Let me think about that."

Tick-Tock, Tick-Tock...

(I took a deep breath and decided—two wrongs don't make a right.)

I said to her, "Okay, put them on the list."

Two weeks later, we were heading for the premiere at the Nokia Theater.

A black SUV arrived to pick up me, my wife, my son, and Cousin T. We rolled up to the theater and stopped in front of the entrance. Before we get out the car, I tell my wife and son, "Remember— no photos for the press. Cousin T will take our own private pics in front of everything."

(I like to keep the family out of this old Hollywood stuff, LOL.)

Then they opened the door, and we stepped out into this little tunnel. There was a girl assigned to me by the film company to give us our tickets and passes.

She said, "You ready?"

I nodded my head and said, "Let's go."

Everything went silent, like slow motion again. We walked out of the tunnel and onto the red carpet. There was a lot of flashing lights. Then I heard the sound of the crowd in the stands on both sides of the red carpet. They got louder and louder.

Ren, Cousin T, and me at the S.O.C. premiere. (2015)

I thought to myself, "Wow, what a feeling with all the fans screaming in the background."

My wife kind of stood back a little. Then I heard her tell my son, "Let your daddy do his thing."

So, I went forward and took pictures with the fans in the stands. The next stop was where all the photographers were taking pictures.

Once all the pictures were taken by them, Cousin T said, "Y'all hold up, I'll take the family pictures now."

After he finished, I walked over to the media area, where all the interviews were taking place.

**(L-R) Dedrick, Derrick, me, and Big Chuck
S.O.C. premiere. (2015)**

After I was done, we finally made it inside the theater. My family took their seats.

Me, Dre, Cube, and Ren were standing backstage behind some curtains. As they announced us and the curtains opened, you could hear all the cheering from the more than 7,000 people in the audience. Dre did his speech, then I stepped up to the mic.

The first thing out my mouth was, "Thank You, God, for everything and everybody."

I will never forget that night. All my brothers and sisters was there. My wife's sisters, her friend Bingo D, some of my childhood friends, Big Chuck, Dedrick, Derrick, my nieces, Pastor Johnson and his wife, Cousin T, Unknown, Lonzo, Cli-n-tel, Money R and crew, RGE, Lil E, E3, and Big Z and his wife were all there. Too bad Big Man couldn't make it. (Whew! I know I forgot somebody. Charge it to my head and not to my heart.)

It was a very beautiful night, elegant, very bougie, and of course, a touch of ghetto and drama. Why do I say that? Inside

274

the premiere, there was low rider cars all around during the reception part. That was a first. Now the drama.

Me and Lil E was standing by my dinner table.

Cube and me at the S.O.C. press junket. (2015)

We was talking. Then all of a sudden, I saw champagne glasses flying through the air.

Me and Lil E said, "What the—"

It was some baby mama drama. (Had nothing to do with me, SMH.) All you could hear was two girls cussing.

One of them said, "You no good b*tch!"

I turned to Lil E and said, "I don't know what's going on over there, but somebody's about to get tossed the blank out. WOOOW!"

The night was almost perfect. But I was kinda sad. If my kids in Atlanta could've been there, it would have been a—perfect— night. Four days later...

It's August 14, 2015— "Movie Time."

Here comes the release of the *Straight Outta Compton* movie. I had already seen the film a couple of times, at the premiere and in the studio.

I wanted to do something very different, so me and Money R came up with this idea.

We would go to a bunch of theaters all weekend and watch the movie with the fans, just to see how they would react to it. Money R called up a few theaters and made the arrangements. They said they would give us free tickets and food.

Me and Dre...This moment was just like old times. (2015)

I said to Money R, "Really? Free food at the movies? They gonna pay for it? You know how high those prices are."

Then I said, "Okay, we gonna do this."

Our first stop? Hollywood, CA—the **TCL Chinese Theater**.

This one would also have a Q & A after the movie played. Let me see...

It was at least twelve of us hanging out that night. There was me, my wife, Bingo D, Allen, Money R, and his wife, and I forgot the names of everybody else. (Don't be mad at me.) Let's move on.

They sneak us up the back way. We all went inside the theater before they let anybody else in. We sat anywhere we wanted—but HOLD UP!

We didn't get any free food this time. We got in for free, but I had to buy all the food. Wow!

The cool thing was they didn't tell people I was in there

276

watching the movie.

When the film ended, the credits started to roll, and then they announced me. I went up to the front of the theater. That's where I did the Q & A, and to my surprise, Lonzo was there also.

Alright. The next day we went to another theater. Where? The Ontario Mills shopping center in California. This time we got favor—God's favor. There was food and tickets for the whole crew.

Did I fail to mention it was all FREE?

Wow! I never got anything free from any theater in my life. God is good. (And I did get two hotdogs, a popcorn, and a large drink!)

The next day was Sunday. I went to church and had a whole new crew. All the church members— well, most of them.

Let me see who was there... It was me, Pastor Johnson, Pastor Nick, Pastor Raymond, and yes, I forgot the other names, LOL. I told them it was going to be cussing and a whole bunch of craziness in the movie. (I warned them— we trying to stay saved here.)

Now, I did that one more time with a smaller crew on Monday. It was the people from the office, and yes, the young one with the goo goo eyes was also there. That was very uncomfortable. I didn't like that at all. The devil is a lie! You got me once. You can't get me twice! 😊

What did I think about the S.O.C. Movie...?

First of all, it was amazing that somebody made a movie about us. Are you serious?

A real full-featured film at the theaters. Not just in the US but all around the world.

I—am—speechless at what God had done for us.

From the **infamous garage** to being the "Number One Movie Three Weeks in a Row."

I can't thank nobody but God and all the fans that have seen it. It was the highest-grossing bio-picture of all time. It grossed over 200 million dollars. (Remember that large chip bag? LOL.) It was a box-office hit, beating out all musicals in history. It was even nominated for an Oscar.

(We was robbed, we should have got that one.)

It got 40 nominations and also won 28 awards. Let me see if I can name some of them:

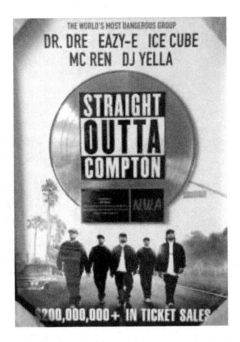

Straight Outta Compton movie plaque (2015)

There was the MTV Award (from the same people that banned us many years ago), NAACP Image Award, Hollywood Film Award, BET Award, AFI Award, African American Film Critics Association Award, EDA Award, All Def Movie Award, BFCC Award, Black Reel Award, and the list goes on and on.

But what did I think of the movie? I thought it was amazing, even though it was only about 70% correct, maybe 60%. Overall, it was a great movie. Am I mad about the crumbs I got? Nope, not really, because it's the way God wanted it to happen. It was all part of his plan. Now for some breaking news!

In December of 2015, after three unsuccessful nominations in a row, we finally did it! N.W.A made it into the **Rock and Roll Hall of Fame for 2016**! I—have—no—words—to—say...

I just cannot believe it. Being homeless just two years ago, and now a hit movie and the **Rock and Roll Hall of Fame**. Wow! God just don't stop. You wanna know some more good news? I just traded in my 2012 Scion XB for a brand-new 2015 XB. I will end the year on that note. Thank you, God!

Billboard cover shoot (2015)

CHAPTER 14: THE FINAL CHAPTER

This year is going to be amazing. It's going to be a fast and wonderful ride. So, put on your safety harness, goggles, and some gloves. Let me take you on this journey...

SOC movie premiere, China (2016)

It's January 2016, and I'm still going to church every Sunday, but now I started going to bible study on Tuesdays. Me and Pastor Johnson would hook up early on Tuesdays and have lunch/dinner, then go to bible study afterwards.

(It's been the same routine every Tuesday up until this day.)

One day, I get two strange calls — one from Cube and one from the **Rock and Roll Hall of Fame** staff. Then I received a message from this guy on Facebook. Let me think of a name for him...

(He's from San Diego, so I'll call him San Diego D.)

But I will get back to that in a little while.

Okay, let's get to Cube's call. He asked me if I wanted to be a part of these two shows he's doing at **Coachella** in April.

I told him, "That will be cool."

Now, for the call from the Rock and Roll people. They was calling to tell me about the arrangements for the inductees' show in April.

I told them, "Just talk to Cousin T about that."

(Man, April's going to be a good month.)

Back to San Diego D.

He said that he watches our bible study all the time on Facebook live. You know something? The funny thing was me and him kept talking back and forth through Facebook about church. He was real hungry for the word.

So, I kept ministering to him about getting baptized. Plus, he wanted to come to check out our bible study.

I told him, "Whenever you get time, come on down."

Back to that story in a bit.

Now it's February 2016. Me and Cousin T are on another 19-hour flight. Where to...?

Dubai once again. We did one show there, then we headed back to LA. A couple of days later, me, Cousin T, Lil E, and E3 met up to do a show in Detroit. We performed at something called **Juggalo Day**. (I have no idea what that meant, LOL.)

On February 24, I had to do an interview for this documentary about Compton. The crazy thing is, we did some of the shots inside the old **Eve After Dark** club.

Wow! Right in front of the old DJ booth—where I used to DJ!

March rolls around, and me and Cousin T are on another plane— this time headed to Tel Aviv, Israel.

Let me show you how good God is. We got there early enough to get some sleep, then hopped on a bus for a 3-hour ride to Jerusalem.

Are you serious? You know how many people would love to go there?

I only been saved for two years, and I got to see **The Last Supper Room**, the **Via Dolorosa** (the road that Jesus walked on the way to be crucified), the burial slab of Jesus, and the tomb where His body laid for 3 days.

Thank you, God! That was an amazing adventure.

We did the show in Tel Aviv, then flew over to Stuttgart, Germany for one there.

Let's move on to April 2016.

281

Via Dolorosa in Jerusalem (2016)

On April 7, 2016, me and my wife started off on a 5 1/2-hour flight to New York for the HOF (**Rock and Roll Hall of Fame**) show. We land, and a black SUV picks us up from the JFK airport and takes us to a beautiful five-star hotel. Cousin T came on a separate flight. Me, Ren, Lady T, and E's mother are at the same hotel. Cube and Dre are at different hotels.

We get inside our room, and there is gifts everywhere. Not just some chocolate on the bed (even though that was there also, LOL), but real gifts, like a nice Bluetooth speaker.

Did I fail to mention that my wife's friend Bingo D came along also? I didn't pay for her flight, but she did stay in our room on the couch. This is my wife's first trip to New York, and what did we do? Well...

Lady T called a couple of black SUVs, and we hit the town. Where did we go? Times Square. From the car it looked beautiful, but we got out and...

Oh, my gosh, it's *FREEZING* out here!

We took a few pics and headed back to the hotel. That's the end of that trip. The next morning, my wife and Bingo D went on an early subway ride (Looking just like tourists— I hope they watch theyself.) As for me, I stayed in the bed.

At about 5p.m., the SUVs picked us up and headed to The Barclays Center in Brooklyn for the 2016 HOF inductees show.

We walked in through the underground entrance. There was a girl assigned to me holding all the passes and tickets.

She showed us to the reception area and said, "I'll be back to get you in 30 minutes."

(Of course, Bingo D had to go sit in the audience, no backstage pass for her, LOL.)

The girl came back and said, "It's time."

Suddenly everything went silent. We went down in an elevator, past a few doors, then through a black curtain. As me and my wife were walking out, I thought to myself...

"This is what all those years of music was all about."

From the Wreckin' Cru to N.W.A...

When I was a kid, I never even heard of the HOF. Now in 2016, we are being inducted along with: Chicago, Cheap Trick, Deep Purple, and the Steve Miller Band. (The ones who made "Fly Like an Eagle.") Wow! I am just so honored. God is so amazing. Oh, was there any drama here? I would say yes because we didn't perform like the other inductees did. I don't know why or whose idea that was. (That's a whole story by itself.)

Me, Cube, Dre, and Ren
Rock and Roll Hall of Fame, Awards Ceremony (2016)

Me and my wife sat down at our table in front of the stage. Dre—he sat to the left of me. Ren sat across from us, and Cube was at a whole different table. The night was beautiful, everything first class. (Including the flights, LOL.)

Kendrick Lamar gives a speech and introduces us. Me, Dre, Cube, Ren, Lady T, and E's mother walk up on the stage. Now I can hear the crowd go nuts. Dre said his speech first, then I walk up to the mic.

I don't remember exactly what I said, but I know I thanked God first for everything. I thanked the group, thanked my late friend E, gave his mother a big hug, thanked Lady T and my wife— that's all I can remember. (Just look it up on YouTube.)

Then I told the guys, "Let's take a quick selfie."

For that split second, it felt like 1989 all over again. You could tell by the picture. There's no money there, there are no managers there, just us...

And look at the smiles. (I think it went viral— check it out.)

That was the biggest night of my music career. I'd like to talk more about it, but there's more to talk about.

Just before we left New York, Lady T asked me if I wanted to go to the **MTV Awards** the next day.

I said, "Cool."

Once we made it back home, I had just enough time to shower and shave, then she had a car service pick me up. I made it to Beverly Hills, then we both went to the awards show. Here I was again, on the red carpet doing that Hollywood stuff. You know, like the photos and all the interviews. After that, we went to our seats. Lady T sat in the back somewhere, and I sat on the front row. I looked to my right, and who do I see? All the actors that played us in the SOC movie.

I said to myself, "That's cool because I have not seen them since the filming days."

As they were getting ready to announce The Best True Story Award for 2016, the ushers came and took us backstage.

As we were standing there, I said to the guys, "Hey, let's take a quick selfie."

(Just like the one I took at the **Rock and Roll Hall of Fame**.)

The stage manager came and said, "Are you ready?"

We nodded our heads and said, "Let's go."

At that moment, they announced the winner—Straight Outta Compton! I was the one told to speak on behalf of the movie. We walked out, and it went silent.

MTV Award (2016)

And you know me...I thanked God first.

Then I heard the cheers from the crowd. That was one heck of a feeling...

From the **infamous garage** to winning MTV's Best True Story Award... God is awesome.

The next day it's rehearsal time for the first **Coachella** show. The soundstage was located in Torrance, California, near the old Audio Achievements studio. All the props for the show was there at the rehearsal. Me, Cube, and Ren went over the songs one time.

Cube said, "We don't need no more practice. For WHAT?"

But him and Snoop had to go over a couple of songs.

The night of the first **Coachella** show happened a week later, on April 16, 2016.

285

Our set would be right before the headliners, Guns N Roses. Cube started his show, then it was time for me and Ren to come out. When Cube introduced me, I walked out. All I could see was the lights and people. I mean a whole lot of people—over 90,000 of them. I don't have to say it, but I will.

From the **infamous garage** to **Coachella**...

Does it get any better than this? Only God knows the answer to that. He already knows what's in store for me. But let's find out right now...

The following week would be a strange one for me. It starts off great, takes a detour, then ends on a somewhat happy note. First, here's the great news.

On Monday, we had another rehearsal for the second **Coachella** show. This time it would be a full reunion with the whole group. Me, Cube, and Ren did our usual one-take practice. Then Dre showed up, and we went over the songs he would be doing. We practiced the timing of the show—how all four of us would end up at the front of the stage for a pic. This will be the money shot that everybody never thought would ever happen again. We got it all together and finished the rehearsal.

Let's skip a couple of days to Wednesday. Big Man called me, so I went over to his place. He told me he'd been acting a little different lately, like real moody. We talked for about 30 minutes.

I asked him, "Do you want to go to the **Coachella** concert this weekend?"

I was wondering this since he didn't go to the movie premiere or to E's hologram show. As usual, he said no. So, I went back to the house. The next day I got a strange call from somebody. (I can't remember who called me.)

They told me that Big Man was in the hospital again.

I rushed down to the Long Beach Medical Center. I got out the car and walked inside, then took the elevator up to the ICU. I walked down the long, cold hallway to his room. (Why is it always cold in these hospitals?) I see his kid's mother, Pastor Johnson, and one of his boys in there.

All I could hear from all these machines was "*Beep, beep, beep...*" There was wires and tubes everywhere.

I said to myself, "What is going on here?"

He was unconscious, but when I looked at his face, it was all twisted, like he was fighting the machines or something. He didn't look very comfortable laying there.

Pastor prayed for him, then I left. I don't like to see people in the hospital, ever since my mother, father, and E was in one. The next day I got a call from Pastor. He told me he had gone back up to the hospital late that night and laid on the floor in Big Man's room and really prayed for him.

He told me, "The Bible says when saints get sick, let them call on the elders in the church so they can pray for them."

When I went back to the hospital and looked at Big Man this time, his face was all relaxed and not twisted up anymore. Looked like he was at peace. Later that night, on Friday, April 22, 2016, Big Man passed away.

I was thinking to myself, "That was my buddy for over 20 years."

We did a lot of stuff together, some good and some bad. Later on, Pastor Johnson told me he had a dream about Big Man. He said that in his dream, he was riding a bike by himself in the Garden of Eden. Sounds to me like my buddy made it to heaven. He will be missed. I was a little bummed out about that, but I had a show to do the next day.

It's Saturday, April 23, 2016, at 6 a.m. in the morning. Me and Cousin T was on our way out to Cube's studio to hook up and catch the tour buses out to **Coachella**.

It was about a 3-hour ride, so we slept all the way there. We got there and hung out around the dressing rooms till showtime.

The stage manager came back there and said, "You guys ready?"

We nodded our heads and walked over to the stage.

The crowd was about 90,000 once again. You could feel the energy of the fans. Soon, it was showtime. Cube went out and did his set, then it was time for the full reunion. The crowd had no idea that me, Dre, Cube, and Ren would all be there together.

First Cube announced me and Ren. The crowd went nuts. We performed songs like "Straight Outta Compton," "Ruthless Villain," "Dope Man," and the "FTP" song.

Then Lil E rode out on a custom bicycle and did his dad's song, "Boys-N-The-Hood."

All of a sudden, Cube said to the crowd, "Is there a doctor in the house?"

Me taking a picture from the turntables... Coachella (2016)

The crowd went nuts again. Dre came out, and we all met at the front of the stage for a photo. Everything seemed like it froze in time. For a split second, it felt like 1989 again—the last time we performed together.

I thought to myself, "Maybe this might be a start to something. But it's up to God and not us."

Dre raised his hand, and the song "Still Dre" started right on the beat.

That was one wonderful night, but I still had the thought of Big Man in the back of my mind.

Time To Hit The Road

God is about to have me moving—real fast. Let me see if I can name all the remaining shows and dates in 2016. I have to take a deep breath because this is gonna be a tough one.

We start off with me and Lil E doing a show in Tulsa, Oklahoma, on April 29. After that, we head back home to pay our respects to my buddy, Big Man, whose funeral is on May 7. Then me and Cousin T jump on a plane to Arizona for a show with W.C. on May 20. Then we head back to LA...

Miss my buddy, Mark "Big Man" Rucker. (R.I.P.)

Remember I told you about San Diego D? Well, he finally came down to our bible study and got baptized on May 24. I also had been ministering to Big Man's daughter about being saved.

So, on May 26, her and her husband came to the church and got baptized. Both of them came out the water speaking in tongues. I'm not trying to take no glory from God, but He just used me to plant a seed in them.

Okay, it's June 3, and we're back on the road again.

Me and Cousin T is on a plane going to a place in South Asia called Sri Lanka. (I had never heard of that country before.) Okay, it's June 3, and we're back on the road again. Me and Cousin T is on a plane going to a place in South Asia called Sri Lanka. (I had never heard of that country before.)

Now, do you remember the movie *Coming to America?* Remember when the daddy walked around, and the girls would throw flowers on the ground?

Well... You may not believe this, but when we got to the hotel in Sri Lanka, after we walked in, guess what was on the floor? Flowers— and the mayor or governor was also there to greet us!

289

Sri Lanka (2016)

Are you kidding me? Wow! They asked me what kind of food I wanted.

I said, "KFC."

And you know what? The staff and the manager came to my hotel room for a little ceremony and autograph signing. The staff gave me flowers and some KFC, but when the ceremony was over...KA-POWW!

The manager of the hotel handed me a bill for the chicken.

I said, "Really?" ☹

After we got back to LA, we flew to Denver, Colorado, for the **Low Rider Car Show**, which was on June 12. Now, let's hook up with the big boys.

On July 30, me, Cube, and Ren did a show in Riverside, California, called the **Hardfest**. When we walked out on the stage, it was 93,000 people there. And I must say, we did rock the house!

One week later, me, Lil E, and Cousin T did the **LA Super Show** on August 7.

Now it was time to go overseas. We headed to England, and on August 11, we did Glasgow. On August 13, we did London, and on August 14, we did Ramsgate, Germany.

And the next day? *Screeeeecccchhhh!*

Wow! 93,000 people! Hardfest (2016)

Cousin T was so tipsy. How tipsy was he? I couldn't even hardly get him out of the car. I had to help walk him up to the counter.

So, you know what happened next? The lady at the counter looked at him, then looked me dead in my eyes and said, "Sir, your friend looks very inebriated. (Other words, drunk as a dead skunk.) He doesn't look like he can get on the plane."

Are you blanking serious? We missed our flight and had to wait about 5 or 6 hours till the next one.

Where was we going? Ibiza, Spain, but this was the cool part. When we got there, they took us up to the top of the mountains to a private resort.

You wanna know what's better than that?

The show got canceled, so we had a few days of nothing to do but kick back in Spain. (Don't get it twisted, I still got paid.)

I guess Cousin T gets to recuperate. God is really good. Now back to the shows.

On August 26, me and Cousin T did Seattle. We met up with Cube and Ren for a show in Denver on August 28. Let me catch my breath...

Now, me, Cube, and Ren headed to Detroit on September 3.

291

Backstage: Denver, Me, Ren, and Cube (2016)

The last time we was here was in 1989 when the police ran us off the stage. This time around, the police had all their lights on, but...

They escorted us to the show! Can you believe that? (They must have watched the S.O.C. movie, LOL.)

The next day, me and Cousin T went right over the border to Canada for a 4-city tour. We played Windsor, Fredericton, Greenwood, and Moncton. After that, we met up with Cube and Ren again, this time in Portland, Oregon, and New York on September 11. Be patient— almost finished with 2016!

A few days later me and Cousin T fly to Des Moines, Iowa. (What is in Iowa? LOL.) We make it back to LA, and on October 14, me, Cube and Ren did a show at the Irvine Meadows Amphitheatre in Irvine, California.

Let me see who else was on that bill...

There was Bone Thugs, Too Short, DJ Quick, and many more.

Early the next morning, we all headed out to San Francisco for a big festival. I had November off, and December would be very—very—very busy. But quite different.

Why do I say that?

Performing in Asia (2016)

New York (2016)

Well, over the next four weeks, I would literally "fly around the world." Hold up! Did I say around the world?

Wait a minute! You telling me I forgot to sign up for the airline mileage programs?

Bahrain (2016)

Oh my gosh! Me and Cousin T flew over 25,000 miles just in December. Woooow! Okay, let me see, where did we go? The first stop was Bahrain. That was a very nice club there.

We hit Dubai again, then flew over to Tokyo, Japan. We was only there for about 12 hours. The next stop was Bali. Me, Lil E, and Cousin T did a show there. (Did I fail to mention— this was my second time in Bali?) Then we all flew over Australia. I think we did 4 or 5 shows there. (Places like Sydney again, Perth, Brisbane, and a couple of other ones.) I'm out of breath right now, so let's switch to the next year.

2017

It's a brand-new year, but the same pattern. That means back on the road.

"Where?" you might ask.

I'm going to tell you. But, before we go there, I finally got my DJ style. How can I describe it? Well, most DJs just mix records back and forth or from side to side. They rarely talk on the mic. But for me, I wanted to be more like a performer or an artist. I would really get involved in the music.

What do I mean by that? I would not just play them, but I would be a part of the music.

I have the crowds sing along with the songs, and it would be like I was the artist for each one. Also, Cousin T would be my "Hype Man." So, it would be more like a concert set than a DJ just mixing. It's better if you see it than me trying to explain it. In other words, we just "rocks the house."

Let's get back to 2017, but before I go there again, I forgot all about these shows from last year.

Me and Cousin T went to Belfast, Ireland (where the Titanic was built), Cardiff, UK, Durham, UK, Düsseldorf, Germany, Edinburg, Scotland, Galway, Ireland (Ireland has some of the loudest fans in the world), Leeds, UK, Manchester UK, Portsmouth UK, Schüttorf, Germany, Auckland, NZ, Christchurch, NZ, Wellington, NZ, Newcastle, AUS, Sunshine Coast, AUS, and Adelaide, AUS. Also, there was Cube's show called the **Riot Festival** in Chicago.

Wow! I just can't get to 2017, but let's go.

Screeeeeecccchhhh!

You know what that sound means. Me and Cousin T are doing a festival in Seattle, Washington, followed by an afterparty, which happened to be at the same place.

Did I fail to mention? When he's on the stage, he walks around with a cup in his hand. The contents of that cup? Straight vodka with a chase of cranberry juice. (Other words, with just a pinch of cranberry juice, LOL.)

And on that particular night, he drank out of the cup one too many times.

By the end of the show, I told the stage people, "He looks a little tipsy. Why don't ya'll just walk him to his room across the street? I'll just stay here and do the afterparty by myself."

Cousin T and me in New Zealand. (2017)

We hit Dubai again, then flew over to Tokyo, Japan. We was only there for about 12 hours. After Seattle, we headed to Singapore, and yes, Cousin T made it to the plane.

As we was driving to the hotel, I was saying to myself, "This is a very beautiful and clean country."

When I say clean, I mean you might get arrested if you throw a piece of gum on the ground. That's how clean this place is. I ain't mad at em.' The club I performed at was on top and outside of a building with a pool and a beach up there.

Don't ask me how they did it, LOL.

Next up was Seoul, South Korea, and Ho Chi Minh City, Vietnam. Did I just say South Korea? Did I just say Vietnam?

Now that was a little different. Most countries speak English, but they're—Naaaw! So, it was very hard to even get food. When you walk up to the counter, they hand you a picture menu, and you point at what you want. Wow!

But the clubs was off the hook. These was some of the best hip-hop heads in the world. They sing along with the songs but didn't speak English. (Now that was a little different, but cool.)

Ren and me (Cube in the back performing)

Vietnam (2017)

Vietnam had a funny name for their club. What was the name? Something we use every day. Do you get it? **The Toilet**, LOL.

At the door, people would take pics with a toilet seat on their heads. Now that's strange and different. The club in South Korea was near the DMZ. (Demilitarized Zone)

Our next stop was Malaysia, Taipei, Taiwan, and then back to Ireland for a few shows.

In mid-July of 2017, we went to Canada, and our tour took us to cities like Toronto, Montreal, Vancouver, and many more. Then, we got back on another plane and flew to London once again. We did 5 or 6 cities there, then we headed to Brussels, Belgium.

Taipei (2017)

Before I close this year out, God had two more miracles planned. One for my wife and me, and one for...

Let's just jump right into it. After all the traveling and stuff, God taught me something. It was so simple. I had all that money and never did it.

You are probably asking now, "What was it...?"

Save money. It was just that simple. Stop spending everything and save something. Well, we did.

God moved us out of an apartment and blessed us with a house. "OMG!"

Buying another house was not in our budget. I was happy with the one-bedroom apartment we had.

But then we moved on up with the two-bedroom, and now we have a house.

I just had to drop to my knees and say, "Thank You, Jesus. Really, thank You."

Do you know what the crazy thing is? Our house is half the size of both of my old houses. But I'm happier now than I was back then. I guess I appreciate it much more, because it never was about the money. I used to do what I wanted to do. Now I do what God wants me to do. Let's get to this last miracle of the year.

I usually get my feet and nails done at a certain shop in Covina. I had been going there for a couple of years. One day I was at the shop getting my feet done. The owner of the shop sat down next to me, and we had a long talk.

I was telling her how I got saved and was going to church all the time. (Not every day, but Tuesdays and Sundays.) As I was talking, she just sat there and listened to everything I said.

I thought to myself, "If I come here one more time, and she sits down and listens, I'm going to invite her to church."

To make a long story short, I came again, she listened again, and I invited her to church.

Pastor Johnson had a good sermon going on that day. Soon it was altar call time. She was a little hesitant to go up at first. But she finally went up.

Pastor laid his hands on her and— "KA-BOOM!" She was on that ground for about 20 minutes screaming. (I guess she had a lot of stuff to get off her chest.)

She got baptized and filled with the Holy Ghost.

God—did—His—thang!

Before we change years, me and Cousin T are doing our usual J-O-B. What's that? Taking more long flights.

Now let's jump into the New Year.

2018

Ireland (2018)

We just had one of those... I would say two flights that equaled 27 hours of flying. Location?

The Peoples Republic of China. Now it was a little different this time. Why? Because people in this country don't speak English at all. (Or they don't wanna speak it, LOL.) This time the promoter traveled with us because he understood their language. Let me think of a name for him...

(I'll call him Compton Kirk.)

He actually lives in Compton or has a shop there or something. I don't know, but he is the homie. We did four cities, Shenzhen, Chongqing, Hong Kong, and Xiamen. I think I got the names right, but "Don't quote me, boy, 'cause I ain't said 'blank.'" (I had E's lyrics on my mind.) All the shows was cool, but...

When we first got to the hotel, there was this girl assistant... Should I say more? Let me REPENT first. (No LOL.)

I wanted to use the internet in the hotel, but you can't just use it. You have to know how to get the signal out of the country.

Guess who knew how to use it? The girl assistant.

So, she followed me to my room to show me how to use the internet. I'm thinking she was coming to my door, giving me the code, and leaving.

(I'm a church boy now—other words, "I'm a little naive.")

The first part was right. She came to the door, but she went THROUGH the door.

I said to myself, "Oh no, she didn't! The devil is a lie! Feet don't fail her now!"

I told her, "Just give me the code, and you gots to go." I was very polite about it.

Then I said, "You ain't gotta go home, but you gotta get outta here." (Sweating and SMH.)

Montebello Rockfest, Canada (2018)

We got back home from that tour, and Cousin T told me about our next trip.

He said, "We going to Georgia."

I said, "Cool, that way, I can see the kids while we out there."

A few days later, Cousin T said, "Bro, we not going to Atlanta, Georgia, but the country of Georgia."

I said, "What? There's a country named Georgia?"

He said, "Yessir."

Well, we was on the next thing smoking, headed to Georgia

301

(part of the old Soviet Union in Europe) by way of Istanbul, Turkey. (Never heard of that one, either.)

God got me going to some crazy places, LOL.

Let's speed through the places I went to this year, and I will stop when I get to Australia. Let me begin.

We went to South Korea again (this time with Lil E), all over London, Singapore a second time, and to the **Montebello Rockfest** in Canada, but hold up!

Me and Lil E also went to Cleveland to do a Q&A at the **Rock and Roll Hall of Fame**.

Then we had another Canada tour. This time, it was 11 shows in 12 days. Now that was a tough one.

Let me think of the cities: Whistler, Nanaimo, Victoria, and Grand Prairie.

We walked off the plane and said, "OMG, it's cold as—I'm saved, can't say that."

We were also in Calgary, Ottawa, Montreal, Branford, and Oshawa. But let's get back to church for a minute.

Wow! What a coincidence!
This is my great-grandfather who was a preacher...

I was starting to be known as the marriage preacher. Wait a minute, did I just say preacher? I am not a preacher, LOL. I'm trying to be like Jonah and hide in a fish. You got to read the Bible and find out about that story.

I just like to talk to young couples that's thinking about getting married. I would always offer to buy their marriage license if they decided to get married. (Up until this day, I have bought about six licenses.) Why?

"The Bible says it's better to marry than to burn."

Other words, they need to get out of fornication. That means shacking up and having a girlfriend or boyfriend, because the names "girlfriend" and "boyfriend" is not mentioned in the Bible.

Wow! God got three of our siblings. There's four more left...
(L-R) My brother Carlos, Pastor Johnson,
my brother René, and me.

Changing the subject, my brother Corky invited my brother René to church one Sunday. I was standing in the back, and Pastor Johnson was in the middle of his sermon. (I don't sit in my favorite chair anymore.)

All of a sudden, he did something he don't normally do. Pastor walked off the pulpit and stood in front of René. He prayed just a little bit, and my brother received the Holy Ghost right then. At the same time, I was in the back praying that God would give him the Holy Ghost. My brother almost fell over all the chairs.

Later he got baptized, and I said, "Thank You, God."

Let's finish 2018. Me and Cousin T are headed back to Australia for the fourth time.

You might say, "You've been there many times. What's so different now?"

Okay, it was an 11-city tour, no big deal: some new and some old places we been, places like Wayville, Maitland, Canberra, Christchurch, NZ, Melbourne, Sydney, Bendigo, Townsville, Gold Coast, Wollongong, and Bunbury.

You might ask, "What's so special about these places?"

Well...Five of the cities was part of the **Groovin' The Moo Festival**. (GTM) This is one of the biggest festivals in Australia.

Groovin' The Moo Festival, Australia (2018)

When I say big, I mean like **Coachella** big. **Coachella** had 90,000 people. GTM had about 30,000. That was big for Australia. Let me describe one of the shows.

All the five festivals looked the same— same sound systems, same lights, same stages, and tents.

Now Canberra was the third show. Me, the sound and light crew, was getting in sync.

They knew my show was 45 minutes long. At the 35-minute mark, the stage manager would give me a cue that my set was almost over. That means everybody's on point. Let's get to the show.

Cousin T and me, Australia (2018)

As I was on the side of the stage, I set my unit up on a riser while this other group was performing. I stood backstage and said a little prayer.

The other artists finished their set. Then they slid my unit to center stage. I had the 4 p.m. slot, which was the perfect set time. That means the people wasn't burnt out yet.

The stage went black, and my video was cued up on all the big screens. All of a sudden, everything slowed down and went silent.

They announced me, and the video started playing, "You are now about to witness the strength of street knowledge..."

I looked at Cousin T, nodded my head, and said, "Let's do this."

I walked out first, stepped in the riser, and stood in front of my unit. The spotlights came on.

I thought to myself, "From the **infamous garage** to the Wreckin' Cru to N.W. A, to the SOC Premiere, to the Hall of Fame, and now... one of the biggest DJ shows I ever done."

I played the song "Hello," and I told the people...

"I Started This Gangsta Sh*t, and This Is The Motha F*cking Thanks I Get." (I did repent for those cuss words.)

The crowd went nuts, and I gots to say...

Thank You, God, for the journey. Let's move to the next year.

2019

I forgot to tell you that something else happened to me towards the end of 2018. God was getting me ready for a couple of things. What, you might ask? Well, I'd rather tell you the story that leads up to them.

One Sunday before church in December of 2018, God put something on my heart.

I asked Pastor Johnson, "Can church members like me baptize people?"

Pastor had to think about that one. We talked about it for a little while and came up with no answer. So, I went home and prayed on it.

Tuesday came around, and me and Pastor met up for our regular lunch. I was a touch late to the restaurant.

I walked in, and soon as I sat down, I looked at Pastor and said, "Do you want me to be a deacon?"

He said, "Brother Antoine, you almost made me fall out the chair. That's the answer you been waiting for. (I still can't get used to that "Brother" stuff, LOL.) God wants you to become a deacon, but only for a short while. Because He's got something bigger in store for you later."

That brings me back to January 2019.

Here are just two of many reasons why God wanted me to become a deacon.

Reason 1: Do you remember the girl I met when Shakespeare brung her around in the Wreckin' Cru days? Her name was Miss Sexy S, and every once and a while, she would give me a call. I would minister to her while we talked on the phone. (No hanky panky stuff.) One night she came to bible study, and she was ready to be baptized.

306

Pastor Johnson said to me, "Brother Antoine, you baptize her."

I looked Pastor dead in the eyes and said, "What you talkin bout Willis?"

He said, "It's time for you to learn, and I will assist you."

To make a long story short, I was nervous, but I did baptize Miss Sexy S in Jesus' name, and she came out the water speaking in tongues. But God wasn't finished with me.

Reason 2: One day after church, me and Pastor Johnson was talking outside. This family walked up and asked a few questions. I wasn't really paying attention.

(I think I was running my mouth on the phone.)

Pastor was talking to them, and the husband of the family said, "Is that who I think it is?"

Pastor said, "Yea, that's DJ Yella."

(He KNOWS I don't like that.)

To make another long story short, God had me ministering to the family, and I baptized them both.

I said to myself, "Go ahead, God— keep on using me."

Since we in this church mode, let's keep it going. Do you remember Money R from the office? This is the conclusion to that story.

Late January 2019... Well, I got a real strange call.

I answered the phone and said, "Hello?"

It was Money R, and it sounded like he was in a deep hole or cave or h*ll or something. He was screaming, but it sounded like a faraway scream—Crazy.

And these was his words...

"Antoine, I need HELP! Come save me!"

Then the phone hung up.

I said to myself, "That was a real strange call."

About 20 minutes later, his friend that used to work at the office gave me a call. He told me that Money R was in front of the emergency room, sleep in the car.

He also said, "Can you come over here and pray for him?"

I asked him, "What's the address? I'll be right there."

After he gave me the address, I got off the phone and called Pastor Johnson. I told him about Money R.

He said to me, "Are you at home?"

I said, "Yes."

He said, "Do you have any anointing oil there?"

I said, "Yes."

Then he told me, "When you go over there, take some and anoint him, but don't lay hands on him."

I said, "You want me to go over there and not lay hands on him? Is there something you want to tell me?"

(I'm thinking, "He don't want them demons on me.")

He said, "You living holy, you'll be alright."

So, I left the house and pulled up in the parking lot of the hospital. I got out the car and walked over to where our friend was standing. He told me Money R had checked out of the hospital. Then he got in his car, and he's been sleep ever since.

(I thought to myself, "How did he call me?")

I walked over to the passenger's side and saw him knocked out.

I said, "Hey... Heeeyyy!"

He didn't move at all. He looked just like death. His lips and face was swollen like he drank 10 gallons of water— all in his head.

Then his mother, who was standing there, told me, "He almost drank himself to death. Near alcohol poisoning."

I said, "Really?"

I took my oil out and put some on his forehead. I said a little prayer and went and prayed for his mother. I put some of the oil on her too. Then, about 30 minutes later, the most incredible thing happened, God as my witness. I saw his lips and face go back to normal form. He looked regular again! All those demons in him just left! He opened his eyes and looked dead at me.

Then he said, "Antoine Carraby? What are you doing here?"

I said, "You called me."

He said, "I did?"

He picked his phone up off the floor of the car and said, "My battery is dead. It's been dead all day."

I said, "You better get on your knees and thank God. Because just 30 minutes ago, you looked like death warmed over."

(Well done, not medium-rare.) He told me later that he had backslid and had been drinking out of control.

I told him, "You need to repent of your sins and come back to God."

Now it's time to get back on the road. Let's start with January

26, 2019.

Me and Lil E are in Dallas. Then me and Cousin T head over to Montreal, Canada, for a Q&A at a university on February 1, 2019. It's a week later and guess where we going? Back to Australia for an 8-city tour. Let me think of some of the places.

There was Brisbane, Central Coast, Sydney, New Castle, Darwin, Townsville, Mackay, and finally Perth.

Okay, that was February. Now we're in March. This time we went to some different places.

Cousin T and me in Sydney, Australia (2019)

Some of these places was even in the Bible, where Paul preached.

The first stop was Athens, Greece. (It was sold out.) Them there was Zagreb, Croatia, (Sold out again.), Stuttgart Germany, (Yes, sold out.), Skopje, Macedonia, (You know it—sold out.), and the last place?

Well... There had to be one.

"One what, you might ask?"

It was zero degrees, cold as "you know what." You get it yet?

Cricket...Crickets... Cricketsss...

That's right— no sell-out—matter of fact, no people.

I have no idea where I am in Australia...LOL...

Europe (2019)

I guess I won't mention that name, LOL.

Afterwards, we headed back home, and I had something different to do this time.

I gave my testimony at Pastor Johnson's church revival called **The Rush Crusade** at the LA Convention Center, featuring Marvin Sapp. Actually, this was my second testimony. The first one was at our church a year ago.

April rolls around, and now we are headed south of the border, to Mexico City. A few weeks later, we traveled to the tropical island of Bali on May 9, 2019. (This was our third trip there.)

We took June off, and then you know where we went. Back to Australia once again. The first show was in Adelaide at the **Beer & BBQ Festival**, then we hit Melbourne and New Zealand. We had a few days off in Surfers Paradise (where the rich people vacation), and the last stop was in Sydney at the **RNB Friday's Club**. I'm out of breath again, but let's keep 2019 going.

We are headed back to the place where people just sit around on the ground and get high. (Which was an all-weekend affair.)

Where is that? The **Hempfest** in Seattle, Washington. It was one of the largest crowds they ever had.

Bali (2019)

The show was cool. I even met Jimmy Hendrix's niece! The hotel was a 5-star plus; I meant plush. But there was a joker in the deck. Let me explain why...

We got to the hotel and checked in. But this time, it's taking quite a while to do that. You usually just walk up to the counter and leave your credit card for the deposit. That's normally how it works, but this time Cousin T had to do some talking because the rooms wasn't paid for. (Most of the time, they are paid for in advance.)

But a couple of months later, the joker showed his face. I got my credit card statement and "A-HA!"

There was a $1,400 charge from that hotel! The promoter never took care of it. Are you kidding me? The show was already like a freebie. So, I had to pay for the rooms— that's $300 apiece, per night, plus tax and some kind of resort fee. The promoter said he would take care of it, and I never thought nothing else about it. That means I got paid pennies on the dollar. And to top it off, I had to pay for those overpriced rooms. (Other words, this is what I get for doing a favor.) Wow, I just got robbed—this time without a gun. Now let's move on.

Australia (2019)

It was October 2019. Me and Dre hooked up for the first time since **Coachella**. I went out to his house, and we talked like it was old times again. He showed me his new house and the studio that he had built. We had a very serious conversation, but I will just keep that to myself.

Okay, now it's time to get back on the road. Where was the flight this time? Seattle again, then Amsterdam, Zurich, Germany, and Brixton outside of London. (The last time I was there was when I was with the group in 1990.)

But let's talk about Amsterdam. This was a very special tribute show to N.W.A, and I was the guest there. This was a unique show. It would be a full orchestra (The Re: Freshed Orchestra) playing our songs.

But it wasn't a normal orchestra. It had the wind section, string section, horn section, and a live DJ. To tell you the truth, they sounded amazing. Where was the show?

In a real concert hall (The Concertgebouw). It was packed wall to wall with...Let me say...

They were people I thought would never listen to our music. (Suits and tuxedos.)

We had rehearsals, and then it was time for the show. I'm backstage looking through some little windows down at the stage. The orchestra played a few songs while different rappers rapped our lyrics. When it got to "Straight Outta Compton," they announced me.

Dre and me (2019)

Everything went silent. They opened these double doors, then the spotlights hit me.

In my mind, I was thinking, "This can't be happening."

From the **infamous garage** to a real concert hall with a full orchestra playing...

I started walking down some stairs, then headed to the front of the stage.

N.W.A Tribute show rehearsal, Amsterdam (2019)

The crowd went nuts. I looked to my left, then to my right. I nodded my head. Then the orchestra played the song, "F" The Police." (The song sounded great!) That was one of the greatest feelings I ever felt. God is so good!

Two weeks later, on December 14, 2019, somebody wanted me to do a private wedding reception. I usually don't do them, but they wanted me to come all the way to Bangkok, China. Compton Kirk hooked that one up. Now I'm getting excited for the New Year. I know 2020 is going to be a good one.

Cousin T and me Europe (2019)

2020

The year is starting off right where the last one ended. Cousin T is making all the arrangements for my upcoming tour.

Where is the destination? The People's Republic of China once again. I think it's going to be about 5-7 cities this time. While we are trying to lock in the shows, I'm still going to church on Sundays, plus I just finished reading the Bible from cover to cover for the second time.

February rolls around, and things are starting to change. A month later, in March, the wife's daughter gave birth to a beautiful and healthy little princess (Tovah).

Then all of a sudden...

WAM-BAM-KA-BOOM!

The world is shut down—No China tour.

No schools, no church, no restaurants, no movies, no sports, not even Las Vegas was open. Who has the power to shut the world down? Nobody but God Himself.

Some might think the devil did it...

Naw! God allowed it to happen. Why?

In my opinion, He is trying to get our attention. We need to get back to God.

"Why?" you might ask again.

In my opinion, we humans are out of control. A lot of people is not thinking about God anymore—even the ones in the church that are supposed to be saved. What did He do? He shut down the church to clean out all the people that was shaking and faking. What happened next? Police brutality got exposed. We talked about it 30 years ago. (Remember the song, "F*** The Police"?) So, in the summer of 2020, protests were everywhere, all around the world, with every race and color.

What happened after that? Infections ran rampant, killing all kinds of people. The Bible says, "the plague came, and the people still did not repent."

Next, we had one of the craziest elections ever. That's a whole book by itself. As the year ends, I thought about something, I have not worked in 365 days. I have not had one ounce of stress about anything. Some people think all of this wasn't real.

Well, let me tell you how real it was. Three of my family members have been infected. That lets me know THIS IS REAL.

Now here we are in 2021. Seems like this country just got exposed again. How might you ask? Some of the people really showed how divided they were. How do we fix these problems? We have to turn from our wicked ways and run back to God. Then we have to get on our KNEES and REPENT!

In my closing, I want to say...

I discovered that I had no one to talk to throughout my life—definitely no one to get any advice from. I mean, nobody sat down with me and told me anything, nothing about life in general. How not to screw up your credit, how to just shake hands (To this day, I still don't like to shake hands.) or how to speak to people— that one I was okay with. No one told me about the birds, the bees, and the fleas, how to treat women (d*mn sure needed help on that one), and no one showed me how not to shoot over 300 adult films for over 15 years. No one told me how to do paperwork in the music industry and not just use a handshake for business deals. I sure couldn't talk to nobody about that **"Black Curtain."** There was no one to talk to about money or how to save, invest, and start a business. No one showed me how to avoid blowing a half-million dollars and have nothing to show for it. Or how not to just walk away from a BRAND-NEW HOUSE, condo, yacht, cars, and then just leave it all. I'm still upset with that one.

I'm just thinking to myself (In my "Old Man" voice...), "YOU BIG DUMMY!"

Also, how not to almost have three babies at one time.

(I learned that one from my two oldest brothers.)

But I did learn one thing from my late brother Keith. (R.I.P.)

I can still hear his voice just like it was yesterday...

"Wash your hands."

Let me speak a little truth. Here it is. The world is a "beast" out there. I mean, a cold beast. The love of money is the root of all evil. People will cut your throat for it. They will lie, steal, kill, rob, or whatever they can do for it. You got to be strong to make it in this world. But you need help with that.

(AND JESUS IS THE ANSWER.)

Why? Because people are chasing after peace and joy. There is only one source for that. It's not money, not fame, not who your mother or father is, or who you think you are. It comes from one place, and that is GOD. There is no other way. Period.

I'd like to thank You, God, for saving me and pulling me out of all of that sin I was in. Thank You for restoring me from being homeless. Thank You for giving me a new lease on life. Thank You for giving me peace and joy.

One thing I learned by reading God's Word is that you can't buy, steal, cheat, or lie your way into Heaven. This next statement might make some people mad. It might even ruffle some feathers. But there is only one way to Heaven, and that is through Jesus Christ. You can't go around Him, under Him, or over Him. He is the only way. He is the Light. He is the "King of Kings" and the "Lord of Lords." He is "GOD," and His name is "Jesus."

For all my wrongdoings, You still forgave all my sins.

Without You, I would have nothing. Without You, I could do nothing. Without You, I am nothing.

I love You because You loved me first.

This is my written testimony. And I give You all the glory and honor. In the name of Jesus, Amen.

I'm done. That's all, folks.

For God so loved the world, that he gave his only begotten Son that
whosoever believeth in him should not perish
but have everlasting life.
John 3:16

@djyellofnwa
On Facebook & Instagram
All bookings and inquiries
Contact: nhousemanagement@gmail.com

Made in the USA
Middletown, DE
07 May 2023

30177374R00179